Negotiating Your Investments

Negotiating Your Investments

USE PROVEN NEGOTIATION METHODS TO ENRICH YOUR FINANCIAL LIFE

Steven G. Blum

October 2015

For Jane,

With good wishes and high
hopes for the future —

WILEY

For general information on our other products and services or for technical support, please contact our Customer Care Department within the United States at
(800) 762-2974, outside the United States at (317) 572-3993 or fax (317) 572-4002.

Wiley publishes in a variety of print and electronic formats and by print-on-
demand. Some material included with standard print versions of this book may
not be included in e-books or in print-on-demand. If this book refers to media
such as a CD or DVD that is not included in the version you purchased, you may
download this material at http://booksupport.wiley.com. For more information
about Wiley products, visit www.wiley.com.

Library of Congress Cataloging-in-Publication Data:

ISBN 978-1-118-58307-4 (Hardcover)
ISBN 978-1-118-58316-6 (ePDF)
ISBN 978-1-118-58315-9 (ePub)

Printed in the United States of America
10 9 8 7 6 5 4 3 2 1

For my beloved Adam, Libby, and Suzie.
To honor my parents,
Harold Blum and Jean Blum.

And in memory of my grandparents,
Adam Spiro, Tonia Spiro, Murray Blum,
and Betty Reichler Blum.

Contents

Prologue xv

Acknowledgments xxi

Introduction xxiii

Part I: What the Best Negotiators Do 1

Chapter 1 **What Is a Good Outcome?** **3**
 Identify Truly Good Outcomes and Don't Get Distracted 6
 What Makes for a Good Outcome? 7
 Chapter Summary 10
 Notes 10

Chapter 2 **Interests, Options, and Goals** **11**
 What Do You Really, *Really* Want? 12
 Shared Interests 13
 Dig Deep to Explore Underlying Interests 15
 Don't Settle for Win-Win 16
 Options 17
 Structure the Deal to Meet Their Needs, Too 18
 Work with Them to Create More Value 20
 Chapter Summary 22
 Notes 23

Chapter 3   **Fairness**   **25**
What Is "Fair"?   25
Move beyond Market Value to Measure Fairness   27
Chapter Summary   27
Notes   28

Chapter 4   **Communication to Build the Kind of Relationship You Want**   **29**
Set Relationship Goals   30
Choose Communication Tools Carefully   30
Work to Create the Atmosphere You Want   32
Focus on What You Want to Tell Them—and How   33
Use Active Listening Techniques   34
Good Negotiating Process   35
Be Aware of the Power Dynamics—and Consider Changing Them   35
Plan a Process That Will Lead to Good Outcomes   37
Chapter Summary   38
Notes   39

Chapter 5   **Thinking about Commitments**   **41**
How Tight Are the Bindings?   41
When Should We Be Bound?   43
Degrees of Commitment   44
Commitment Is Not Just about the Ending—Consider It throughout the Process   46
Many Little Agreement Steps   46
Chapter Summary   47
Note   47

Chapter 6   **Best Alternative: Where Your Power Comes From**   **49**
Step 1—An Inventory of Your Possible Alternatives   50
Step 2—Identify Your BATNA   51
Step 3—Strengthen Your BATNA   51
Step 4—Estimate What the Other Side's BATNA Might Be   53
Step 5—Consider Whether You Can Weaken the Other Side's BATNA   53
Work to Shape Their Perceptions   55
Be Careful Not to Rely *Too Much* on BATNA, Especially Where Relationships
    Are Important   56
Chapter Summary   57
Notes   58

Chapter 7   **The Preparation Phase**   **59**

Where Do We Hope to End Up?   59

Consider the Substantive Issues   60

Then Consider the Relationship Issues   60

You Want Good Substance and Good Relationships—But Don't Trade

   One for the Other   61

Set High, Achievable Goals   62

Who Are These People Who Will Soon Be Sitting Across from Us?   62

Chapter Summary   63

Notes   64

Chapter 8   **The Exchanging Information Phase**   **65**

Ask Lots of Questions   66

Strengthen Your Bonds with the Other Parties   67

Gather Up All the Facts That They Are Willing to Share   68

Managing the Danger That They May Lie to Us   69

Chapter Summary   70

Note   70

Chapter 9   **The Bargaining Phase**   **71**

Work to Increase the Pie—and to Claim a Fair Slice   72

Use Conditional Language to Explore Trades That May Create Value   73

Propose Terms Favorable to You—But Defensible as Fair   75

Make Small Concessions Slowly and Deliberately—and Insist on Fairness   75

Be Resolute about Claiming Your Fair Share   76

Chapter Summary   77

Notes   77

Chapter 10   **The Closing and Commitment Phase**   **79**

You Want Promises They Are Sure to Keep   80

Create Scarcity to Enhance Their Enthusiasm for the Deal   80

Prepare to Be Patient   82

Chapter Summary   82

Notes   83

Chapter 11   **The Problem with Agents**   **85**

Sometimes Employing an Agent Is Wise   85

Often Employing an Agent Is Foolish   86

Are the Agent's Interests the Same as Yours?   87
Chapter Summary   89
Note   89

Part II: Applying Negotiating Principles to Investing 91

Chapter 12   **Why Is Investing Really Just Another Type of Negotiation?**   **95**
Investing Is Similar to Other Big-Ticket Negotiations   95
Do Not Be Fooled into Thinking It Is Something Other Than a Negotiation   97
Different Types of Investing Negotiations   98
Chapter Summary   101

Chapter 13   **What Is a Good Outcome Regarding Your Investments?**   **103**
The One Investment Goal That Almost Everyone Shares   104
Your Investment Good Outcome Is Uniquely Your Own   104
Should You Narrow Your Investment Goals?   108
Chapter Summary   109
Notes   110

Chapter 14   **The Problem of Conflicts of Interest**   **111**
Incentives Matter   112
Some Conflicts Other Than Money   113
Chapter Summary   114
Note   115

Chapter 15   **The Problem of Asymmetric Information**   **117**
They Know Much More Than You Do about the Tricks of the Trade   117
Knowing More Creates Tremendous Opportunity to Take
     Advantage of Others   118
Chapter Summary   120
Notes   120

Chapter 16   **Whom Can You Trust? And Why?**   **121**
Be Extremely Careful about Whom You Trust—and How Much   121
You Can Work Well with People without Trusting Them   123
You Can Trust Those Whose Best Interests Make Them Trustworthy   123
Chapter Summary   125

Chapter 17   **Professionalism: Who Is a True Professional and Why?**   **127**
The Traditional Professions' Struggle with Society's Need for Trustworthy Help   127
The Traditional Professions Don't Always Succeed—but They Must Always Try   128
Reclaiming Professionalism   129
Chapter Summary   130

Chapter 18   **Use the Power of Your Alternatives**   **131**
Alternatives When Making Direct Investments in Actively Traded Securities   132
Alternatives When Investing Through Intermediaries   133
With So Many to Choose from, You Can Demand What You Want with Confidence   136
Chapter Summary   137
Notes   137

Chapter 19   **Knowing Your Interests and Theirs**   **139**
Understanding Your Own Interests   139
Thinking about Their Interests   142
Interests That Can Lead You Astray   146
Chapter Summary   148

Chapter 20   **Many Different Possible Options for How to Structure the Deal**   **149**
Trade Their Interests for Yours   149
Work Together to Create Packages of Interests   150
Find the Best Investment Deal among Many   151
A Few Cautions   153
Chapter Summary   154

Chapter 21   **Insist on Using Objective Standards of Fairness**   **155**
Gather Your Measures of Fairness   155
Beware of What They Call Fair   156
Keep Your Eyes on Profitability and Transparency   157
Demand a Fair Division of All the Value That the Deal Creates   158
Do the Math on Fees and Costs   158
Pay Only for Services That Provide You with Value   159
Chapter Summary   160
Notes   160

Chapter 22   **Plan the Type and Tone of Communication You Want**   **161**
Communication to Enhance Your Understanding   161
Communication to Make Things Clear to Them   162

Create the Tone and Atmosphere You Want   162
Chapter Summary   163
Note   163

Chapter 23   Think about Relationship Goals   165
A Good Working Relationship Need Not Be Personal   165
Pay Attention to Power Dynamics   166
Special Concerns about Financial Advisors   167
Chapter Summary   167
Notes   167

Chapter 24   When to Commit—and to What   169
Avoid Getting Locked In   169
Pay Attention to the "When" of Commitments   171
Chapter Summary   172

Chapter 25   The Four Phases of an Investment Negotiation   173
The Preparation Phase of Investing   173
Gather New Data Continuously   175
The Exchanging Information Phase of Investing   177
Plan to Put Them at Ease   178
The Bargaining Phase of Investing   180
Propose Ways for Them to Meet Their Most Important Interests   181
Let Them Know the Things on Which You Cannot Compromise   182
Be Aware of Their Salesmanship Skills   182
The Closing and Commitment Phase of Investing   183
Build In Your Ability to Check on Them and to Get Out   183
Get Everything in Writing   184
Chapter Summary   187
Notes   187

**Part III: The Economic Truths You Need to Know
              to Be an Effective Investor-Negotiator   189**

Chapter 26   Nobody Can Consistently Beat the Market   191
The Markets Are, for the Most Part, Rational   191
Don't Confuse Random Chance with Skill   192

Stock Research Offers Little Value   195

Chapter Summary   198

Notes   198

Chapter 27   Past Performance Does Not Guarantee Future Results   201

No One Can Predict the Future   201

Chapter Summary   202

Chapter 28   The Concept of Present Value   203

What Is Tax Deferral Worth?   204

Present Value and Life Insurance   204

Present Value and Money-Back Guarantees   205

Present Value and Comparing Investments   205

Chapter Summary   206

Chapter 29   There Is Really Only One Interest Rate   207

Higher Rates Reflect Higher Levels of Risk   207

Risky Investments Involve a Danger of Losing Much of Your Principal   209

Chapter Summary   210

Chapter 30   There Is No Such Thing as a Free Lunch—Except Diversification   211

Why You Want to Diversify   212

Chapter Summary   212

Chapter 31   Diversify Across Every Asset Class   213

Be Honest with Yourself about Your Risk Tolerance   214

How to Achieve Diversification of an Investment Portfolio   215

Diversifying Asset Classes beyond Stocks   216

Use Time to Further Diversify   219

The Efficient Markets Hypothesis   220

Some Practical Advice on Choosing Specific Categories of Index Funds   221

Chapter Summary   222

Notes   222

Chapter 32   We Know What Has Happened in the Past   223

The Historical Average Return on Stock Investments Is a Very Good Result   223

Seeking Higher Than Market Returns Is Called Gambling   224

Chapter Summary   225

Notes   225

Chapter 33   **Costs Are Important—They Reduce Your Returns**   **227**
Higher Costs Result in Lower Returns   227
Many Investments Carry Expenses That Are Just Too High to Be a Good Deal   228
Figure Out How Much You Are Paying to Those Who Lay Hands
    on Your Investments   229
How You Can Minimize Costs   229
Chapter Summary   231
Notes   232

Chapter 34   **Investments to Avoid**   **233**
Variable Annuities   233
Hedge Funds   233
Derivatives   234
Callable Bonds   235
Convertible Securities   236
High Costs, Complexity, and Creative Geniuses   237
Chapter Summary   238
Notes   238

Chapter 35   **How Much Is at Stake?**   **241**
The Impact of the Fees You Pay for Advice   243
The Need for Action   245
Chapter Summary   246
Note   246

Afterword: What Is a Good Outcome in Your Financial Life?   247

Selected Bibliography   249

About the Author   253

Index   255

Prologue

I have been negotiating all of my life. So have you. Negotiation is what happens when we want something from someone else or they want something from us. Thus, from our earliest moments to our dying day, we are negotiators.

Of course, we may not think of it that way. In my case, I had already become a lawyer and was busy trying to settle cases for my clients before I first had the chance to give much thought to the process. The young lawyer just did what many people do: shouted and threatened and waved his arms. (Of course, many other unskilled negotiators just accede to the other side's demands, make every effort to avoid the conflict, or just propose to split the difference.) There is a world of difference between being someone who negotiates and being a skilled negotiator.

Several years into my career as a lawyer, I got lucky. My supervising attorney handed me a copy of the book *Getting to Yes*. I found it amazingly helpful and, even more, deeply satisfying. There really were ways to think about, organize, plan for, and execute negotiations so as to do much better in them. My luck was a lot greater than just the book, though. I had already been admitted to a graduate program at Harvard, and, when I arrived on campus, I headed straight over to the Program on Negotiation at Harvard Law School to find out what other wonderful things they might have to offer me. As it happened, they invited me to take a series of courses culminating in what they called the Specialization in Negotiation and Dispute Resolution. By jumping at this offer, I had the opportunity to study with some of the greatest thinkers and teachers of negotiation in the world.

As I worked my way through classes taught by Roger Fisher, Bill Ury, Bruce Patton, Lawrence Susskind, Frank Sander, and David Kuechle, my understanding and skills got palpably better. Almost every teacher there was extraordinary. About one course, though,

I cannot help boasting. The instructor in Conflict, Cooperation and Strategy never failed to amaze. His insights were astonishing, and his far-reaching mind took us to places we would never have been and understandings we would never have accomplished. That course was taught by then professor, now Nobel laureate, Thomas Schelling.

As an academic exercise, studying negotiation at Harvard was sublime. I loved the topic and got to think and write about it with some of the greatest teachers at a pinnacle of academic thought.

To my amazement and delight, though, the real-life part of the exercise was also bearing remarkable fruit. I was getting better as a negotiator. A lot better. My entire life started looking up as I built healthier relationships, planned more effective communication, worked to meet my own underlying interests as well as those of the people around me, and began to focus on and strengthen my BATNA. I was also introduced to the question that has come to be something of a guiding light in my life: What is a good outcome? I had become a genuine expert in what the world calls "the Harvard method" of negotiation.

It was a little bit like finding a magic genie in a bottle. "This stuff really works," I remember telling a friend. I began to have stronger friendships, better alliances, greater satisfactions, and more money. Perhaps of even greater importance, I learned to focus on what I really wanted and on how to guide other people toward providing it to me. Of course, they tended to offer it in exchange for what they really wanted, but I began to see that not as a problem but as a huge new set of opportunities. Everybody wants something, and I can help them get it. In the process, I can get a great deal of what I want. It felt a bit like a new life.

A few years later, I got lucky again. After working for a number of years at Dartmouth College, I was asked to take a position at the University of Pennsylvania. My practical negotiating skills came in handy as I was able to persuade Wharton to let me teach a version of what had so delighted me at Harvard. (To be more accurate, I negotiated my way into taking over a class for Professor Edward Shills when he fell ill.) I have been teaching there ever since.

With intellectual leadership from Chairman Richard Shell, pedagogic development by colleagues such as Maurice Schweitzer, Adam Grant, and Jennifer Beer, and extraordinary promotion by

Stuart Diamond, a remarkable core of thinking and writing about negotiation has grown at Wharton. And, of course, I have been one of its greatest beneficiaries. In teaching negotiation and conflict resolution at Wharton for over 20 years, I have also been a continuous student of the techniques, methods, skills, and habits of mind that make a negotiator successful. My own proficiency has improved continuously through teaching, thinking, practicing, and paying attention to colleagues. I am deeply enriched by the process of guiding new students through the stages of learning about what negotiation is, how it works, and how to do it better. It continues to be true that I learn something new every time I teach.

The subject of my classes has the power to change lives. It changed mine, and students regularly report that it changes theirs. Part I of this book, along with the writings of some of the teachers and scholars I have mentioned, can start you on the path to making such changes in your own life. You can become a better negotiator and apply those skills to almost every sphere of your interactions with other people.

The intention of this book, though, is to focus on a single area where application of these powerful negotiation methods can bring extraordinary results. Using the tools and techniques of negotiation in your financial life can bring remarkable monetary rewards. The first step is to recognize that your finances are a series of negotiations. Having mastered the mind-set and skills of an excellent negotiator, you will view your financial interactions in a completely different way. The financial services industry and its representatives sit on the other side of the negotiating table from you. A skilled negotiator will act very differently than does a passive client. Your new proficiency will help you more than you might believe possible.

This book centers particular attention on investing. As you will see, making an investment is best understood as a process of negotiation. You are seeking to obtain an ownership interest in something on the most favorable terms possible. Someone else is trying to sell that interest to you, and, naturally, they are trying to get the best of the deal. When scrutinized from this perspective, certain wise moves become apparent. Investing, it turns out, is just as subject to negotiation methods as are buying a car, asking for a raise, or selling a franchise.

As with negotiation, generally, my understanding of investment as negotiation comes from both the academy and the real world.

Not only have I been teaching at Wharton for two decades but I have also simultaneously been a working practitioner. After completing law school, including a second law degree in taxation from the renowned Graduate Tax Program at the New York University School of Law, and practicing for a number of years, I came to realize that I didn't enjoy being a lawyer. I longed to work more closely with individuals around their real-life problems. When questioned by loved ones, I often expressed my desire to become "a counselor, or minister, or rabbi; someone with a flock of real people I could guide." After some years in the vocational wilderness, a stern friend took me by the shoulders. "Listen," she said, "you know taxation, estate planning, investments, law, and money, and you can't figure out how to help people? Those are the very things about which most people desperately need guidance." So, with her voice ringing in my ears, I hung out a shingle. That is why I love to claim, with tongue in cheek, that I invented what is now called "wealth management." The idea of putting tax and estate planning advice together with investment guidance eventually dawned on the financial services industry as a more efficient way to sell their products. It had come to me, years earlier, as a way to transition from lawyer to useful counselor.

I have been guiding my clients through their financial lives for many years. My colleagues and I get very good outcomes for each of them. Why wouldn't we? We apply the tools of a world-class negotiator to each aspect of a client's financial needs, and ask the appropriate questions. We prepare fully, learn and gather all relevant information, look for opportunities to align interests with those who work on our client's behalf, and avoid binding commitments unless they are tremendously to the client's benefit. We also search for better alternatives, insist on fairness, communicate clearly, never try to take advantage of others, and use time to our client's advantage. We know what relevant experts (economists) believe to be true and what they know to be nonsense. We study those subjects where study bears fruit. We are always trustworthy but not necessarily trusting. In other words, we guide our clients through financial life as befits a thoughtful negotiator trained at Harvard and Wharton.

As Part II of this book will demonstrate, you can do that, too. I will show you how to approach the financial portions of your life as ongoing negotiations. You can apply the tools, skills, and knowledge of the best negotiation experts. And you can come away with dramatically better outcomes that will leave you far richer than you would have otherwise been.

Among the things that top-flight negotiators do without fail are preparing fully, knowing their subject matter, claiming their fair share of value, and getting advice from the right people. In direct contrast, they meticulously avoid bargaining in relative ignorance, paying too much, being maneuvered by those with conflicting agendas, and getting played by those who have access to better information. There are certain basic truths you need to know if you are to succeed in negotiating your investments.

Part III of this book is designed to teach you what you need to know to do a great job as an investor-negotiator. It will supply you with much of the information, knowledge, and insight required to prepare, gather, understand, and judge potential agreements. You will go to the bargaining table armed with, among other things, the knowledge accumulated from a century of economic study. A top negotiator would be sure to have this information at hand—you will do the same.

The skills this book will teach you are worth a remarkable amount of money. Part III offers you tools for figuring out just how much is at stake in your unique situation. You may be as astonished as I was at the beginning of my studies. This book can, quite literally, be worth a fortune to you. I certainly hope it will be.

Feel free to let me know how you do with this. I am, first and foremost, a teacher, and I want to know how my students are doing. You can write to me at: stevengblum@negotiatingtruth.com and let me know what works, what doesn't, what needs improvement, and what is just right. You can also let me know what amazing (or horrible) things you see out there as you negotiate your way to a brighter investment future.

Acknowledgments

I am grateful to many people. Like most things of value in life, this book would not have been possible without the help of numerous colleagues, friends, and loved ones.

My gratitude to Marcia Layton Turner is immense for all her help with writing, motivation, and navigation. I am also thankful to Tricia Jain and Matt Crespi, two former students who contributed greatly to this project.

I am deeply indebted to Judy Tanur and Jennifer Beer for their help in transforming earlier writings into a final draft. Both of them are extraordinary teachers and writers as well as respected academics.

Moving from idea to expression is not always easy. Thank you to Dr. Diane Roston and Dr. Phineas Baxandall for guiding me. Marianne Weingroff commented on an early draft in very helpful ways. Just as he did when I was in college, my old professor Richard Ohmann keep me thinking straight and refused to let me get away with too much nonsense.

Mary Bonfini and Dr. Dirk Holden were invaluable in keeping the ship steady while I searched for my muse. Similar thanks to Henry Bartechko, Joan Multer, and Annmarie Sheehan. I am also grateful to Gil Stein, David Miller, Paul Harris, R. Scott Taylor, Ina Shea, and Anne Shehab. Margy Klaw, a superb lawyer, blazed the trail as a writer.

My students have taught me a tremendous amount over the years, and I wish to acknowledge them all. As for my teachers, I owe them so much and can hope only to make partial repayment by giving others some small measure of what they gave to me. I am particularly grateful to the professors, scholars, and practitioners with whom I worked at the Program on Negotiation at Harvard Law School. I also want to thank my teachers at Wesleyan University,

Northeastern University School of Law, New York University School of Law, and Harvard University.

Everyone in the Department of Legal Studies and Business Ethics at Wharton deserves my gratitude. Faculty colleagues have been extraordinary. The department staff has been kind and helpful. Tamara English and Lowell Lysinger merit particular appreciation for their tireless assistance. Richard Shell is not only a leader in the theory and pedagogy of negotiation as an academic subject but also our chair. Amy Sepinwall, Alan Strudler and Bob Borghese come in for special thanks. The Wharton School of Business and the University of Pennsylvania generally have been a professional home for two decades. The support of those institutions has been a gift.

My thanks to everyone at Wiley for shepherding this project into print. In particular, Judy Howarth, Laura (Walsh) Grachko, and Tula Batanchiev have been lovely to work with.

I am a part of all that I have met.

Steve Ritz, Alvin Peters, Angelo Bellfatto, Dic Wheeler, Liza Baron, Peggy Grodinsky, Karen Bleich, Marcia Tanur, and Donna San Antonio are dear to me and deserve part of the credit for anything I ever accomplish. I could not have done this without you.

Finally, I am most grateful of all to Adam, Libby, and Suzie for supporting the writing of this book, even when it wasn't easy to do so. And for loving me almost as much as I love each of them.

Introduction

A primary tenet of this book is that the actions necessary to take good care of your financial life, including making investments, are a series of negotiations. The world's most sophisticated investors know this very well. It is a recognition that is ignored only at one's peril.

When Henry Kravis entered into a deal to buy RJR Nabisco through a leveraged buyout, he understood that his company was entering into an epic negotiation. Two years earlier, though, when Sam Rizzo bought a few shares of RJR Nabisco as an investment for his family's future, he had not the slightest thought that he was entering a negotiation.

As Facebook prepared to go public by issuing stock in 2012, Mark Zuckerberg, Sheryl Sandberg, and all the attendant lawyers and investment bankers behaved as if they were getting ready for one of the biggest negotiations they would ever be part of. On the other hand, many thousands of investors and speculators who bought those shares failed to see themselves as negotiators on the other side of the table.

When Goldman Sachs created the ABACUS CDO investment product to facilitate an investor's plan to short the mortgage market, Vice President Fabrice Tourre and his team knew they were engaging in a complex multiparty negotiation. The German bankers who bought the product as a long-side investment did not seem to share the same realization.

Failing to understand your financial transactions as acts of negotiation sets you up as prey for those who do. Almost everyone you know recognizes that one must negotiate skillfully to buy a piece of property. Those same people, though, buy investments (also a kind of property) with the trust and passivity of lambs being led from the barn.

To the RJR Nabisco, Facebook, and ABACUS examples can be added a hundred more drawn from everyday financial transactions. Let me offer a few:

- Choosing to work with a brokerage or investment firm
- Selecting an independent investment advisor
- Buying a mutual fund
- Looking at homes with a real estate broker
- Buying a bond that is callable by the issuer
- Choosing a type of checking account offered by the local bank
- Selecting a credit card and then using it
- Deciding on an insurance broker and then buying life insurance through her from a given underwriter

Even buying a book full of investment advice is a negotiation.

When lawyers from a major accounting firm suggested a tax shelter to some of their clients, it would have been savvy to compare the charges being levied with the anticipated tax savings.

"Tell us," the clients might have asked, "about how you guarantee your work. Will you pay all costs and penalties if the IRS rules the shelter abusive and illegal? Under what circumstances will you return your fee?" Thereafter, they might have considered getting all those answers incorporated into a written client agreement.

Furthermore, when Bernie Johnson was sold a variable annuity product that he didn't fully understand and would cost him over a million dollars of lost return in his lifetime, he did not see the transaction as a negotiation. Rather, he thought it more akin to purchasing medicine prescribed by his doctor. The gentlemen who sold him the annuity, however, understood all too well that they were on one side of a bargaining table and Bernie was on the other.

At the time when Jack Dunphy bought shares in Hudson Technologies, Inc., online through a discount stockbroker, it would not have dawned on him in a million years that he was involved in a negotiation. Rather, he thought, the deal was quite like going to Walmart and buying a large and expensive loaf of bread. Jack attached no significance to the fact that he paid the "ask" price, which was over 10 percent more than the "bid" price for the shares. The market maker, somewhere in Manhattan, who pocketed the spread was far more cognizant of the parameters of the transaction.

Indeed, she may well have examined it through the lens of a negotiation framework.

How much might be at stake? As you will see in Chapter 35, the amounts to be gained or lost over a lifetime are huge. While failing to negotiate may not leave a fortune on the table in every single transaction, the amount in question is sometimes more than you would imagine. Furthermore, when you gather together all the investments you make in a lifetime, many millions of dollars are at stake.

That may sound a little crazy. The first time I reread that sentence, I had to do a double take. It's true, though. This book is full of information that will teach you to negotiate cost cutting and improved returns and, amazingly, those will be worth literally millions of dollars to you over your lifetime. Thus, my plea to you is simple. Take this seriously, read carefully, and don't put off the learning and actions that are called for. Far too much money is at stake.

PART

I

WHAT THE BEST NEGOTIATORS DO

Becoming a better negotiator can improve your life. It can help you get more of what you want, attain a greater share of your goals, and better develop the ways you spend your days on this earth. Improving your negotiating skills is an effort worth making.

The hill you must climb to strengthen your negotiating is not too steep. Part I of this book can guide you. Other books will be mentioned, and I encourage you to pick up a few of those as well. Read and think; it will bring good results. Beyond reading, the best way to become better is to practice. Happily, your life affords you almost endless opportunities to try out the methods and techniques this book will suggest. I urge you to supplement the book with practical application. As you learn about something new in these pages, give it a try.

If I were somehow allowed to offer you only one thing to improve your negotiating, it would be this: If you prepare fully for each negotiation, you will do better. It is that simple. As a general rule, the more prepared you are, the better your outcomes will be. In any important negotiation, you should prepare as if it matters. Prepare as would an actor before a big performance, an athlete before an Olympic match, or a lawyer before a major trial. Preparation is something within your reach that can directly improve results. It is there for the taking. Take it. Do your homework.

You will do even better if you develop a framework around which to organize your preparation. The following pages will help you with that. Part I of this book offers you a way to think about negotiating. By breaking down any negotiation into its elements and stages, you will have a structure around which to build your preparation. Of course, as will be stressed, this preparation is not something you do only at the beginning of the negotiation process. On the contrary, you will be working on it right up until the end.

Many of my students enter our class reporting that they are frightened or intimidated when they must negotiate. As the semester progresses, most feel those fears lifting away. At the very end of our work together, some tell me that negotiating has become fun. It is something I am always delighted to hear. So that is my goal for you, dear reader. I hope that Part I of this book strengthens your confidence, increases your skill, and leads you to see negotiation as both helpful and fun.

CHAPTER 1

What Is a Good Outcome?

We start by thinking about the end. Why are we negotiating? What do we hope to achieve? What do we *really* want?

This book begins, as do all my courses, with a question. Indeed, it is my favorite question in the world: What is a good outcome? It's a playful double entendre, referring both to a specific situation, such as the negotiation you are currently working on, and to the question itself. What does the phrase *good outcome* really mean? This is the most serious question a negotiator could ask. After all, what is the point of negotiating if you end up with less than a good outcome? How, in turn, can you end up there if you cannot define it in advance? Understanding what a good outcome is generally and identifying what it will look like in any given situation are critical components of negotiating success.

My second favorite question has a familiar ring: What is an even better outcome? Once you have identified a series of potentially good results, the next step is to start thinking of ways to improve on them. There is always something just a little bit better than what you have already identified, even if it means simply adding the words "even better" to the current thinking. For example, a medical school dean I worked with defined a good outcome of his negotiation with the university president as increasing funding for research and maintaining a solid working relationship. We worked toward envisioning a better outcome by leaving the funding aim unchanged but expanding the affiliation goal to "building a stronger relationship with the president."

Professor Howard Raiffa[1] used to challenge businessmen with this claim: "Bring me any commercial agreement and I will improve it by more than my fee." He always followed by teasingly noting that his fee was quite substantial. Raiffa was reminding us that skillful examination can almost always reveal better ways to structure a deal and create more value for the dealmakers. Economists talk about getting closer to Pareto optimality, and ordinary folks mean the same thing when they say, "Don't leave money on the table."

In thinking about getting to good or even better outcomes, it is useful to identify what we do not want. In other words, what is a bad outcome? Obviously, failing to get the terms you desire, being taken advantage of, feeling you lost, or ending up with less than you started with are all examples of bad outcomes. What I call a bad outcome can also occur, though, when a negotiator wins the battle in a way that takes him away from the direction he really wants to go.

Imagine a university president who has a deep need to always be seen as the smartest guy in the room. He has won world renown for his brilliance and served at the highest levels of government. Nevertheless, he must continually demonstrate that he is the brightest man alive, and he has a habit of showing contempt for those just a little bit less sharp. In faculty meetings, he spends too much time getting into little one-on-one intellectual contests. In small negotiations over minor matters, he often uses his power and intellect to wrestle his opponent to the ground. Over time, his desire to one-up his colleagues gets a whole lot of professors pissed off. They begin to conspire against him. They start a whisper campaign to discredit him with the board of trustees, and attempt to vote no confidence in him at the university senate. After a while, he is unable to govern the university, and eventually he is forced to resign. This brilliant man brought himself down by insisting on winning tiny battles. He consistently entered into small contests in which he would triumph, but the ultimate result was a bad outcome for him.

One of the most important things a negotiator can do is figure out what she is trying to gain or achieve. As simple as it sounds, the key is to then take actions that will move things in the prescribed direction and be scrupulous about avoiding measures that point things the other way.

The road to a fuller exploration of this idea always leads back to Pyrrhus.

> The Greek King Pyrrhus of Epirus led an army that suffered irreplaceable casualties in defeating the Romans at Heraclea in 280 B.C. and Asculum in 279 B.C. during the Pyrrhic War. In both of Pyrrhus's victories, the Romans suffered greater casualties than Pyrrhus did. However, the Romans had a much larger supply of men from which to draw soldiers, so their casualties did less damage to their war effort than Pyrrhus's casualties did to his. He is often quoted as having said, "Another such victory and we shall be utterly ruined."[2]

As a young lawyer, I saw case after case that could be described as Pyrrhic victories. People in difficult disputes would turn to their attorneys for advice about how to proceed. Being lawyers, they would recommend litigation: We'll sue the bastards. By the end of that process, often years later, the loser of the lawsuit was bitter and impoverished. In many cases, so was the so-called winner. One can almost imagine the lawyer calling the client to read the verdict and congratulate him. "One more such victory," the client might mumble, "and we shall be utterly ruined."

If you look carefully, you will see examples of Pyrrhic victories all around, situations where someone can accurately say, "I won" yet must acknowledge that winning actually took him in the opposite direction from what he was trying to achieve.

In June 2013, the U.S. National Highway Traffic Safety Administration (NHTSA) recommended that a major automobile manufacturer recall one of its models because of an alleged defect that made the cars prone to fires in rear impact collisions.[3] The manufacturer decided to dig in its heels and declined to issue the recall. In light of the NHTSA's lack of power to force the issue, the manufacturer may believe that it won the battle. A negotiation professor would point out some other ways to look at the situation. What is the manufacturer really trying to do? (Sell cars.) What do they need to do it? (Customers who have confidence in their products.) How much do they spend on advertising to gain those confident customers? (Hundreds of millions.) How badly does this horrible publicity drive them in the opposite direction? (Very badly, indeed.) The ancient King Pyrrhus would surely recognize the point and label this a bad outcome for the car company.

Many aspects of the U.S. war in Vietnam might fit under this rubric. There was so much death, destruction, and loss, so much human suffering. And, of course, that faraway war caused a grave breakdown in social and governmental institutions in the United States. The situation in Asia got so bad, and the American war effort so estranged from its own goals, that eventually an unidentified military official was quoted as saying of the village of Bên Tre: "It became necessary to destroy the town to save it."[4]

Sometimes there is a world of difference between winning and getting a good outcome. Opt for the good outcome.

Identify Truly Good Outcomes and Don't Get Distracted

Of course, most negotiators believe they are working toward the best possible outcome in every case. Where do they go wrong? There are two major stumbling blocks to achieving best outcomes. The first is that a negotiator fails to identify what really good outcomes are. The second is that she gets distracted by other things—side issues that are irrelevant, or worse, to the good outcome being pursued.

Failing to think through what a really good outcome looks like may be a function of inadequate training, time pressure, or poor preparation. Taking the time to think through where this negotiation is headed and where I *really* want it to go is effort well spent. The law of unintended consequences usually works against us, but with forethought and careful attention, we can often avoid its ill effects. Indeed, if we pay close attention to all the likely results of our efforts, we may be able to create a cascade of happy side effects. Chapter 2 of this book focuses on interests that can guide you in thinking hard about your true desires and the negotiated outcomes that can actually move you toward them.

Getting distracted by small battles and side issues is a mistake that can be remedied through practice and careful planning. We live in a competitive society, and it is easy for us to get carried away by the idea of winning. Many people pride themselves on a competitive tenacity that leaves nothing on the table. If possible, they take the table as well. But research has consistently shown that many of these winners end up regretting their victories. Indeed, it happens so often that economists have termed the phenomenon "winner's curse." Competition is a natural and necessary motivator, yet it does not always bring a happy ending. What goes awry here? "People . . . pay far too much money, spend too much time, or sacrifice too many other interests for the privilege of saying they have won," Professor Shell explains.[5] The desire to win represents a dangerous shift in focus: Besting the competition becomes the primary goal, and the outcome itself becomes secondary. Paradoxically, the strategies and behaviors that follow are usually self-damaging. Avoid hurting your own efforts by keeping your eyes firmly fixed on where you really are trying to go.

What Makes for a Good Outcome?

So, what does a really good outcome look like? It tends to leave you with most of the things you want, both substantively and with regard to the people you are negotiating with.

For many years, I taught in a business school in Athens. There is a quarrel so common among Greek families that students came to me with what seemed to be different versions of the same story. It has to do with ownership of an olive tree. Imagine that two families live side by side in that fertile Mediterranean land. A small grove of olive trees grows along the border between them. Or, to make the story even more dramatic, a single olive tree sits astride the property line. Both families claim the tree, and its fruit, as their own. A dispute breaks out that grows angrier with the passing years and, eventually, across generations. Nobody wants to yield on the olive tree. Nobody wants to compromise. It is a matter of high principle. But what does each member of each family really want? Everyone seeks to live a good and peaceful life in the shade of the olive trees. The resentment, fighting, and bad feelings are all directed toward their closest neighbors. I would argue that to win the battle of the olive tree is to reap a bad outcome. A good outcome is defined in part, I believe, by friendly relations and peace among our neighbors. After all, when you grow more olives than you can use, there is great joy to be had in sharing them with those we live among.

An angry customer (one of my best students) approaches the airline, demanding compensation for delays that caused her to miss her connection. She will have to spend many hours in this hub airport waiting for the next flight. When she demands compensation, the airline's first instinct is to deny, stonewall, and stubbornly

refuse. In declining to budge, the representative cites internal policy. That policy is designed to save the airline a few bucks, which,
multiplied by the millions of delayed passengers, adds up to millions. As the student points out, though, a lifelong customer is
worth many thousands of dollars. A great deal more is spent each
year on advertising to offset terrible word of mouth. What might a
good outcome look like? Suppose the airline gives the stranded student a free membership in the First Class Club Lounge? It actually
costs them nothing (the lounge is already there), and it meets the
traveler's need for a little comfort and soothing in the middle of
the long trip. Note, too, that it may actually instill a kind of brand
loyalty in her, since to conveniently use their lounges may necessi-
tate flying their airline.

As I frequently urge when teaching business executives, companies work hard and spend millions to build their reputations.
Negotiated outcomes that leave that reputation intact are valuable
for them. Those deals that actually improve the company's reputation are truly golden. Their adversary in the consumer complaint
or lawsuit is actually their once and future customer.

Consider this wonderful, if apocryphal, tale of an encounter
between an American businessman and a Mexican fisherman.

As the story goes, an American investment banker is on vacation
in a small coastal village in Mexico and happens to notice a little
boat just pulling into the dock. In it is a man and several large fish
he had caught. Seeing the fresh fish, the American asked how long it
had taken to catch them. "Only a little while" was the reply. "Why
didn't you stay out a little longer and try to catch more fish?" the
banker asked. The fisherman replied that he didn't need more fish,
that his catch was plenty to feed his family. "But then what do you do
with the rest of your day?" the banker asked. The fisherman replied,
"I sleep late, swim, play with my children, take a siesta with my wife
each afternoon, and spend evenings in the village drinking wine and
playing my guitar with my friends." The American grew excited. "I
could help you with your fishing business," he almost shouted. He
began sketching out a plan to help the fisherman become successful
and wealthy. First, the fisherman would need to fish for a few more
hours each day to enable him to catch more fish and then use the
extra money earned from selling the fish to buy a bigger boat. With
a larger boat, he could then catch even more fish and buy more
boats, ultimately amassing a fleet of fishing boats. Eventually, the

investment banker told him, he could own his own fish-processing plant. Of course, he'd have to eventually move to Mexico City, then Los Angeles, and finally New York City to more effectively manage his growing fishing empire. "How long would all this take?" asked the fisherman. "Oh, 15 to 20 years" was the reply. "And then what would I do?" asked the fisherman. "Then you would announce an IPO, go public, and make millions. You'd be a very wealthy man!" said the banker excitedly. "And then what?" the fisherman asked. "Then you can retire, move to a small fishing village where you could sleep late, swim, play with your kids, take a siesta with your wife, and spend your evenings in the village drinking wine and playing your guitar."

My favorite example of all would probably make a good script for a Hollywood movie. Two students of mine were negotiating against each other in the most important case of the semester. Both of them knew that a high score would earn an A but a lesser performance was going to doom the negotiator to a lower semester grade. It was a zero-sum case with no opportunity to create value, so they could not both get good scores—and they knew that, too. It was a kind of fight to the death (Wharton grading edition). There was one other factor in this negotiation that needs mentioning. After deciding that they hated each other in the first week of the course, they had been slowly going through a process of falling in love. They didn't quite know it yet, but one of them felt overwhelming attraction, and the other's heart started to race whenever they were together. As these two sat down across a big oak table, one of them suddenly heard the professor's voice echoing across memory from the first days of the semester. "What is *really* a good outcome?" he bellowed. "And what might seem good on the surface but is actually a bad outcome?" Their eyes met, and their slightly trembling hands reached out to each other for the handshake that was to begin the case. What do you think would be a good outcome? How about a better outcome? What is the dangerous very bad outcome that looms in this situation?

There are many paths to the best possible outcome. Some involve getting more money or increasing wealth. Others have to do with strengthening relationships, increasing personal happiness, following ethical or religious codes or ideals, gaining renown or admiration, building or strengthening reputation, and generally becoming more of the kind of person we really want to be.

In the end, what is truly a good outcome of a negotiation for you? I suppose it is the result, in all its consequences, ripples, flapping butterfly wings, and unanticipated side effects that leads to a significant increase in your well-being. And I will define your well-being as including, but not limited to, your happiness, fulfillment, pleasure, achievement, delight, contentment, and peace.

Chapter Summary

- Understanding what a good outcome looks like *for you* is critical to negotiating success.
- Once you identify a good outcome, work to improve it.
- Avoid Pyrrhic victories that take you farther away from your ultimate goals.
- If your negotiating partner is left worse off or feels victimized, it may not be the best possible outcome for you.

Notes

1. Howard Raiffa, *Negotiation Analysis: The Science and Art of Collaborative Decision-Making* (Cambridge, MA: Belknap Press, 2007).
2. Adrienne Mayor, *The Poison King: The Life and Legend of Mithradates, Rome's Deadliest Enemy* (Princeton, NJ: Princeton University Press, 2009).
3. Bill Vlasic, "Chrysler Rejects Regulator's Request to Recall Jeeps," *New York Times,* June 5, 2013, B1.
4. Guenter Lewy, *America in Vietnam* (New York: Oxford University Press, 1980).
5. Richard Shell, *Bargaining for Advantage: Negotiation Strategies for Reasonable People* (New York: Penguin, 2006), 38.

2

Interests, Options, and Goals

Interests motivate people; they are the silent movers behind the hub-bub of positions. Your position is something you have decided on. Your interests are what caused you so to decide.
—Fisher, Ury, and Patton, *Getting to Yes*[1]

Good negotiators pay a great deal of attention to underlying interests. They seek a deal that meets their own interests very well, satisfies the interests of other parties sufficiently, and adequately addresses those of all important players who are not part of the actual negotiation. To do otherwise is a mistake. If the agreement does not meet the needs of the other negotiation parties, they will not agree to enter into the deal. If they are somehow tricked into signing a contract that does not really work for them, they will seek ways to sabotage, escape, or otherwise not comply. That is not good for anyone.

In any important deal, there are third parties who are not part of the negotiation at all, yet have the power to subvert it. Governmental regulators, interest groups, and courts come quickly to mind in a major industrial agreement. If we are talking about a deal between brother and sister, though, important parties not at the bargaining table include mom, dad, other siblings, and the babysitter. All of these nonparticipants have tremendous power to help make the negotiated deal succeed. They also have the power to sink it. As a result, any good negotiator will be sure their interests are met to at least an acceptable degree.

What Do You Really, *Really* Want?

What are we talking about? How can we usefully define "interests"?

Your interests are comprised of every preference, want, need, concern, and fear that affects how you feel about the deal on the table. The number and scope of your interests are much broader than you might realize. There are the interests that brought you to negotiate in the first place and the interests with which you justify your position. But beyond those, there are many, many others that extend past the completely relevant or fully rational. Because all of these interests are also silent movers behind what you seek, your positions are more flexible than they seem.

To a chorus of groans, I tell my students that the answer was best expressed by the British pop girl group, the Spice Girls, in their debut single "Wannabe." They cried out, "Tell me what you want, what you *really, really* want." Interests are those things a negotiator *really, really* wants. They stand in stark contrast to what she says she wants, which are best described as her positions.

The difference between positions and interests is something you grasped even as a child. When you were a kid, you sometimes took a position diametrically opposed to that of your parent. As a toddler, you may have staunchly refused to eat greens; perhaps as a teenager, you hitchhiked. In the heated negotiations that ensued, you knew on some level that, regardless of the positions you were holding firm to, your interests and your parent's interest were mostly shared. While there was much shouting over the small number that differed, the vast majority of your interests were never diametrically opposed to those who acted primarily out of love and concern for you. Even back then, you had at least a slight inkling that diligently separating positions from interests is a strong basis for building solutions.

We sense the power of interests over positions in family interactions. She wants to go to a movie, and he wants to eat pizza. After a short period of conflict, they find a way to pursue the interests of both. Perhaps they do both in one long evening, or they agree to the movie theater tonight and the pizza place for next week's date night. Maybe they stay in, watch a movie on Netflix, and have a pizza delivered. In any event, they both understand that the underlying interests of mutual affection and a pleasant time together are important and the seemingly opposed positions are not.

However, in a formal negotiating context, we often decide that because the other side's positions are opposed to ours, their interests must also be opposed. It's a natural inclination, Fisher, Ury, and Patton state: "If we have an interest in defending ourselves, they must want to attack us."[2] Assuming this of the other party is costly and limiting in any negotiation. While his desire to go to the pizza joint is not critically important, his tendency to take the most obvious position that satisfies a motivating interest is to be expected. We all do that. If we remove ourselves slightly from declared positions and instead identify the underlying interests, we have much better chances of reaching agreement.

Shared Interests

In any given negotiation, we have certain interests that we share with the other side, some interests that are different from (but compatible with) theirs, and a number of interests that conflict with their interests. Of course, the proportions vary greatly by situation; we share more interests with our children than we do with a warring country. It is never the case, though, that all our interests are in conflict with theirs. Although conflicting interests are important to consider, they need not become the focus. If we give both shared interests and different but compatible interests greater attention, conflicting interests become far more manageable.

When shared interests are met, all parties are happier with the bargain. Consider Google's innovative deal with its engineers. Google has an interest in innovation for the sake of advancing the company. Many of the engineers working there, who tend to be highly intelligent and self-motivated, have an interest in innovation for the sake of self-fulfillment. For many years, Google allowed each of them to spend up to 20 percent of their working hours on a pet project of their own choosing, unrelated to their assigned work. A number of Google's products have been the brainchildren of this program.[3] Furthermore, building on such a shared interest paves the way for alliance and good feeling between the parties. Highlighting their shared interests is an effective way to make both parties more receptive to agreement.

It is tremendous fun to watch students who are learning these negotiating concepts begin to deploy them in their lives. One student recently demonstrated his mastery of using shared interests to create value and close the deal. After graduating, Trevor continued to live in housing near campus, where the majority of tenants were students. He paid his rent on time each month and got to know his landlord personally, distinguishing himself as responsible and respectful. During a friendly chat, Trevor discovered that the landlord wanted to renovate some properties but couldn't do so while they were occupied. Trevor seized on this as a shared interest; he knew he would be living there for a while, and he, too, wanted to make some changes to his apartment. He proposed the set of renovations that he had in mind and said he'd be happy to coordinate and oversee them. The landlord was thrilled that the apartment would increase in value while occupied, agreed to cover the cost of Trevor's renovations, and also discounted Trevor's rent for "tenant improvements." Trevor, in turn, got to live in an improved apartment for less rent than he'd previously been paying.

In most situations, the parties to a negotiation have many interests that are neither shared nor opposed. These are different but compatible interests, and they present wonderful opportunities for making a deal. The chance to meet the other guy's interests without interfering with your own is an advantageous situation. You create value for them at no substantive cost to yourself. This will make the deal more valuable to them, resulting in greater leverage for you. You get paid your share of this value either by their increased commitment to the deal or by asking them to share the value in some other trade.

It's the concept that underlies bartering. What's valuable to you that the other side can provide at little cost? What's important to them and easy for you to give? The idea can be reinforced by a nostalgic trip back to our elementary school lunchrooms. Kids trade what their parents made for them in exchange for more desirable items. Tom's peanut butter and jelly is exchanged for Jane's baloney. Since Tom loves baloney and Jane is slightly more partial to PB&J, both children are enriched. My college students do this once each term with candy bars: Can you bring in one type of sweet and leave class with a different one you like better?

Should we focus more on our interests or theirs when we negotiate? The answer, of course, is both. In the classroom, I put up on the board a long list of things that a negotiator might think about. So, I ask, how many things are you thinking about in total? The least cautious students simply count up the items on the board and call out that number. The warier ones, sensing a trap, hold back reluctantly. Then I draw three columns to the right of the list. The first column is labeled "me or us." Above the second, I write "them." The third column gets labeled "other interested parties." Indeed, depending on the number of people or institutions involved, there could be a dozen or more such columns. The point is that each item gets considered from the point of view of each negotiator.

What are my interests? What are the interests of Jane, who is sitting across the table from me? What about those of Jane's boss? Is it wise to assume they are all the same? (Hint: no!) And who else is involved or affected by the outcome of this negotiation?

Dig Deep to Explore Underlying Interests

I challenge my students by telling them they are in a big negotiation with me. What do you want? I ask them. First come the obvious answers: to learn, wisdom, insight, a good grade. What else? Eventually, we are able to dig deeper. Some of my students seek a helping hand, a caring teacher, and someone who will listen. A few hope I can offer assistance someday in the future. A number want a professor who will fight off sexist assumptions, will acknowledge the cultural norms of their upbringing, or won't call on them if they look unprepared. Many seek the professorial kindness of not embarrassing them in front of their peers. A lot of my students hope to be entertained. A few even admit to anticipating that I will be funny. Almost all hope not to be bored.

Like most negotiators you will encounter, my students have a list of goals and underlying interests that is fuller and deeper than might be imagined at first glance. They are multifaceted and complete human beings, and so they hold a complex mix of interests. Learning a good deal about the interests of the person sitting across the table is one of the most important jobs a negotiator has.

There are a number of interests that almost everyone shares. Some of these are material—most people seek the path that will bring them greater comfort and financial security. Beyond that, though, is a list of things that almost everyone wants. On that list are respect, affection, dignity, and saving face. People want to be seen in a positive light. Almost everyone wants to be treated fairly. Nobody wants to be taken advantage of or look like a fool. This list is tremendously useful to a negotiator because the best way to get what we want is to give our partners what they want in exchange.

Somehow, life conspires to make almost all of us look in the mirror every morning. Folks have very different needs regarding whom they see staring back at them. We all share, though, an aching need to see in that mirror the kind of person we believe we are. Nothing is more crushing than to gaze into that reflecting glass and realize you are looking at someone who does not meet the image or standards you have set for yourself. This is important to a negotiator; it can be used to help or deeply hurt the partner on the other side of the table. My own thought is that the best negotiators offer the gift of creating a path for their partner to live up to all they hope to see in their reflection tomorrow morning. In doing them that kindness, they open the door for mutual exchange of consideration and helpfulness and a joint search for ways to get everyone what they need.

By the same token, good negotiators do not back their partners into corners. Like a snake who cannot escape, an adversary who has no good choice but to lash out will do so ferociously. Do yourself, and your partner, the good deed of not putting her in that situation. Think hard about how the choice looks from the other's point of view. Search continuously for the doors she can easily walk through, and build a path right up to them.

When people think of successful negotiation techniques, they often draw on the term *win-win*. Indeed, that is often used as shorthand for the Harvard negotiation method we are exploring. As with many shorthand expressions, though, it is worth some further thought.

Don't Settle for Win-Win

A criticism of using the term *win-win* is that it may cause a negotiator to aim too low. After all, every rational deal that is consummated is really a win-win deal; both parties leave better off than they were before. As a result, this mentality may cause us to stop trying for better deals as soon as some plausible solution that improves everyone's position comes into view. G. Richard Shell addresses this in the second chapter of his book, *Bargaining for*

Advantage. He advises us to choose optimistic, justifiable objectives. He wants us to set and reach for high goals.[4] This will get us past the trap that win-win might set for us: settling for the lowest outcome that meets the requirements of making everyone a little bit better off.

By setting a goal above what you expect to have happen, you are creating a way to improve your own outcome. Be careful, though, not to choose goals that have no basis in reality; they are likely to leave you feeling disappointed when they do not come to fruition. Realistically high goals set you up for greater success; pie-in-the-sky goals lead you to disillusionment and failure.

Goals provide direction, a path of sorts, to guide your negotiations. Shell explains that expectations form a lower boundary and goals form an upper boundary in negotiations—higher goals are something to shoot for.[5] Many negotiators breathe a sigh of relief when they get what they expected. Great negotiators know, however, that expectations are the lowest acceptable result and that you should raise the bar by pushing to achieve a well-thought-out goal.

No matter what the endeavor, set high but realistic goals for yourself. Set goals that are too low, and you will achieve only a minimally acceptable outcome; set goals well beyond the realm of possibility, and you will give up even before you begin. But set higher goals, just outside your comfort zone, and you will get more from each negotiation.

Options

How many different options have the parties for how they might structure this deal? What is the number of different combinations and rearrangements and trade-offs? Good negotiators know that there are hundreds, if not thousands, of possibilities for just about every agreement they prepare to make. The job becomes one of identifying the very best option among all those possibilities.

How might we define the very best option? At first, we might be tempted to choose that agreement in which I get the most. As we learned in Chapter 1, a negotiation professor would express it as the deal that best meets my interests. The problem, of course, is that there is someone on the other side of the table who also seeks to get more. It turns out the very best option is going to be the arrangement that best fulfills the interests of all the parties involved.

Skilled negotiators are in a search for that series of exchanges, trade-offs, and mutual promises that maximize the attainment of interests. When nobody's situation could be improved except by making somebody worse off, economists say that the deal is Pareto optimal. It is the same thing my daughter meant when she squealed delightedly after her birthday party: "Everyone was happy with her stuffed animal. Nobody could have been happier unless she took another girl's animal—but that would have made her cry." It is that arrangement that best meets the overall needs and interests of everyone involved.

Of course, when negotiating, we try to obtain the best advantage for ourselves. We want to get all of our interests met and let the chips fall where they may concerning the goals, needs, and aspirations of our partners and adversaries. Or at least that's the first thought. After we study negotiation for a while, though, it becomes apparent that getting more for us and little or nothing for the others is not actually a very good outcome for us.

Structure the Deal to Meet Their Needs, Too

What happens when we take the other guy to the cleaners? Or, as the Greeks would say in translation, when we "take their underwear?" In most instances, they are mad at us. They tell their friends and relations that we are not very good to deal with. They are resentful and start to avoid us. They do business with our competitors and take a certain delight in our failures. Furthermore, they try to get out of the deal we made with them. Perhaps they sue us. If not, though, they drag their feet and are slow and surly about every required step of the process in fulfilling their promises to us. The whole thing becomes unpleasant, difficult, and costly. Does this sound like a good deal for us?

This is one of the magical things to emerge from a careful study of negotiation practice and techniques. It turns out that getting the better of them is not really very good for us. Rather, getting a great deal for ourselves while also hammering out a pretty darned good deal for them is the path that leads to our greatest success. What is a better outcome than getting everything I want? Getting everything I want, and having all the other people involved feel satisfied, happy with the arrangement, and maybe even a little bit grateful to me.

How do good negotiators go about the process of exploring all the options and deciding together to choose the very best one? Fisher, Ury, and Patton suggest that we "separate inventing from deciding."[6] In their book, they lay out a process for brainstorming ideas and possibilities. Indeed, they challenge negotiators to consider setting up such a procedure with the other parties. In any event, though, negotiators need some method for uncovering as many possible ways to solve the puzzle as they can.

Ultimately, the question to be resolved is which of the many possible structures for this deal best meets the underlying interests of the folks involved. Remember that a deal that satisfies everyone serves you best. As a result, it is a mistake to take the attitude that solving their problem is their problem. (See Chapter 4.) Rather, a wise negotiator digs right in and helps design an agreement that meets their interests and addresses their constraints.

Roger Fisher delighted in telling a story from his youth that made this point while amusing his audience. As a young man, he was an airman who served during World War II. He was part of a squad testing engines on bomber aircraft. As Fisher related the tale, the crew usually became bored flying over Canada in an elderly B-29 with three old trusted engines turning and a brand-new fourth engine being run for the first time.

One day the crusty old test pilot, satisfied that engine number 4 was hale and hearty, decided to shut down and feather engines number 1, 2, and 3. The relative quiet in the northern sky was amazing to the squad, and they expressed astonishment and delight. Egged on by that reaction, the pilot shut down and feathered number 4. With no engine running at all, the only sound was of the wind whishing by. The giant bomber was now essentially a huge, fat, inefficient glider. The eerie silence was miraculous. Now the pilot, having gotten his kicks and achieved the reaction he wanted, reached down to restart the engines. Only at that point did he realize that a B-29 requires an external power source to start an engine. Such a power source was normally available from another running engine. Now, however, with all the engines off, nothing on the wings could offer any help.

Everyone among the crew became frantic. The pilot himself tried furiously, although in vain, to push against the starter. Other crewmen were strapping on parachutes. The plane was losing altitude at about 20 feet per second, a rate that would cause a terrible rendezvous with the ground in a matter of minutes. Every face was grim, and every palm sweaty.

Suddenly the copilot, sitting shoulder to shoulder and elbow to elbow with the pilot, began to laugh. What began as a snicker grew louder and turned into a bellow. Angrily and in disbelief, the pilot turned to him. "What are you laughing about?" he asked. The copilot replied, "Boy, oh boy, have *you* got a big problem!"

Fisher's point was that when partners are involved, the trouble of one is actually the problem of all. To the extent that we are all in it together, one person's failure has bad consequences for others. To get good outcomes for yourself, help your partners solve their problems.

A critically important part of addressing everyone's interests and concerns is through a process of creating more value. Negotiators who tend to see the process as dividing a fixed pie have a very hard time with this. Rather, it is essential to stop thinking of negotiating as a zero-sum game and become highly proficient at making the pie bigger before we start to split it up.

Work with Them to Create More Value

Which options offer the most opportunity for creating mutual gain? In essence, what can I trade to you that you value more dearly, and what can I receive from you that holds greater worth to me? Inventing options is the process of discovering where these trades exist. Remember back to the grade school lunchroom; your grilled cheese for my turkey sandwich, your cookie for my chips, and both of us happier.

The art of creating such value is truly a skill that can be developed and strengthened with practice. Begin to look around, seek out everyday examples, and you'll find it becomes more intuitive over time. The opportunities really are all around us. Just ask the two women in the kitchen who were squabbling over the last egg in the refrigerator. Each was working on a recipe, and each declared the absolute necessity of using that sole egg. Old friends that they were, a bargaining session broker out. Annie offered Betty homemade cookies, hand delivered, for a week. Betty shot back with four days of complete dinners. Only as they approached exchanging a firstborn child for that coveted egg did Annie think to ask why Betty needed it. "For the yolk," Betty replied. Annie began to laugh. "I need only the egg white," she giggled.

Practice makes perfect in many things, including finding ways to create more value. You should be continuously on the lookout for situations that allow for the dovetailing of interests. As a practice tip, it is worth noting that win-win is very often win-win-lose. A great many of the wonderful ways to create mutual gain involve cutting somebody else out of the deal and then dividing the spoils that they would have claimed. We do not feel bad about this because the person or entity left out is usually nameless, faceless, and of no concern to us. Furthermore, they may never even know about the deal or the role they might have played in it. For example, when I persuaded the house seller to write my mortgage in exchange for a higher sales price, some undetermined bank was cut out of the deal. A dairy cooperative that allows farmers to sell their milk for higher prices eliminates some unnamed middleman. A family utilizing grandparents to babysit their beloved grandchildren is inadvertently taking employment from some enterprising teenager who will not get a child care job.

Creating more value can sometimes seem a little abstract. How a person measures worth is as unique as the individual herself. It can involve not just economic value but sentiment, ideals, ethics, hopes, and dreams. On the other hand, sometimes the process can be measured in dollars and cents. Consider the example of a local theater and the rising star lured to perform on its stage. Each had a tremendous interest in the success of the one-time-only performance. Each would be willing to pay dearly to ensure a packed house. When the time came to negotiate over the star's fee, the theater owner gently inquired as to whether perhaps a lower fee paid to the star could be supplemented by more money spent on advertising. Suddenly, from stage right emerged an itinerant professor. "Watch this," he said. "For every dollar effectively spent on advertising, you get two dollars of value." He took a dollar out of his pocket and held it out. "If we spend this on your marketing campaign, how much value do you get?" He turned to the theater owner. "One dollar's worth," said the owner. Then he turned to the young star, who also replied, "One dollar's worth of value." The professor smiled and explained, "You have spent this single dollar, and yet you have derived two dollars of value from it. Magic!"

Exploring, talking, and finding out are critical to this process. Good negotiators ask why a hundred different times in as many ways. Listening, gathering information, and learning are prized skills. Research has shown that most skilled negotiators ask questions and test for understanding more frequently than do merely adequate bargainers. Learning the nuances of the other side's goals, desires, needs, and impediments is the way to begin creating greater value. "Tell me what you want—what you *really, really* want."

The more inquiring and perceptive you are, the more possibilities you have to offer your negotiating partner. A factory, for instance, needs to get rid of excess steam; located next door is an office building using a coal furnace to warm the building. A health food company is looking for a steady supply of wheat germ to sell; a maker of breakfast cereal removes wheat germ before processing wheat into cereal flakes. A state transportation department is getting rid of old, useless railroad cars; that same state's fish and game department is planning to buy trash that can be sunk offshore to create artificial reefs.

As you learn more about the other side and their interests, you can explore possible trades with them. A good way to work through this process is by the using if-then statements. For example, if your factory provided steam to the neighboring office building for heat, would the landlord be willing to pay a small fee for it, based on the savings from not having to purchase more coal? Or, as the health food CEO, could you offer to cart away the wheat germ at no cost to the cereal manufacturer?

In most cases, those options that create the most value will be the very best ones for meeting the underlying interests of the parties. Once the maximum amount of value has been created, when no piece of the pie remains unclaimed on the table, then and only then should negotiators begin to worry about forging the final terms of an agreement. The task that Lax and Sebenius call "the negotiators dilemma: creating and claiming value"[7] is made dramatically easier when the parties have worked together to bake a big, full, and rich pie before they begin to worry about dividing up the slices.

Chapter Summary

- Work to create deals that meet your own interests very well and the other side's at least sufficiently.

- Do not ignore third parties to the negotiation; take their interests into account as well.
- The interests that lie below each party's stated positions can be the key to creating deals that meet everyone's real needs.
- Most negotiation situations include some interests in common, some that are different but compatible, and others that are in conflict. Explore shared interests and work to dovetail compatible interests.
- Options are the many ways that a deal could be structured.
- Think of a negotiation not as a fixed amount of value to be divided, but as a pie that can be enlarged before it is cut. The creation of more value usually makes agreement easier.

Notes

1. Roger Fisher, William Ury, and Bruce Patton, *Getting to Yes: Negotiating Agreement Without Giving In*, 3rd ed. (New York: Penguin Group, 2011), 43.
2. Ibid., 44.
3. Bharat Mediratta and Julie Bick, "The Google Way: Give Engineers Room," *New York Times,* October 21, 2007.
4. G. Richard Shell, *Bargaining for Advantage: Negotiation Strategies for Reasonable People* (New York: Penguin Books, 2006), 34.
5. Ibid., 29.
6. Fisher, Ury, and Patton, *Getting to Yes*, 62.
7. David Lax and James Sebenius, *The Manager as Negotiator: Bargaining for Cooperation and Competitive Gain* (New York: Free Press, 1986), 29.

CHAPTER 3

Fairness

Nobody likes to be treated unfairly. Not you and not those you negotiate with. Nobody enjoys realizing that they got a less than fair deal, either. Both being treated in a legitimate manner and getting a deal that is basically just are important to everyone.

Good negotiators refuse to be part of a process, or outcome, that is anything less than fair. You should do the same. Just as a skilled negotiator will never agree to a deal that does not do a good job of meeting her interests or that is not better than her best alternative, so, too, she should decline one that is perceptibly unfair.

What Is "Fair"?

Clearly, we are headed straight toward the problem of defining "fairness." What does it mean, and how are we going to measure it? Leading negotiation professors urge us to look to authoritative standards and norms to help delineate fairness. What Fisher, Ury, and Patton call "objective criteria"[1] can be thought of as outside measures of fairness that can be used to anchor a negotiation in principles rather than as a test of will.

These outside yardsticks for measuring fairness will help us in two ways. First, they guide us in forming the upper and lower boundaries of a fair solution or deal. That leaves us with a range of potentially fair outcomes. Once these are established, we can safely bargain, knowing that any agreement inside that range can be justified as fair. By the same token, we will commit ourselves to refusing a deal that falls outside that range. The authoritative standards have created a kind of safety net for us to avoid ending up with a deal that does not measure up as legitimate.

Second, we also use such standards and norms as a means of persuading our partners as to the general equity of the proposals we are making. Can we overcome their doubts by pointing to the norms of their profession, the standards of their beliefs, or the principles of their faith? Can we show them that what we are proposing is something they would readily agree to if not involved in a negotiation? Objective criteria can help demonstrate that a proposal meets their need as well as ours to be treated fairly.

A recent graduate of the University of Pennsylvania Law School was offered a position with the largest law firm in Philadelphia. When he learned of the starting salary they were offering, though, he became discouraged. He knew for a fact that many of his Wharton MBA friends would be starting at higher amounts. His professor encouraged him to talk with the hiring partner at the law firm. The partner was surprised that he was unhappy. "We pay every starting associate that same salary," he said. "You are getting what everybody gets." "Furthermore," he went on, "we raised the starting salary last year. It is fair to say that nobody has ever started at this firm at an amount higher than what you will be receiving." The new graduate had to agree that was a pretty convincing standard. And the implied standard, that a new lawyer should get as much as an MBA, was probably less appropriate than he had originally thought.

In addition to using norms and standards to persuade the other side about fairness, a good negotiator should remain open to be persuaded in like manner. Is it possible that they are being much fairer than I understood them to be? What criteria are they basing their proposals on? How does the situation look from their point of view? Professor Fisher always used to ask his negotiating partners, "Where did that figure come from?" He was challenging them to justify their offers and show how they were grounded in fairness.

The admonition to never accept a deal that is not fair, no matter how attractive, can occasionally be gut-wrenching. What if a proposal is clearly not legitimate yet extremely attractive? Still, the wisest negotiator I know likes to set the boundaries early in the process. "I will accept any offer that you can show me is fair," he says, "but I will not accept any offer—regardless of value—until you show me why it is fair." He is insisting from the outset that fairness will be a requirement that must be met.

What specific authoritative standards or norms can we use to show fairness? Fisher, Ury, and Patton give us a wonderful list to start us thinking:[2]

Market value	What a court would decide
Precedent	Moral standards
Scientific judgment	Equal treatment
Professional standards	Tradition
Efficiency	Reciprocity
Costs	Etc.

Move beyond Market Value to Measure Fairness

Because I spend a lot of time at Wharton, it is typical to see market value used a great deal in discussions of standards. Certainly it is a strong and legitimate standard. It is valuable, though, to broaden our practice by becoming skilled at using other criteria.

To be playful, when we study this topic, I tell my students that I intend to shoot and kill anyone who does not turn in their homework on time. Why is that not a legitimate punishment? The list of reasons includes moral standards, precedent, court decisions, equal treatment, and professional standards. When I ask what might be an appropriate sanction for late homework, the replies include (1) how other professors handle it, (2) fairness to those students who did turn it in on time, (3) what I have done about this in past years, and (4) an attempt to correlate the infraction with the harm it does. Once that whole list is on the table, students begin to gravitate toward the standards that result in the lowest penalties to advance their interests.

Fisher, Ury, and Patton famously urge that negotiators should "separate the people from the problem."[3] What is the problem they are referring to? After years of study, I have concluded that in an ideal negotiation, all parties work together, as one team, toward resolution. The problem they are resolving, in the end, is the answer to this question: What is the *fairest* solution we can find to the issue we are negotiating about?

Chapter Summary

- Good negotiators insist on both a fair process and a fair outcome.

- In using objective criteria to determine what is fair, it helps to offer criteria that will be credible to the other side.
- Justify your proposals by showing how they are grounded in legitimate standards. Ask your negotiating partners to do the same.
- Work to make the negotiation process an exercise in joint problem solving. The problem to solve: What is the fairest solution?

Notes

1. Roger Fisher, William Ury, and Bruce Patton, *Getting to Yes: Negotiating Agreement Without Giving In*, 3rd ed. (New York: Penguin Group, 2011), 82.
2. Ibid., 86.
3. Ibid., 19.

4

Communication to Build the Kind of Relationship You Want

Top negotiators almost always want to create a good relationship. That term is generic, though, and needs to be carefully fitted to the situation. You probably don't want a loving relationship with your accountant or a businesslike relationship with your daughter. So defining the scope and type of relationship with each person in each negotiation is an important first step.

It helps quite a bit to know a great deal about the people you are negotiating with. You can start by trying to identify each one's negotiating style, as explained in the first chapter of G. Richard Shell's *Bargaining for Advantage.*[1] From there, it is well worth discovering whether those you are working with are takers, givers, or matchers, as those three types are explained by Adam Grant in his book *Give and Take.*[2] Beyond that, though, it is good to learn about their personal characteristics. Some people are kind, and others are abusive; some are talkative, and others are taciturn; some are adventurous, and others like to follow a well-worn path. Furthermore, most people are at least partly defined by their past and their experiences. Who is this person? Where has she been? What influences have deeply affected her? What is she proud of? What are her likes and dislikes? You get the idea. The more you can know about the other people, the better off you are likely to be. As will be discussed later in greater depth, attempting to learn all you can about the other people in a negotiation is an effort well worth making.

Set Relationship Goals

Among the reasons you are gathering all this information about the other people involved is to guide you in thinking about your relationship goals. Early on, you set a general idea for the kind of relationship you are trying to fashion. As you work together, though, new data may allow you to refine or amend these targets. Think about what the relationship is like right now, what it might be like as the negotiation progresses, what you need this relationship to be once this negotiation is concluded, and what long-term potential this relationship might hold if you can move it in a desirable direction.

The first time Joe Biden worked with Barack Obama on a bill as colleagues in the Senate, it is surely true that he had no idea that this man would be president, would chose Biden as his vice president, and would embrace him as a key member of his presidential inner circle. Relationships are full of potential, and the best negotiators are always looking ahead at the same time they are working hard on the current deal. Keep an open mind about where the new relationship might go once the negotiation is concluded.

Furthermore, a positive relationship is likely to create a virtuous cycle of good feelings between and about the people involved. Research shows us consistently that goodwill fosters goodwill, even in the short term. You will get more of what you want by working alongside the other party to find a solution than by working against him to wrench one out. And, of course, the opposite is also true. A poor relationship, or one filled with bad feelings, is likely to hamper efforts or, at the very least, will not produce the good feelings that sometimes make the difference between agreement and failure. People are simply willing to go a little bit further for those they feel good about.

Communicating successfully is critically important for more than one reason. It is necessary to conduct the current negotiation on its merits. It is also the most important tool you have for maintaining and building the negotiating relationship you want. Furthermore, as we will see later, it is the cornerstone for defining the negotiation process you wish to establish.

Choose Communication Tools Carefully

How do we communicate? There are a great many decisions to make. We tend to make our communication choices subconsciously when negotiating; a path to improved practice is to give them great thought and make our choices purposefully. Which communication methods and preferences are going to make a good outcome more likely?

I am always amazed when I surreptitiously observe students from other countries negotiate the cases we use for practice at Wharton. Which language will they choose to speak in? Particularly fascinating is the decision to use English in situations where the two negotiators share a different first language. For example, why wouldn't two Korean students conduct the case in Korean? Is it a conscious choice or just habit that flows from having spoken English in class for weeks? Did they consider which language choice would serve them best? Would working in Korean advantage one more than the other? Or is it merely so that I, their instructor, can understand?

By analogy, a craftsman should use the best tool for the job at hand. The proper wrench or saw or plane will surely result in a better work outcome—even if it means a trip out to the truck to get the correct device.

Should you negotiate face-to-face or use a more convenient or anonymous method? While there is no single correct one-size-fits-all answer, we may have some default preferences. The telephone offers great convenience at the cost of losing face-to-face cues and nonverbal messaging. In recent years, I've noticed more and more negotiation being done by e-mail. This takes away the advantages of voice as well as face-to-face. On occasion, I am now engaged in bargaining with companies where I suspect that no human being is involved—that the partner on the other end is a computer or some sort of bot. Such situations do not make me too happy. The question that serves as a starting point for what medium to use is an old one. What are you trying to accomplish? Then you must examine which communication methods are most likely to assist you in that attempt.

If part of your plan is to win over the other person with your warmth and charm, do not try to do it over e-mail. While in-person negotiation techniques have much to offer, it can be very inefficient when compared with the ease and time savings of telephony or Internet-based communication. So, as with many other things in life, we must make a cost-benefit analysis. If the stakes are small or the results unimportant, we may choose ease instead of opting for the most effective method. Of course, it warrants some examination of just how much less effective the easy way is. Don't give up too much advantage just because you feel lazy. On the other hand, where the stakes are important or we deeply value our connection to the people involved, it may be worth the effort to choose the absolutely best communication medium for getting the job done right.

Work to Create the Atmosphere You Want

What kind of tone and atmosphere do you want to establish in any given negotiation? There are a hundred choices, but each one will subtly affect what happens between the parties. For example, bargaining with neighbors over property borders could call for a warm tone and being conducted over chocolate chip cookies. The sorority meeting to address everyone's negligent failure to do their chores might benefit from a more sober tone, and a decision to refrain from serving drinks might help. Official diplomatic negotiations are often held in highly stylized ways to set a serious and formal tone. A meeting of the Teamsters Union bargaining team with railroad management is often stylized as well and for the same reason: to set a particular tone. But that tone is quite different from the one at the United Nations. The recruiters coming to campus in an attempt to recruit our best students to their multinational companies set one kind of tone. My wife and I set a very different one when interviewing potential babysitters. The important message here is that there is great value in considering what tone a negotiator wishes to establish and then taking a series of ongoing actions to make it happen. The mistake a negotiator must avoid is to simply figure that the tone will somehow take care of itself. Be purposeful.

We send all kinds of messages through our speech and written words. Most of us realize, though, that we also send a plethora of messages through nonverbal means. Our bodies speak, our actions speak, and even our absences tell a story. Eyes and haircuts and torsos and feet and clothing all send cues to those around us. So do furniture and automobiles and gift-wrapping and jars of jellybeans. Khrushchev even took off his shoe and pounded it against the desk.[3] Pay attention and send messages consistent with what you want your partners to receive. Be very careful that your nonverbal messages do not contradict the verbal ones you have planned so carefully.

Whatever messages we want them to get, it is our job to make sure that they *get* them: that they receive the message and they understand it in full. Lots of effort should be put into making sure that the sending and receiving you intended actually succeed.

Some funny or outrageous examples may help make this point. Beach-going consumers can be better messaged by a sign pulled behind an airplane than through paper flyers. A scorned wife lets her husband know that she will shame him for his infidelities on a center city billboard. A number of Ivy League college hopefuls have sent their applications by balloon or carrier pigeon. This may be a great strategy if the message conveyed consistently through the application is "I'm creative." On the other hand, if the applicant's strong point is rigorous academic analysis, the balloon thing may fall flat. Furthermore, if it is the third balloon application this week, it may not strike the admissions committee as all that creative. Even in more everyday situations, good negotiators plan their communication with message reception in mind.

Focus on What You Want to Tell Them—and How

An important threshold question in most negotiations revolves around how much openness or withholding there will be. As discussed elsewhere, there are tremendous strategic considerations to how much information you will share and how much should be carefully guarded. As a communication matter, though, careful consideration should be given to how the decisions in this area will be implemented. How will you let them know what you want them to know? In what way will you make sure that they are sharing important information in return? No negotiator wants to be in the position of telling everything and learning nothing. How to ensure information give-and-take is essential. Careful planning around saying what you want to say, not releasing that which you intend to keep secret, and learning all you can from the other side is worth a great deal of effort.

What is it that we want to communicate to those we are negotiating with? Probably we want them to understand a great deal of substance: prices, terms, bottom lines, parameters, specifications, and on and on. Also, we want them to appreciate our needs, interests, goals, and limitations. Beyond those things, though, a skilled negotiator will wish to get across a great deal more. As we study the subject of negotiation, we become versed in a great many *ways* that we wish to negotiate. Techniques, cautions, methods, and areas of concern are all things that we want not only to execute but also to communicate to our partners.

Here are some examples. Do we want to be soft on the people and hard on the problem?[4] We should let them know about that intention. Will we separate inventing from deciding?[5] We need them to join us in that effort. Will we refuse to bargain based on any metrics other than fairness? If so, we want them to know it. Is it our plan to meet relationship problems with relationship tools but solve substantive disagreements only with substantive tools, as G. Richard Shell urges?[6] Surely we want them to be fully informed of that intention. And perhaps most important, are we open to reason? Can they persuade us? If so, what kinds of arguments will we be receptive to and which we will reject outright? These are things we need them to know fully and clearly.

Use Active Listening Techniques

Your communication, and therefore your results, will be better if you continuously strive for improvement. You should be constantly monitoring your communication efforts for purpose and effectiveness. Are they hearing all you want them to hear? Do they understand? As fully as might be possible? What might you do to improve the interaction? The very best negotiators use the techniques of active listening more than do average bargainers. In particular, they ask far more questions and test for understanding by summing up and getting confirmation. You will frequently hear such an expert say something like "What I understand you to be saying is . . ." and then asking you, "Do I have that right?" Such active listening techniques can go a long way toward minimizing misunderstandings and reinforcing effective communication.

Communication failures can cost us dearly even in situations where all our intentions were good. Consider O. Henry's well-loved story "The Gift of the Magi." A poor young couple approach Christmas, each resolved to buy the other a meaningful gift. Each is determined that the special gift will be a surprise. Della sells the only thing of value she has, her long, beautiful hair, to pay for a platinum fob chain for Jim's prized possession, his pocket watch. At the same time, though, Jim sells his watch to afford jeweled combs for Della's hair. The symmetry of their bad outcome is almost perfect.

I have come to the conclusion, after several decades of study, that misunderstanding and miscommunication are actually the biggest places where negotiations go wrong. Confusion, misinterpretation, mistrust, language problems, errors, mix-ups, double meanings, and failure to fully understand one another are where things go awry the most. Thus, they form the area with the greatest potential for improving negotiation outcomes. If we can communicate more effectively, we can get better outcomes. And, of course, the good feelings that flow from such better outcomes can facilitate even better communication in the future.

Good Negotiating Process

In addition to communicating effectively, negotiators are interacting with each other in an ongoing and continuously changing process. The means and methods by which we interact in the negotiation invariably play a tremendous role in what ends up occurring and what outcome results. As a mindful and careful negotiator, you want to plan the *process* with a sharp eye on what kinds of interactions are going to lead to the best results for you.

There is a tremendous amount going on between the parties to a negotiation every time they interact. This is amplified when they are meeting together. A very incomplete list of issues includes the method of conversation, choice of language, ways of presenting and receiving data, positioning in the room, nonverbal messaging, gender dynamics, eye contact, and seating arrangements. In a one-on-one negotiation, the number of such issues is huge. As we begin to add the complexity of other parties, the number of things to pay attention to can become staggering.

Be Aware of the Power Dynamics—and Consider Changing Them

Consider the extremely important matter of personal power dynamics. In most human interactions, one person is given or takes more of the authority and control over the interaction. Sometimes this is a natural consequence of people's roles, such as a parent's superiority to a child. In some cases, this is the result of social structures: When you are introduced to the president or the queen, you automatically act deferentially. There are many situations, though, where the question of power gets resolved by one party simply being aggressive and seizing control.

To teach these ideas to my students, I use the classroom dynamic itself as a demonstration model. Where does the power reside in a university classroom and why? As professor, I usually possess overwhelming power and authority in the room. Let's think about how this comes to be. My students almost invariably defer to me. I have great power over them because I give them grades. But they also give me authority because the university has told them that they should. They think me knowledgeable without really checking that out because the entire university system sends them consistent messages that this is so. They tend to believe I am always right, in part because they are spending an astronomical amount of money to learn from me. Were I to be wrong, or full of bull, it would create massive cognitive dissonance and suggest that they have made a terrible mistake in their choice of spending, time and effort applied, school, and general direction in life. Unless I do something terrible, they will continue to grant me extraordinary authority, respect, and deference.

Consider, too, the physical setup in the classroom. I stand at the front of the class, and they all sit (metaphorically) at my feet. I control the information flows in the room: blackboards, screens, computers, and handouts. I set the agenda of what will be discussed, and I call on them to speak. On the other hand, I talk when I wish and cut them off as I deem necessary. I roam the room as I teach; directing their attention where I think it will best enhance learning. I make all the rules. I can even dismiss someone from the room, and, I am sure, they will leave without protest. In the classroom, the professor is pretty much a king.

I am not criticizing the power structure of the classroom. Not only do I enjoy its fruits, but, more seriously, I recognize it as being constituted and implemented to advance a worthwhile cause. Indeed, we could imagine a university president defending all that goes on at her college by pointing out the wonderful good outcomes of successfully educating younger people. And I would agree. I teach about these structures not to urge students to rebel against them but to notice and be fully aware of them. Where they lead to best outcomes, they can be observed and then followed. On the other hand, the world is also full of power dynamics put in place to serve less admirable goals or simply to advance one person's or organization's agenda. In such circumstances, passive acceptance is a mistake. Good negotiators are well advised to ask whether the power structures and processes in current use are the best ones to advance our goal of reaching a best possible outcome.

Where the process in place is neither a necessary consequence of larger roles and relationships (such as deferring to a government official) nor a good one for advancing a negotiator's interests, you should not accept it. In plain English, as a good negotiator, you should try to change it to your own advantage.

- Who controls the conversation?
- Is one person treated deferentially or as having authority?
- Where do the discussions take place?
- Are you going to play dirty tricks (example: one chair high above the other), and how are you going to react to such tricks if used against you?
- What interpersonal atmosphere do you want to create (friendly, businesslike, mildly intimate, standoffish, cautious, gung ho)?
- Should food or recreation play a role (restaurant, golf)? If it does, who gets advantage from that?
- Who controls the data presentation (controlling the blackboard)?

Plan a Process That Will Lead to Good Outcomes

Clearly, part of good negotiation practice is considering in depth the kind of process that is going to lead to a good outcome. Thereafter, you should implement a plan and take a series of actions to maximize the possibility of establishing that process.

You can be guided in thinking about process issues by the old journalists' guideline of who, what, when, where, why, and how. To these I would add tone, pace, and atmosphere.

In one of the books that followed from the initial success at the Harvard Negotiation Project, *Getting Together*, Fisher and Brown instruct the reader on how to create a relationship that can deal well with differences.[7] They suggest that a negotiator learn how the other side sees things. Thereafter, they suggest that the parties negotiate side-by-side, the idea being that a process in which the parties work together, as teammates, to solve the problem of finding an outcome good for all involved is a superior process. Consider how different it might feel from the more traditional procedure of sitting across the table from each other as adversaries.

Fisher and Brown go on to recommend that negotiators always consult before deciding[8]—and listen carefully to the response that such consultation brings. Letting the other side know what you are going to do, before you do it, is a wise practice. Don't present them with an unpleasant surprise that it is too late to undo. Rather, be up front about your alternatives and what they should expect. Then pay close attention as they respond. You are simultaneously building the relationship while working through the specific negotiation problem. Paying close attention to what—and how—they are communicating with you is important to both.

In their recommendation that a negotiator be "wholly trustworthy but not wholly trusting,"[9] Fisher and Brown are coming down strongly on the side of creating a process that is honest and forthright. Some negotiators believe that a certain amount of puffery, bluffing, and misleading is acceptable as long as all bargainers are aware of and playing by the same rules. Although such a process is common and can work, it may be inferior to establishing right up front the expectation of reliability and honest communication. Of course, as Fisher and Brown remind us, the mere fact that we have insisted on forthrightness, and unwaveringly offered it, does not mean we should entirely trust the other parties. We do not want to fall victim to their failure to follow through on an agreed-upon process. Neither, though, do we want them to find us less than completely reliable.

As with other aspects of negotiation, the most important thing with regard to process is to be purposeful. Plan for it, notice it, and try to influence it in the direction that will best serve you. Consider being open and forthright in discussing with your partners the kind of process you seek. Do not, however, ignore it or assume that it will somehow work out fine without your serious efforts to steer it in the best direction.

Chapter Summary

- Think about the type and scope of relationship you want to have with your negotiation partner during and after this negotiation.
- A positive relationship can create good feelings. An adversarial relationship risks tension. As you build an appropriate relationship, consider its effect on reaching good agreements.
- Communication is the most important tool you have to build the kind of relationship you want. Choose the communication

method most advantageous for your discussions, with an eye toward the kind of relationship you are seeking to fashion.

- Use active listening techniques to reduce misunderstanding. Miscommunication is a common reason negotiations break down. Improving communication provides an opportunity to strengthen negotiation outcomes.
- Pay attention to power dynamics. Question whether the current understandings and processes are likely to lead to best possible outcomes. If not, try to change the situation.
- Consult before deciding by letting your negotiation partner know about your plans and alternatives.
- Don't trust them imprudently, but act in such a way that they will never be disappointed by having trusted you.

Notes

1. G. Richard Shell, *Bargaining for Advantage: Negotiation Strategies for Reasonable People*, 2nd ed. (New York: Penguin Books, 2006), 3.
2. Adam Grant, *Give and Take: A Revolutionary Approach to Success* (New York: Viking, 2013), 4.
3. William Taubman, "Did He Bang It?: Nikita Krushchev and the Shoe," *New York Times*, July 26, 2013.
4. Roger Fisher, William Ury, and Bruce Patton, *Getting to Yes: Negotiating Agreement Without Giving In*, 3rd ed. (New York: Penguin Group, 2011), 9.
5. Ibid., 62.
6. Shell, *Bargaining for Advantage*, 67.
7. Roger Fisher and Scott Brown, *Getting Together: Building Relationships as We Negotiate* (New York: Penguin Books, 1988), 3.
8. Ibid., 84.
9. Ibid., 107.

5

Thinking about Commitments

Good negotiators are at all times keenly aware of what they are being locked into, how tight or loose the constraints are, and when such bindings are occurring.

In one of our oldest stories, Odysseus seeks the best of all possible worlds; he wants to hear the sirens' song yet live to tell of it and return home with his ship. He instructs his crew to tie him fast to the ship's mast while they stuff wax in their ears. The clever Greek has figured out a way to pre-bind himself to staying aboard ship. His commitment rests not on promises or contracts, but on strong rope. Make no mistake, once he heard the sirens calling to him, he begged, cursed, and demanded that his men untie him. It is no wonder that we consider Odysseus among the great negotiators in Western literature.

How Tight Are the Bindings?

Consider this question. Do you wish to be more tightly bound or more loosely bound? A strange query, indeed, particularly since the answer must be that it depends on the subject at hand. In some things you want to be bound up as tightly as possible—for example, the snugness of your seat belt on a roller coaster. In others, such as the dinner menu for the coming year, you probably want to be as loosely obligated as possible.

Think of commitment in negotiation as a series of questions about how snug or loose are the bindings of promises, obligations, requirements, guarantees, and assurances. Are we locked in? Can we change our mind? How bad are the consequences if we renege? What if a better opportunity comes along?

As with all things in negotiation, these questions apply both to us and to those with whom we are negotiating. How tightly are we tied in? How binding is their promise? What if we break our word? Will they follow through on all they said they would do? Can I skip out on my girlfriend? Can she walk away from me? How we experience levels of commitment as they apply to ourselves may differ wildly from our feelings about how they apply to those we negotiate with.

While it is not always true, a general rule is that negotiators seek to bind their partners as tightly as possible while leaving themselves as much wiggle room as the situation will allow. For example, after a long and grueling national search, a top Ivy League university has decided to offer its presidency to a leading politician. She is the former governor, and her name has come up as a leading candidate to run for the Senate next year. A member of the search committee approaches her privately and asks if she will accept the position if it is offered. The university does not want to make a binding offer to her unless she is willing to be tightly bound, in turn, by accepting it publicly. On the other hand, the candidate is quite interested in the possible Senate seat. She knows her chances of winning it will be much clearer after the close of the legislative session several weeks from now. She tells the university that she would like to be able to hold off acceptance for a month. She is hoping to have the offer be fully binding on the university while she draws out the time she has to choose.

Many students, upon learning this concept of commitment in negotiation, relate it to the problem of roommate division of chores. One woman wrote this:

> You and your college roommates have crafted the mother of all agreements. It took about three hours in someone's bedroom for it to come to fruition, but all of you stayed engaged, actively offering and exchanging interests. Together, you've drafted up calendars for bathroom cleaning and kitchen cleaning. You've started a rotation for toilet paper purchase. You've established standard practice for dishwashing and food labeling. Every aspect of this agreement has been labored over, and the result is pretty comprehensive.

All of you agree to it. All of you scan the calendars, nod your heads. "Looks good to me." Two weeks into the semester, there are flies buzzing over an overrun sink.

What happened? Brilliant and meticulous as your agreement was, it was anchored to nothing. So it drifted away. That is to say, you reached agreement, but there was nothing to create real commitment. Without strong commitment, agreement is little more than an empty formality.

I usually teach commitment by insisting that students never use that word when writing about it. To prepare for this communication challenge, we compile a long list of synonyms that can be used to describe what we are talking about. The class often comes up with several hundred different words and phrases. After all, a great deal of the language of contracts, agreements, and promises is a series of descriptions of how bound the parties are, how much leeway they may have, and when the various obligations come into effect.

When Should We Be Bound?

The second part of analyzing commitment, after considering the level to which each party is bound, involves thinking about *when* the binding takes place. The potential college president knows she will have to make a binding choice eventually, but she hopes to put it off until she has more information about her alternative. The university is aware that, once they make a formal public offer, they cannot take it back. As a result, they search for a way to secretly know their candidate's decision, preserving their own wiggle room, before they announce the offer.

In what situations is the flexibility of being *not yet bound* advantageous? On the other hand, when does a total lack of discretion work to your benefit? Consider the example of a U.S. president who wishes to deter the use of chemical weapons in a faraway Middle Eastern nation. While he may threaten a bombing campaign if those weapons are not removed, it seems wise to retain an ability to call off such hostilities if a peaceful accord can be reached. The American leader will be best served by not locking in a course of action until all avenues have been exhausted. In contrast to this, think about the Cold War procedure of having nuclear bombers turn off their radios after receiving an order to strike. So great was the fear of an enemy subterfuge designed to turn the jets around that an absolute lock-in was considered prudent. The plot of the 1964 movie *Fail-Safe* turns on this protocol. In retrospect, though, we may decide that the flexibility to turn back from a single course of action is often most sensible. In many cases, the least binding options are desirable until very late in the negotiating process.

Eventually, though, there comes a time when binding yourself tightly to a course of action is the key to forward movement. Sometimes this is necessary to discourage counterparties from dragging things out in the hope of further concessions. This is often referred to as creating a closing window of opportunity. For example, while I am usually generous in granting extensions of due dates for students' work, there is often a straggler who needs to have a firm deadline imposed. In that case, I eventually tell her that work later than a set date will be marked down a grade—and that there will be no flexibility in this regard.

A process of brainstorming ideas with your counterparts can be extremely fruitful in a negotiation. This is essentially the concept of "separating inventing from deciding," so important to Fisher and his colleagues for creating mutual gains.[1] Its success, however, necessarily depends on finding a way to get partners' agreement that ideas will not bind until the proper time. It turns out to be quite difficult because as soon as someone mentions a possible option favorable to one player, she tries to tie everyone to it. Often called *anchoring*, this tendency to affix the discussion to one desirable outcome must be circumvented for the brainstorming process to work. In a teasing irony, the Harvard professors challenge us to find a way to forcibly prevent ourselves from latching onto the ideas prematurely—a kind of commitment not to commit.

Degrees of Commitment

When considering this element of any negotiation, it is important to realize that commitment is not an all-or-nothing proposition. It is easy to mistakenly think of a negotiator as either bound or not bound. The concept is more subtle than that. Rather, think of there being many degrees of bindingness and join me in wishing for an instrument, like a gauge, to measure them.

A former student came to my office hours to share joy over her recent marriage. She told me the entire chronological tale of the courtship. She and her boyfriend met on a blind date. She knew right away that he was going to be very special to her. The boyfriend, on the other hand, was not as sure. When he didn't call for several days, she worked up her nerve and asked him for a second date. A third date followed, which ended with kissing and holding hands. A month later they were going steady. About a half year later, he got down on one knee and asked her to marry him. She was not too sure and actually replied, "maybe." Almost a month passed before she whispered in his ear, "I do." To which, of course, he replied, "You do *what?*," since he was not clear what she was talking about. Their engagement lasted a year. In the middle of it, she got cold feet and had a long discussion with her sister about whether she could get out of it. Her sister insisted that she did not have to marry him if her heart wasn't 100 percent. Her fears eventually passed, though, and she became very excited and full of love for her betrothed. On their wedding day, they exchanged rings, said "I do," and the clergyman declared them husband and wife. So did the State of New York. Sitting in my office, a strange *Mona Lisa* smile crossed her face. "There's no going back now," she said, placing her hand on her slightly rounded belly and giving me a wink of her eye.

Thinking back on this happy story, I thought it perfect for teaching the many degrees of commitment. Consider the level to which each member of the couple was bound after the first date, after the third date, and during the period of going steady. There is some tie at each of those points, but the level is different. Compare the level after the marriage proposal with after the ceremony and when the legal documents were signed. Or when her sister pointed out that, notwithstanding her acceptance, she did not *have to* marry him. Sitting there in my office, I saw that her commitment to her husband had just recently risen to a new and more powerful level.

It is my intention to install on my desk a commitment meter that will measure the level to which a party is bound at any given time. It will use colors to indicate those different levels and will be highly sensitive to subtle changes. After all, if another student comes to tell me a story of true love, I don't want to miss the chance to teach about this critical element of negotiation.

Commitment Is Not Just about the Ending— Consider It throughout the Process

This concept of commitment, of tight or loose bindings and when they begin to fasten, applies not only to final agreement but also throughout every step in a negotiation process. It is relevant when we agree to start discussing a deal and when we concur to keep trying, when we decide to sit down together and when we mutually agree to seek help. Every step is a mini commitment that can be examined in this light.

Two titans of industry, hugely powerful men with egos to match, had been negotiating all day over whether a takeover was going to be hostile or friendly. As the dinner hour neared, voices were raised, and tempers began to flare. One of the moguls put up his hand. "Tell you what," he said. "Let's just stop for today. Even though we were scheduled to keep talking after dinner, let us just agree to put this whole matter to rest until Monday morning at 8 A.M. Will you agree to that?" The other man agreed, and they shook hands.

The two men have made an agreement. They have bound themselves. At first glance, they seem to have settled nothing. They have simply postponed their heated attempt to find an acceptable deal. But they have agreed to postpone and to resume at a date certain: a tiny little mini agreement. We expect much good to come from this small joint decision; heads can cool and sleep can soothe. When they meet again at the agreed upon time, they will be better able to work toward a resolution that all parties desire.

Many Little Agreement Steps

The negotiation process is made up of a series of little steps. At each juncture, there are decisions to be made. At every step, a negotiator encounters questions as to how much to be bound and to what. Furthermore, the question of *when* to be bound comes up continuously. Instead of agreeing to meet on Monday morning, the businessman might have responded that he would call tomorrow to set up a time. That response would have been less binding and might allow him more time to decide what level of obligation should come next in the ongoing process.

A series of smaller commitments is very often the way that leads to a big agreement. In international relations, these are often referred to as confidence-building measures. The concept applies to small negotiations as well as big ones. Who hasn't laid out a chain of such agreements when bargaining with a child? If you will eat your spinach, we will go to the ice cream stand. If you are good on the trip, you can get sprinkles. After the ice cream, we are going to brush our teeth and get ready for bed. . . .

As you negotiate, pay attention to these commitment issues. Attend to them not only as they affect you but also with an eye toward their impact on your negotiating partners. At every stage, there are forks in the road that require decisions about whether and how much to be bound. Help pave the way for those across the table to easily agree to the next step. Before you know it, you will find yourselves marching confidently, arm in arm, toward agreements that ensure good outcomes for everyone.

Chapter Summary

- Negotiators usually prefer to bind their partners as tightly as possible while leaving themselves maximum freedom and flexibility.
- From the beginning, you should consider how tightly each party is bound to the agreement and when that binding takes place.
- In seeking to brainstorm possible solutions, be careful to avoid the tendency to anchor the discussion on ideas favorable to one side or the other.
- Issues of commitment are measured in degrees; they are not "all or nothing."
- These commitment issues should be considered throughout the entire process, not just at the conclusion of the negotiation.
- A series of small commitments or a planned chain of agreements can build confidence and help lead to a larger agreement.

Note

1. Roger Fisher, William Ury, and Bruce Patton, *Getting to Yes: Negotiating Agreement Without Giving In*, 3rd ed. (New York: Penguin Group, 2011), 62.

CHAPTER 6

Best Alternative: Where Your Power Comes From

In negotiation, power comes from alternatives. One of the first things a skilled practitioner explores is what course she will take if the deal being worked on completely falls apart. If I can't make this arrangement with this person work out at all, what will I do instead? Answering this question lays the foundation for increasing negotiating strength. And greater strength presents the potential for increased control, influence, and authority.

In studying negotiation, we refer to "alternatives" as all the things you might do completely outside of the negotiation you are currently working on. Think of being in a restaurant and discussing the menu with your waiter. You ask for a salad instead of the side of fries. When he says, "No substitutions," you can continue to negotiate with him, or you can walk out and go to the café around the corner. The latter choice is an alternative—no further negotiation; I will go deal with someone else.

"People think of negotiating power as being determined by resources like wealth, political connections, physical strength, friends, and military might," say Fisher, Ury, and Patton. "In fact, the relative negotiating power of two parties depends primarily upon how attractive to each is the option of not reaching agreement."[1] The less you mind walking away from an agreement, the more power you have relative to your negotiating partner.

49

Once an attractive backup plan has been put securely into place, you needn't settle for a negotiated agreement that's less appealing to you than your alternative. On the other hand, if you realize that the consequences of not settling are dramatically worse than the agreement you are seeking, acknowledging that your alternative is weak may prompt you to consider terms of agreement that you hadn't previously entertained.

Now let's learn how to derive significant power from this concept. Proper analysis and use of alternatives requires a number of steps. Good negotiators start by assessing all of their alternatives to the deal currently being discussed. It can be a lengthy list. All the possibilities should be included.

Step 1—An Inventory of Your Possible Alternatives

The next step is to take a critical eye to all possible other paths with the goal of identifying the very best one. Of all the things you could do if this current negotiation falls apart or cannot be concluded, which is actually the best one for you? It is very important to consider all factors; this is not just a question of money or most toys or number of beans. Don't fool yourself into choosing an alternative that is not really best but might seem so to the outside world.

A young Wharton graduate whose lifelong goal was to work for a prestigious investment bank on Wall Street got an offer from Greatman Stocks & Co. and dearly wanted to go there. He got into a bargaining tiff with their personnel office over moving expense reimbursement, though, and pointed out that he had an "even better" offer that paid more money from a prestigious consulting company. In addition to a high salary, the consulting firm would give him an unlimited relocation allowance. He decided that this alternative was very strong, and, when no agreement on moving costs could be reached with the folks at Greatman, he broke off negotiations and signed with the consultants. Sadly, though, he was soon in my office, weeping and depressed, to decry the terrible mistake he had made. "I badly wanted to work at Greatman," he moaned. I had to explain to my former student that he had deceived himself by confusing "more money" with "better offer." Alternatives should be ranked by taking into account all factors that matter, including those that are personal, psychological, and abstract.

Step 2—Identify Your BATNA

Once the very best alternative is identified, it gets labeled as your best alternative to a negotiated agreement (BATNA). Knowing exactly what your BATNA is gives you a powerful floor to support your negotiation effort. You will *never* accept a deal unless it is better than your BATNA. It forms a minimum acceptable level for you. As you will see, this is incredibly useful.

Step 3—Strengthen Your BATNA

Once you know what your current BATNA is, your next step is to try to improve it. Believe it or not, making your BATNA better is rather easy, and, with practice, you will become a master at it. There are two general categories of BATNA improvement. Let's examine each in its turn.

A negotiator can always try to take the BATNA already in hand and strengthen it. For example, a family decided to sell their home because they felt uncomfortable living in it. The old place had a number of defects, and everyone wanted something newer and more functional. A single buyer showed interest, but his bid was far lower than was hoped for. Some haggling took place over a period of weeks, but, in the end, the buyer seemed unwilling to pay a fair price for the house. All family members decided that their BATNA was to not sell and continue living there. To strengthen that BATNA, the father decided to repair the leaky roof immediately. The slow drip in the kitchen was one of the most annoying problems in the old place. Although it would not make it a paradise, fixing the leak made the home feel far more comfortable and pleasant to live in. As a result, the best alternative to selling—staying in the old home—was a better prospect than it had previously been.

The second category is to go out and get another alternative that is even better than your current BATNA. Once this is accomplished, the new and better alternative becomes your new BATNA. By the way, your former BATNA is now another alternative but no longer your best one. With a stronger BATNA, your negotiating power has improved. Consider how much stronger would have been the negotiating position of the young grad whose goal was to work for a prestigious investment bank if he had gone out and gotten a job offer from another Wall Street firm. Even if the offer was significantly inferior to Greatman's, as long as it was stronger than the one from the consulting firm, he would have improved his bargaining position.

Here a little explanation may help. It is said that a strong BATNA provides the negotiator with both a sword and a shield. In other words, it allows her to be more aggressive (offense) while also protecting her from making bad deals (defense). Let's consider the case of the young Wharton graduate more closely. He really wants to work at Greatman, but he also wants to be treated fairly and to be able to negotiate for the maximum possible advantage. Now let's use a simplifying trick: Imagine that we could quantify the value of all his offers on a scale of 1 to 100. We will say that the offer from Greatman, all things considered, was worth 90 to him. Now we consider his alternatives. Before he was asked to work at the consulting firm, he thought his best alternative to accepting Greatman's offer was to go to law school. He knew it would make him miserable, and so that choice gets a value of 30. He was excited to receive the consulting offer, even though it paled in comparison to working for Greatman, so it can be assigned a value of 75. When he goes out and gets a firm offer from Greatman's competitor, a Wall Street investment firm we shall call Money Standard, his situation improves. The offer from Money is better for our grad, and so it gets a value of 85.

Consider how this improved situation affects the Wharton graduate's negotiating behavior. The defensive shield of a stronger BATNA protects him. Without it, the failure of the Greatman deal would see him falling from a situation worth 90 to one he values at 30—a long and painful fall that he will do almost anything to avoid. When his BATNA was strengthened to something he valued at 75, though, he had not that far to fall in the event of not reaching agreement with Greatman. He is much safer if losing the Greatman deal costs him only a little instead of a lot. We can see, as well, that when he improved his BATNA to one worth 85, he was in an even more comfortable position.

Think, as well, about the aspect of a stronger BATNA that we referred to as a sword. Just how assertive or bold might our young grad be when he risks losing his offer worth 90 and falling all the way to an alternative he thinks is worth 30. He dare not take a risk. When he strengthens his BATNA to a 75, however, he may be less fearful and more able to negotiate forcefully. After his best alternative is further improved, all the way to something he valued only a little less than the Greatman offer, he had little to lose. He might have the courage to bargain without fear. His confidence, skill, and cleverness can all be let loose, now that he knows there is a solid safety net right below him.

It is worth noting that not every value or benefit can be reduced to a number. The "simplifying trick," to assign everything a quantitative value, was employed solely to teach the concept. In a real-life negotiation, you must find a way to value, weigh, and compare every single aspect of the primary deal and its alternatives. Don't overweight those that can be easily measured or give short shrift to the ones, like comfort, feelings, or personal well-being, that are hard to calculate.

Step 4—Estimate What the Other Side's BATNA Might Be

Make an intelligent guess as to the other negotiator's BATNA.

Once you have assessed your current BATNA and worked to strengthen it, the time comes to begin thinking about your negotiating partner's best alternative. While you cannot know exactly what she sees as her best choice if agreement with you cannot be reached, you can make an educated guess. You are already thinking hard about her situation and how things look from where she stands. Furthermore, you are asking as many questions as possible to gather even more data. Consider asking her. Of course, you must treat her answer with care since she has strong incentives to lie about this. Clever questions, though, can shed a great deal of light on how the other side may be evaluating its own situation.

Having some idea of what the other side sees as their BATNA will be of real help to you. Do you expect them to be comfortable with no deal or to dread that outcome? Will they try hard to find agreement with you, or can they afford a take-it-or-leave-it attitude? These are questions you really want answers to, all the while reminding yourself that you are working with estimates and educated guesses, not hard facts.

Not only will an idea of what their BATNA might look like help you approximate relative negotiating strength but also it will give you the opportunity to alter it. Just as you worked hard to strengthen your own best alternative, so can you think about weakening theirs.

Step 5—Consider Whether You Can Weaken the Other Side's BATNA

Can you weaken their BATNA? Sometimes. While strengthening our own best alternative is fairly easy and should be done in just about every case, reducing the value of theirs can be challenging. It is even harder to make their alternative weaker in an ethical way. Nevertheless, there are occasions where it can be achieved, and a good negotiator always gives the matter due consideration.

A university-based pharmacology group developed a new process for a certain drug and was negotiating its sale to a multinational pharmaceutical company. Their only concern was a scientist known for his skepticism about the particular pathway the new process used. He was creating a whole new mechanism, and, while his method was several years from completion, waiting for this alternative might well be the buyer's BATNA. Could they weaken this alternative? The group decided to hire the doubting scientist as a consultant on their project. They paid him a hefty fee, but, as part of his contract, he could not compete with them or discuss their method publicly for two years. Effectively, they had taken the alternative away from the pharmaceutical company, leaving them with their next best alternative to serve as a weaker BATNA.

A more gruesome example comes from Francis Ford Coppola's *The Godfather*. In that movie, the consigliere is sent to Hollywood to negotiate getting a particular movie role for the godson. The movie producer, who will make the decision, is offered help with some labor troubles he is having on his movie set. "The Godfather would like to do you a favor," the consigliere tells him. Of course, in return he expected the favor of the role going to the godson. After a day of low-level negotiating, the producer went to bed believing that he would reject the deal. As anyone who has seen that movie well remembers, the producer awakens to find the severed head of his favorite racehorse in the bed with him. Before retiring the previous evening, the producer believed that his BATNA looked something like this: He would have a strike on the movie set, and the Godfather would not be pleased with him. The producer believed that, while not pleasant, he could live with that BATNA. The message sent with that severed horse head was this: "You have misunderstood your BATNA. It is much worse than you have been assuming. Now that you understand it correctly, do you care to proceed with it? Or would you rather make the deal?"

As this example suggests, it can be quite hard to actually weaken the other side's BATNA. You do not have the kind of resources that the fictional Godfather could muster. Furthermore, few of us would even consider the use of such brutal, illegal, and immoral tactics. The concept, though, is clear and useful. If you can weaken the other side's best alternative you will have, in effect, made yourself relatively stronger.

Here is a slightly silly example but one that a group of my undergraduates tried out. An agreement hinged on a fraternity's supplying ice cream to the neighboring sorority. When the negotiation got heated, the young woman made clear that they could simply bypass the brothers and go to the local ice cream shop and buy the "moose tracks" flavor in question. While the discussion dragged on, one fraternity member was secretly dispatched to buy out all the "moose tracks" ice cream from the shop. When the deal was done, the fraternity's negotiator challenged this counterpart that her BATNA was not as strong as she thought. Of course, this story turns on the fact that rivalry between these two groups was so intense that no expense would be spared in trying to best each other. Woe unto the businessman who tried this particular technique.

Work to Shape Their Perceptions

Having identified our best alternative, strengthened it, made an educated guess about the other side's BATNA, and considered weakening it, we have one more thing to consider. The leverage that comes from having a stronger alternative than the other side hinges on *perception*, not facts. You are in the better position as long as the person sitting across from you *thinks* you are. Of course, this can be a two-edged sword in that you may actually have a stronger alternative, but they may not know it.[2] It may be necessary to find ways to show her your willingness to walk away from the deal because you have something else available that is of almost equal value to you.

Mother Nature has incorporated this idea into the defense systems of some animals. In a confrontation between two elephants, the smaller one may flare its ears in an attempt to look bigger than it really is. In a similar vein, the Wizard of Oz urges Dorothy to focus on the giant apparition before her and "pay no attention to the little man behind the curtain." Notwithstanding the maxim that "size doesn't matter," it may sometimes be important to convince the other negotiators that yours is bigger. Sometimes perception can play a bigger role than underlying facts, particularly when some of the facts are subjective or not readily apparent.

In the end, though, your BATNA is as strong as your own true preference to use it. If you will gladly live with your alternative, you are in a strong position regardless of what anyone else might think about it. If John Lennon was happy to forgo another record deal in favor of just sitting in his apartment and "watching the wheels go round and round," he was in a very strong position, even though anyone else in the world would have jumped at the chance for the music contract he was turning down.

Be Careful Not to Rely *Too Much* on BATNA, Especially Where Relationships Are Important

Understanding and harnessing the power of BATNA is one of the most important things a negotiator can do to increase her power in a negotiation. Indeed, it can be so potent as to blind us to some negative effects. I have long studied the mismatch between self-evaluation and third-party ratings of negotiators. Or to put the matter in plain English, why do some folks think themselves superstar negotiators when everyone else finds them ineffective and unpleasant to deal with?

In particular, those with a competitive negotiating style are far more likely to rate themselves good or excellent while outside evaluators see them as less effective. What might explain this anomaly? It took me a long time to discover that the self-evaluators were not taking into account deals that they were never offered or that they unwisely walked away from. They were ranking themselves based only on the outcomes of those deals they completed. In other words, they got good numbers when they made an agreement but lost out because many good prospective deals were not being made.

The confidence that comes from knowing you can walk away from a deal, with only slight diminishment in your results, can become a strong internal motivator. Why should I work hard to persuade you, compromise with you, or build a better arrangement with you, when I can just go on to my alternative? It becomes a little too easy to just walk away. Indeed, strengthening one's BATNA and then just moving on to it can become something of a habit. This might work fine for my magnificent Wharton students who are juggling four job offers. Consider, though, how destructive it could be in a marriage or a partnership. When people are strongly bound together for reasons that transcend a mere financial relationship, walking away should probably be something of a last resort. Although a commodities dealer might think BATNA is the greatest thing since sliced bread, a marriage counselor might find it distasteful. Remember that really good negotiators, as opposed to those who merely delude themselves, do not substitute a strong BATNA for doing the hard work of finding a way to make the primary deal succeed in a way that is good for everyone.

Until now, this book has offered skills and techniques for you to use throughout a negotiation. The next four chapters lay out the four stages of a negotiation and explain what you should be thinking about in each successive phase.

Any serious negotiation begins long before the parties take a seat at the metaphoric negotiating table. In his *Bargaining for Advantage*, G. Richard Shell refers to the first phase as the strategy preparation stage.[3] He goes on to outline the three subsequent stages of negotiation: the second is exchanging information, the third is opening and making concessions, and the final phase is closing and gaining commitment. Shell clarifies that "in complex bargaining encounters, people vary the sequence and pacing of these steps." Skilled negotiators, he says, are "alert to their counterpart's pace, striving to stay 'in step' as the process moves along." Keeping this requisite flexibility in mind, Shell's four basic stages give us an organized and thorough framework for making our way through a negotiation.

Chapter Summary

- The relative negotiating power of each party comes from how easy it would be to walk away from the deal being discussed. The less you mind walking away—the less you need the deal—the more power you have relative to your partner.
- Good negotiators first assess all of their alternatives to the deal at hand, taking into account all factors, including personal, psychological, and abstract concerns.
- Once every realistic alternative has been considered, the one currently judged best is assigned the label BATNA—your best alternative to a negotiated agreement.
- BATNA is dynamic. Indeed, it changes frequently based on both actions you take and circumstances beyond your control.

- Never accept a deal unless it is better than your BATNA. In effect, your BATNA forms a minimum floor below which you will not go.
- Once you are clear about your BATNA, you should try to improve it. Successfully doing so strengthens your relative negotiating position.
- An intelligent estimation of your partner's BATNA helps you assess your relative negotiating strength.
- Consider whether you can weaken the other side's BATNA.
- Negotiating strength hinges on perception. It is not the actual relative strength of the parties' alternatives that determines power but their perceptions of it. Work to influence this perception.

Notes

1. Roger Fisher, William Ury, and Bruce Patton, *Getting to Yes: Negotiating Agreement Without Giving In*, 3rd ed. (New York: Penguin Group, 2011), 104.
2. G. Richard Shell, *Bargaining for Advantage: Negotiation Strategies for Reasonable People*, 2nd ed. (New York: Penguin Books, 2006), 110.
3. Ibid., 117.

CHAPTER

The Preparation Phase

As is often the case in life, thorough preparation is fundamental to success in negotiating. Research shows that our habit and method of preparation prior to a negotiation is the single most important determinant of our performance when actually engaged with our partners. To do it well involves devising a plan of action that's tailored to the situation at hand. To structure our preparation, though, we need a solid understanding of the negotiation we are entering.

Where Do We Hope to End Up?

Begin by trying to assess where you want to end up. To a great degree, we are revisiting my favorite question: What is a good outcome? In particular, consider: What will be a good outcome for me? What will be a good outcome for my team or group? (Sometimes these are very different.) What will be a good outcome for the folks on the other side? This inquiry can be broken down into several parts.

Substance and relationship each deserve careful consideration. G. Richard Shell tells us, "Every negotiation . . . combines some measure of conflict over substantive issues with a degree of sensitivity to the way people should treat each other."[1] These two dimensions— the substance and the relationship between parties—form the basis of a thorough situational analysis. So we can consider good outcomes from both substantive and relationship aspects. In the end, the best possible outcomes blend these and other pieces back together.

Consider the Substantive Issues

In sizing up the substantive issues, we ask: How significant are the stakes in this negotiation? How essential is this thing to us? Is the specific subject being negotiated over critically important to me? This is, of course, highly subjective. We can imagine two standby passengers negotiating with an airline employee over the last seat on a flight. One needs to get home to be at the bedside of a critically ill spouse; the other has an important professional paper to deliver that evening in the destination city. They will surely see the stakes quite differently, even though the substantive issue is identical. What's important here is that we're as honest as possible with ourselves. What are we really after, and what interests lie deep below the position we have initially staked out?

Once we have asked ourselves these questions, we should put on the other party's shoes and revisit them. How important do *they* perceive the substantive issues to be? How badly do they need agreement? Critical to our effectiveness is an understanding of not only their perceptions but also the disparities between their perceptions and ours.

Then Consider the Relationship Issues

Having considered the substance from each side's point of view, we begin thinking about relationship issues. How central are these to a good outcome? To us? To them? How great is the importance of the relationship between the parties when compared with the weight of the substantive issues?

There is a story told in certain business circles about a sales representative who was invited to Bentonville, Arkansas, to meet with Walmart. He had worked long and hard to convince the giant retailer to sell his company's products. Now he was finally getting a shot at nailing down a contract. He knew all the rumors detailing how fierce Walmart can be about demanding price concessions, so he decided to lead with his toughest hardball negotiating stance. He determined at the outset that he would not go below a price of $3 per unit. The Walmart representatives demanded that he come down 20 percent below that. He held his ground. Finally, the Walmart people agreed to $3 per unit and said they would start with a relatively small contract and see how well the item sold. The sales representative was elated. He had stuck to his guns and won a great victory on price. As he was leaving the building, though, he overheard some of the Walmart buyers whispering among themselves. "Yes, that's him. He's the jerk. We gave him a contract, but I don't ever want to deal with him again. We don't need his product that badly."

Walmart is the largest retailer in the world. Building a solid working relationship with that company may be far more important than winning an initial skirmish on price.

Our relationship with the other parties may well change as a result of the negotiation. At the outset, we should ask ourselves how important we perceive our future relationship with the other side to be. What do we want that relationship to look like after this negotiation is concluded? Is this a one-time transaction where we expect little or no further interaction with the other parties? At the other extreme, is this akin to a marriage? More often than not, the parties' dealings with each other don't end abruptly with the negotiated agreement. And as with most things that require some measure of trust, relationships are far more easily damaged than they are repaired.

You Want Good Substance and Good Relationships—But Don't Trade One for the Other

Notwithstanding their relative weightings, a good outcome in most negotiation situations involves a good substantive result and maintaining or improving the kind of relationship we want. There is a great danger, though, if you can be coerced into trading the one for the other. Good negotiators refuse to concede on substance in exchange for an improved relationship. Just as we have long-ago memories of a schoolyard promise to be your best friend in exchange for some lunchroom concession, so, too, we remember a recent insistence on a substantive concession to preserve the relationship. Any time someone demands a compromise on price or terms in exchange for strengthened relations, your reply should always be the same: "I deeply value your friendship, and I offer you all the aspects of good friendship that I can. As for the substance, though, that has to be decided on the merits based on fairness." Remember to use substantive tools for deciding substance and relationship tools to build relationships. And refuse to trade the one for the other.

Our preparation for good outcomes weaves substance and relationship goals together. Once we get clear on what a good outcome looks like in the matter we are preparing for, we go on to considering better outcomes. Can we raise the target? What might the best possible overall outcomes look like?

Set High, Achievable Goals

Shell urges the importance of setting high but attainable goals as part of good negotiating practice.[2] This process begins during the preparation phase. You want to set tentative goals. It is worth noting, though, that in the early stages of a negotiation you probably will not have enough information to appropriately determine your final goals. Rather, you continue to gather information throughout the negotiating process and, as you do, reset your goals as you learn more.

Gathering information begins during the preparation phase of a negotiation and continues beyond it. You will want to know all you can about the other negotiators, parties not present, the situation as they see it, and what they are trying to achieve. Your initial research begins before you sit down with others. As you plan, you begin to both gather information and understand what further information you will need.

Who Are These People Who Will Soon Be Sitting Across from Us?

Among the subjects you are learning and gathering information on are the people who will be sitting at the negotiating table. Who are they and what individual characteristics are important for you to know about them? In the first chapter of Shell's book, five distinct bargaining styles are identified. Avoiders, compromisers, accommodators, problem solvers, and competitors are each explained.[3] In his final chapter, Shell gives useful advice for how people in each style can be become more effective.[4] There is significant advantage in knowing which of these most closely fits each of the negotiating partners you will soon be sitting down with. And, of course, having more self-insight about where you fall on this scale and how your style can be most successfully deployed will be tremendously useful.

Adam Grant delineates between givers, takers, and matchers in his book, *Give and Take*.[5] Here again, knowledge of who you are dealing with, along with self-insight, is of great utility. We begin gathering these understandings in the preparation phase.

Of course, there are limits on how much we can learn about other people through indirect evidence. Our knowledge of the bargaining style, personality, generosity, and mannerisms of negotiating partners will be greatly enhanced later in the process. Then we will be able to both observe and question them directly. For now, though, as we prepare, we gather what we can. We also make lists and take notes on what we will need to learn in the later stages.

In light of the type of relationship we expect and the style and personalities of the negotiators, preparation should include choosing the most appropriate setting and means of communication. Where should the talks take place, using what media, over what time frame? Can you alter the mood and tone in ways that will be advantageous? Will you want to brainstorm with these partners? If so, where and when? Might you set things up to facilitate separating inventing from deciding? The best negotiators put real thought into every aspect of the process, as being deliberate with procedure can have very real implications for both the negotiated agreement and the negotiated relationship.

Preparation for any negotiation is not complete without initial consideration of what path to take if a deal cannot be reached. This is the analysis of alternatives and BATNA discussed in Chapter 6. It must begin during the preparation phase. Like many of the areas discussed here, though, further consideration will be needed in later stages. BATNA is a dynamic and constantly changing thing, and consistent attention to it throughout the various parts of a negotiation is the way to improve outcomes.

Chapter Summary

- Being fully prepared is one of the most important determinants of success. Don't skimp on preparation.
- Every negotiation consists of substantive issues and relationship considerations. Your preparation should consider each in its turn.
- The best negotiating outcomes involve a good substantive result and a relationship that has been improved or at least not harmed or weakened.
- Setting high but achievable goals will help improve outcomes.
- Good preparation includes increased understanding of whom you are dealing with. Learn as much as you can about the other people involved, and prepare to adjust your negotiating approach based on the type of negotiator sitting across the table.

Notes

1. G. Richard Shell, *Bargaining for Advantage: Negotiation Strategies for Reasonable People*, 2nd ed. (New York Penguin Books, 2006), 121.
2. Ibid., 22.
3. Ibid., 10.
4. Ibid., 229.
5. Adam Grant, *Give and Take: A Revolutionary Approach to Success* (New York: Viking, 2013), 4.

CHAPTER 8

The Exchanging Information Phase

With the commencement of the information exchange phase, we are for the first time metaphorically sitting down together with the people with whom we are negotiating—even if we are on opposite ends of the earth. We are beginning to interact directly with them.

This stage of the negotiation process offers us a number of critically important opportunities. First of all, we want to gather information from the other parties. They know a great deal about a whole lot of subjects we would like to learn more about. They can share with us information we did not previously have, data that we gathered in an incomplete fashion, and things we did not even know about. They can also straighten us out on subjects we learned of but misunderstood.

Some of the things we want to learn include everything about them as people, all about their business and their industry, and as much as possible about their character and their ethics. We will seek to find out what they know, what they don't know, and what they are trying to learn. We will attempt to find out as much as we can about their goals, targets, and objectives as they see them. We will also ask questions to uncover their underlying interests—even if they are not fully aware themselves. We seek to know what they really, really want.

We also want to explore with them their understanding of fairness as it relates to the negotiation at hand. What are they going to experience as fair? Which authoritative standards and norms are going to resonate with them? Later in the negotiation process, we may very well need to close the deal by showing them that we are being fair. Every insight we can now gather up as to how we might do that will be very valuable. Furthermore, the fair deal we will eventually try to put together will need to meet their legitimate interests and needs. Now is our chance to find out in detail what those are.

Ask Lots of Questions

Our method for learning all of this is to ask them questions. Get them talking. Seek clarification of what they share with us. Show interest in what they have to say, and ask them to tell us more. Much of the discussion is about their very favorite subject—themselves. Since most people are delighted to talk about themselves and their situation, all we need do is give them a little bit of encouragement.

Good negotiators ask more questions. A much-cited study reinforces this.[1] It found that skilled negotiators spend almost 40 percent of their time acquiring information (asking questions) and clarifying information (restating and reframing what they've heard to verify that they've understood correctly). Average negotiators spend about 18 percent of their time on the same behaviors. In other words, average negotiators ask half as many questions as skilled negotiators. The key here is to ask questions and listen well enough to pose precise follow-up questions. The latter is just as important as the former. Although you can prepare a good set of queries ahead of time, probing and clarifying the other party's position requires you to listen carefully and continue to formulate good questions. Good listening skills, along with good preparation habits and the ability to express thoughts clearly, consistently show up in the research as among the top traits of the most effective negotiators. Talk less, ask more, and keep your ears perked up.

Our ideal situation in this second phase of a negotiation is that we just ask question after question, and they happily give us answers. The problem with this plan, though, is that no skilled negotiator is going to let us get away with that. Just as we want to learn everything possible about them, so, too, they want to learn about us. As a result, a sharing of information and details usually results. Very often, good negotiators end up in a sharing back and forth that looks almost like a dance. You tell me some things, and I will tell you some things. You elaborate, and then I will elaborate. Such a negotiation ballet is a very good thing.

Strengthen Your Bonds with the Other Parties

A separate but important function of the information exchange phase is to attend to the relationship between parties. Do not underestimate the importance of building rapport with the other people; setting the tone of ongoing interaction will pay off nicely. Not only is it a means of ensuring that the relationship remains intact for future interaction but also, as research has confirmed, it makes it more likely that a negotiated agreement is reached at all.

Consider a study of MBA students wherein half the students were provided only with the other party's name and e-mail address. The other half got a photograph of their counterpart, as well as explicit instructions to exchange information on hobbies, families, job plans, and hometowns prior to discussing anything related to the negotiation at hand. Although the rapport-building measures in the experiment were forced, 94 percent of the socializing groups reached a deal, and only 70 percent of the other pairs made it to agreement. A similar study conducted among law students brought similar results: "Negotiators who shared a getting-to-know-you telephone call before initiating e-mail negotiations were more successful than those who did not."

Regardless of method of communication or choice of location, good negotiators begin their interactions with getting-to-know-you conversation with the people involved. They make sure to strengthen the relationship between parties as much as possible before introducing any matters that might strain it.

If you have good social skills and people tend to like you, do not hesitate to let your personality shine through. Be yourself. Being personable costs you nothing. On the other hand, maintaining a pretense of stiff or detached formality in a negotiation is unhelpful at best and counterproductive at worst. You want the other side to see you as a person, and you'll do best if they like and trust the person you are. In the period of initial discussion, it is unwise to discuss anything of substantive importance. Rather, use those encounters as a means of breaking the ice. Set a conversational tone, and engage in an open and accessible way.

Psychologists refer to the similarity principle when explaining why people place greater trust in those they perceive as like themselves. We are more comfortable with someone when we feel that person shares something—an experience or affiliation, an interest or attitude—with us. This tendency should not be ignored.

Look for common ground, and introduce it as soon as possible: bring up a shared alma mater, a mutual hometown, a son or daughter, or a love of baseball. Even if the common ground itself seems trivial or superficial, the benefit of finding some solidarity with your partner is proven and consistent. Even the most seasoned negotiators won't balk at a genuine connection. It is important, though, to be genuine. Be careful not to suggest an ulterior motive by overdoing flattery, stretching the truth, or attempting to link commonalities to some substantive purpose. Such tactics are bound to backfire. No one wants to feel manipulated, particularly not under the guise of building an alliance. By the same token, be on your guard if the other party tries to exact a concession from you based on the success of their schmoozing. Remember that your goal here is to open channels of communication and create an environment conducive to *later* negotiation.

Gather Up All the Facts That They Are Willing to Share

You will, at some point, turn from casual rapport-building conversation to exchanging substantive information. When you do, pay close attention to how you ask questions. Your counterparts are likely to be on their guard and fearful of giving away information about vulnerability. Seeking information on facts is far less likely to set off alarm bells than asking about their needs. You will get a more honest and useful answer if they don't fear giving something away by providing it to you.

As the other parties provide more factual information, ask questions that clarify and confirm what you've heard. Being attentive helps you avoid miscommunication, and it also gives the other side the satisfaction of being actively understood.

It's critical, however, to listen and absorb with discernment. The information you receive will not all be accurate. There is usually an incentive for the other parties to misrepresent certain needs or interests. As mentioned, you can preempt bluffing by asking questions of a factual nature; it is psychologically much harder to falsify numbers than it is to mislead about the severity of a situation or the importance of an issue. There is usually a way to check up on factual information. Asking others who have negotiated with these folks from a similar position and doing some rigorous research on the matter can help to clear up factual misstatements.

Managing the Danger That They May Lie to Us

Nevertheless, there is a danger we must deal with in taking in all we are told. As my students are quick to point out, they have a tremendous incentive to lie to us. How should we deal with that problem? Here is my suggestion. As we gather the data they are telling us, we sift it into two separate piles in our head. The first pile is labeled "no reason they should lie about this." The other pile is marked "Here is what they said, but they had strong incentives to lie." Although care is required, we may go forward assuming that all the information in the first pile was provided truthfully. As for the second pile, whose information may well be tainted, we analyze what they offered under the microscope of "here is what they said, but they had strong reasons to mislead." Such information may not be useful as truth, but it is still full of information.

For example, former baseball star Pete Rose was eventually banned from the sport for gambling on ball games. When directly confronted with this accusation, he is reported to have told investigators that he did indeed gamble but not on baseball games. This is very valuable information for anyone seeking to take the measure of Pete Rose. He told his inquisitors that he gambled and implied that he took risks, had impulse-control problems, and was not afraid to lose money. He didn't tell the truth, but he did reveal a great deal about himself.

One final note on the second stage of a negotiation: Most negotiators are impatient. They want to get to the bargaining dance. As soon as either party proposes a term or a price, the exchanging information phase comes to an abrupt end. Almost always, this happens too early—sometimes *way* too early. I urge all my students: Stay in this second negotiating stage much longer than your gut tells you to. Stay and learn about the situation, the other parties, and their point of view for as long as is humanly possible.

Note as well that while the description of the four stages of negotiation is presented as a linear progression, you may want to go back and forth between them. Sometimes you learn something in one stage that significantly alters your understanding or your plans. Don't hesitate to take a break and go back to the previous stage, adjust what you have done, and come back better positioned to continue. This is particularly true of the data-gathering opportunities afforded you by the information exchange phase.

The more time and effort you spend exploring and understanding the other side's perceptions—learning what makes them tick—the more momentum you build for the phases of the negotiation that still lie ahead.

Chapter Summary

- The second stage of the negotiation allows you to gather information on a firsthand basis from your negotiating partner. Of course, your partner will seek the same from you
- The more you can get your partner to talk about himself, the more useful information you will be able to gather.
- Among other things, you want to learn what your partner knows, wants, and perceives to be fair.
- While exchanging information, you should be trying to build rapport. Getting-to-know-you conversations are very valuable. Creating a bond based on common interests, hobbies, or experiences, for example, can strengthen the relationship and make agreement more likely.
- Don't try to present yourself as someone you are not. Let your own personality shine through. Sincerity has its own power.
- Not all information your partner shares will be true. As you collect data, assess whether your partner had an incentive to lie about each statement. Separate the reliable statements from those liable to be untrue.
- Work to avoid bringing the exchanging information phase to a premature close. Negotiators are anxious to move on to bargaining and often miss the opportunity to learn important facts. Try to keep gathering information, and refrain from bargaining, for as long as possible.

Note

1. N. Rackham and J. Carlisle, "The Effective Negotiator—Part 1: The Behaviour of Successful Negotiators," *Journal of European Industrial Training* 2, no. 6 (1978): 6–11; N. Rackham and J. Carlisle, "The Effective Negotiator—Part 2: Planning for Negotiations," *Journal of European Industrial Training* 2, no. 7 (1978): 2–5.

CHAPTER 9

The Bargaining Phase

Having done everything possible to plan, prepare, learn, gather information, and try to see things from our negotiating partners' vantage point, we proceed toward the next step. We have planned and set a tone for the interaction that we believe will contribute to the creation of a good outcome. Much thought has gone into improving communication to facilitate understanding, reduce miscommunication, and permit good work and good feelings. That thought encompasses a sophisticated consideration of relationship that considers not only the interaction within this negotiation but well beyond that to the long term. What might the bond between these parties have the potential to become? It assumes, as well, that we have considered and are familiar with our strengths. This means knowing our BATNA and having made educated guesses about it relative to what their BATNA might be. We have considered how badly they may need this deal and how burdensome it would be for us to just walk away. Finally, having gathered from the other parties as much information, clarification, and perspective as possible, it is time to move into the third phase of a negotiation.

G. Richard Shell calls this third stage "opening and making concessions."[1] In lectures, I have sometimes teased my audience by referring to it as that which, only an hour ago, they would have called "negotiating." This is the phase where offers are considered, counteroffers are made, and the outlines of an agreement take shape.

Work to Increase the Pie—and to Claim a Fair Slice

This third phase involves two distinct types of bargaining that we examined in earlier chapters. Negotiation scholars call these two strategies integrative bargaining and distributive bargaining. The former is about creating more value. We often refer to it as making the pie bigger. It involves trading interests in a way that generates value and leaves all parties better off. The latter, on the other hand, is about dividing whatever value there is between the negotiators. It is the search for acceptable divisions of the value that exists. We take the pie and divide it into the various slices that each party will receive. Both integrative bargaining and distributive bargaining are essential to reaching agreements that create real value for all involved.

To say it another way, the bargaining phase of a negotiation is about both creating value and claiming a fair share of the value that has been created. Good negotiators work continuously to sharpen their skills at doing both things simultaneously.

The idea behind integrative bargaining may sound familiar to you. It is the same concept as creating options that we discussed in Chapter 2. To review briefly, the premise behind inventing options is that there are certain things you need that cost me little to give you, and there are things I want that you could give me easily. There exist opportunities to trade and benefit us both. When we exchange information and perspectives in the second phase of a negotiation, these opportunities are what we are looking for.

At the very nadir of the 2008 financial crisis, Goldman Sachs was in trouble, and they badly wanted a deal. At the very least, they needed a capital infusion to shore up their balance sheet. Beyond that, though, they would benefit from some public display that reinforced confidence in their solvency. They wanted a big vote of confidence from a source that mattered. Someone who could offer all of that was one of their best customers, Warren Buffett of Berkshire Hathaway. Buffett, however, is a shrewd negotiator who does not give something precious without getting a thing of great value in return. He knew that while any cash investment would help Goldman in its time of need, such an investment from the most admired investor of our times would be worth *dramatically* more to them. Buffett offered to make a $5 billion investment in Goldman Sachs but required a custom-made and extremely favorable structure for the deal.[2] In exchange for the money, Berkshire received $5 billion in preferred shares and a warrant that would allow them to purchase an additional $5 billion in shares at a price of $115, even though the shares were trading at $125 at the time. For the preferred shares, Goldman agreed to pay Berkshire a yearly 10 percent dividend, with an option of buying back the stock at any time for 10 percent more than Berkshire had paid. As for the warrants, they were valuable enough that in March 2013 Goldman agreed to buy them back for $1.4 billion in Goldman Sachs stock. All told, Berkshire made a $3.2 billion of profit on their 4.5-year-old investment in Goldman for a return of 64 percent. It was a magnificent integrative deal because both sides got what they valued most. Goldman got an infusion of cash at the moment of their greatest danger from the most admired—and deepest pocketed—investor in the United States. Buffett got a sweetheart deal, structured by the master himself, which was almost sure to make a handsome return with relatively little risk.

Use Conditional Language to Explore Trades That May Create Value

The process of inventing options in the third stage begins with conditional terms. We explore possible trades without committing to anything. Good negotiators are continuously looking for a trade that might exist and then testing to see if it is achievable. This process is creative and should be treated as such—all possibilities are worth considering. Even bad ideas often give rise to good ones. What trades or deals can we come up with that build on the interests we share, or interests that are different but compatible? Eventually, we work together to package the best trades into viable options.

How can we explore such trades without getting locked into proposals? How might we, as Fisher, Ury, and Patton suggest, separate inventing from deciding?[3] A simple but effective way to structure a trade, and to indicate to the other party what you're doing, is to use the formulation: If you consider A, then we might be able to do B. For example, if you consider reducing the price by 10 percent, then we might be able to buy three bushels instead of one. When you identify an area of high value to you where they can move, that is your *if.* Link that to something they value highly, and you have your *then.* The two together form a potential trade.

For example, a client of mine was getting married and needed floral arrangements. Her florist had a wonderful aesthetic sense, but her work was quite costly, and the planned reception was large. My client knew that carnations were in season and tended to be less expensive. In fact, she was very fond of carnations. Her proposal to the florist was "If you would be able to make more bouquets within our budget, then we'd consider replacing some of the more expensive flowers with, say, carnations. What do you think?" From there, the open structure of the trade left room to settle on the exact number of bouquets and the exact proportion of carnations.

Trades structured this way derive legitimacy from the norm of reciprocity. There's an implicit fairness in the if–then formulation; by using it, we signify that this exchange is good for both parties: "If you make dinner, I'll do the dishes." "If you'll work in the satellite office, we'll give you a higher signing bonus." "If you call right now, we'll double this offer!" These statements imply mutual concession and mutual benefit, each contingent on the other. You are saying to the other person that if you can give me this (high priority for me and not that important to you), I'll give you that (low priority for me and rather important to you).

Consider the problem if my client had said to the florist, "I like carnations! I'd love for you to use more of them instead of the peonies." In this formulation, she has made no indication that this is a concession of value. Consequently, the florist would feel no reciprocal obligation to make a concession of his own. In fact, the florist may even try to charge extra for accommodating her personal flower preferences.

Typically what happens during successful integrative bargaining is that a period of brainstorming is followed by each party expressing interest in different possible options for structuring the deal. Each then proposes an ideal set of trades. To reconcile these, the parties use a series of if–then proposals to indicate their most important interests and discern those of others.

Even if the integrative trading is very successful, however, there will come a point at which some distributive bargaining is required to settle on specific terms. This is the back-and-forth of offers and counteroffers that we know so well. Haggling at an open-air market, bargaining over souvenirs in a touristy port of call, and wrangling with my son about his bedtime all come to mind. How do we go about opening up the numbers game?

Propose Terms Favorable to You—But Defensible as Fair

Research tells us that the best approach is to propose the most optimistic offer that does not harm our basic credibility. In other words,
start out with an ambitious first offer but not a wild one. Begin with
a proposal that can be justified by some reasonable standard. It may
not be the *very fairest* standard, but it allows you to defend the offer
as arguably legitimate. From there, expect to make concessions.

Why start high and concede, as opposed to making a more
moderate offer and holding fast to it? A recent study compared
three concession strategies. In the first, negotiators started high
and didn't budge; in the second, they started moderately and didn't
budge; in the third, they started high and gradually conceded to a
moderate point. The last strategy was significantly more successful.[4]
"Concessions are the language of cooperation," explains Shell.[5] Every
time you concede something, you acknowledge the legitimacy of the
other party's demands. The value derived from this social exchange
is a powerful factor in reaching agreement. In the study, not only did
the third, high-concession strategy yield more agreement and better
outcomes for the negotiators but also "the people facing the negotiators . . . reported much higher levels of satisfaction with their agreements than did people who faced those who refused to move."

Make Small Concessions Slowly and Deliberately—and Insist on Fairness

Make concessions, but make them slowly and carefully. What we
obtain too cheaply, we esteem too lightly. Do not make sweeping,
magnanimous concessions without comment. The other side will
actually think less of a concession that you've made easily or casu-
ally. Give things up little by little, and every time you do give up
something, talk about it. Be sure that the other side recognizes
your concession and ascribes to its due value; that's the only way
they'll feel pressure to reciprocate in kind.

Finally, as you approach agreement, try not to concede solely
because the other side is digging in their heels. Concede only on
principle and for a reason; constantly substantiate your position,
and ask for justification of theirs. Haggling tends to degenerate
quickly into a tug-of-war that ends, often bitterly, with one side exert-
ing sheer power over the other. To avoid a contest of wills, defer to
objective standards and norms of fairness wherever possible.

For example, we can imagine that the florist preparing bouquets for the wedding might have been slow to agree to a smaller flower budget. Her profit was probably proportional to the amount spent on bouquets. The bride's proposal to use less expensive carnations was initially rebuffed. She held her ground, though, while bringing in outside measures of fairness. "Several of my friends have had large numbers of carnations in their wedding arrangements; in fact, you did one of those weddings. Furthermore, *Bride Magazine*, which I know you think highly of, has featured them twice this year." Rather than create a power play, the young woman is inviting the florist into the "if–then" conversation with standards of fairness from outside this conversation.

We should stop here to note that this process is not easy. Lax and Sebenius refer to the tension between creating value and claiming it as "the negotiator's dilemma."[6] Few negotiators want to make concessions easily, and many are defensive and fearful of giving out too much information. The challenge, faced by each negotiator, might be put as simply as these two thoughts: "How can I possibly give you what you want if you won't tell me what it is? On the other hand, if you do tell me what you want, I may well raise the price for it."

Be Resolute about Claiming Your Fair Share

Good negotiators, though, insist on claiming a *fair* share of the value created. How can we start to measure what might be fair? In Chapter 3, we considered authoritative norms and standards as well as objective criteria. In other words, what *outside measures of fairness* can we muster for the effort? With diligence, we will find many such measures and use the best ones to guide us toward a fair, legitimate, and workable solution.

Think of Warren Buffett and Goldman Sachs bargaining over the exact terms of Berkshire's investment. Even though it was going to create a great deal of value for each side, they did not simply make things up or pull numbers out of the air. While there is no public record of their secret negotiations, we can assume that both sides invoked precedent, industry standards, and economic facts as they searched for mutually acceptable conditions and stipulations. Neither side would let the other claim all of that value. Their discussions can be seen as an effort to find a fair division of it. In the case of Buffett and a top Goldman negotiator, their experience and skill allowed them to ensure that the other side was not walking off with too big a slice of the newly created pie. You must be alert to making sure of the same thing. Keep in mind that nothing less than a fair share of the mutually created value can be considered a good outcome.

Chapter Summary

- During the bargaining phase, offers are considered and counteroffers made. This phase is about both creating value and claiming a fair share of the value that has been created. Good negotiators do both things simultaneously.
- Trade those things you want that cost the other side little to give in exchange for things they want that you can give at little cost. These trades benefit everyone. They create more value.
- Such trades should be explored with conditional language. Good negotiators hunt for trades that might be acceptable and test for terms that might be agreeable, without committing to them. Such proposed deals are framed using if–then language to test what is possible.
- Begin by exploring offers that are at the most favorable end of the range of arguably fair agreements. Be sure you can justify your proposals with an objective standard.
- When offering concessions, make it clear that you are doing so. Make each concession slowly and carefully.
- Insist on claiming at least a fair share of the value that the deal creates.

Notes

1. G. Richard Shell, *Bargaining for Advantage: Negotiation Strategies for Reasonable People*, 2nd ed. (New York: Penguin Books, 2006), 156.
2. Tami Luhby, "Buffett's Berkshire Invests $5B in Goldman," CNNMoney.com, September 24, 2008.
3. Roger Fisher, William Ury, and Bruce Patton, *Getting to Yes: Negotiating Agreement Without Giving In*, 3rd ed. (New York: Penguin Group, 2011), 62.
4. Alan A. Benton, Harold H. Kelley, and Barry Liebling, "Effects of Extremity of Offers and Concession Rate on the Outcomes of Bargaining," *Journal of Personality and Social Psychology* 24, no. 1 (1972): 73–83.
5. Shell, *Bargaining for Advantage*, 164.
6. David Lax and James Sebenius, *Manager as Negotiator: Bargaining for Cooperation and Competitive Gain* (New York: The Free Press, 1986), 29.

CHAPTER 10

The Closing and Commitment Phase

The bargaining stage of a negotiation draws to a close as you and your partners prepare to enter into an agreement. Now you arrive at the final phase of the process, in which you are looking to memorialize what has been decided, shake hands, and start implementing all that has been promised.

From the very first chapter, this book has argued that you should be focused on what you are really trying to achieve. That concept makes a good guide to thinking about the final phase of a negotiation. What you are really seeking, in any deal, is an agreement that is durable, realistic, and helpful for all parties. As you come to the close of a negotiation, you are seeking to structure the agreement to ensure those characteristics.

Let's take a minute to think about what you are *not* trying to do. Surely you are not seeking merely to make and listen to a lot of promises, get signatures on a piece of paper, or have everyone voice assent to some deal they have little intention of following through on. In one of the most infamous agreements in the twentieth century, British Prime Minister Neville Chamberlain returned from shaking hands with Adolf Hitler and declared that he had secured "peace for our time." History recalls that the German had no intention of keeping his word. Chamberlain had gotten an agreement but had not forged any kind of durable commitment. He got what he sought but failed utterly in achieving what he, and his country, really, *really* wanted.

You Want Promises They Are Sure to Keep

As a skilled negotiator, you are seeking commitments that are likely to be fulfilled by everyone involved. You seek promises that you can have every expectation will be kept. What this means, of course, as discussed in Chapter 2, is an agreement that meets the other parties' interests. They will keep their promises, and complete their part of the deal, if it is in their best interest to do so.

Thus, the target for concluding a negotiation is an agreement wherein it makes perfect sense that they will keep all the promises they made. If you put yourself in their shoes, does the deal look like a good one that *they* would be willing to defend to their friends and colleagues and even to their critics? Do they have a lot to lose if the deal later falls apart? Examining these questions from their standpoint, rather than your own, is a powerful technique for understanding the impediments to strong commitments.

As negotiators approach the close of a long and challenging process, they may be hesitant to put the finishing touches on the deal. For reasons of uncertainty, fear, or greed, those last few steps can be hard to walk. G. Richard Shell instructs us on several ways to get over these difficulties.[1] Understanding the scarcity effect, overcommitment, and loss aversion (discussed later) will assist you with your own reluctance and in dealing with your partners' foot-dragging.

Create Scarcity to Enhance Their Enthusiasm for the Deal

Both economists and psychologists study scarcity. Just as a shortage of something drives up its price in economic terms, so, too, does it increase how badly most people want it. Simply put, humans place a higher value on a thing that is scarce and a lower value on something plentiful. Among the situations that create such an effect are time, popularity, and the risk of loss. Thus, negotiators respond to what is referred to as a closing window of opportunity. Students finishing their MBA know this all too well, as many recruiting firms make exploding offers that terminate on a certain date. As we learned in Chapter 2, most negotiators wish to bind the other side while keeping their own wiggle room. When a proposal or offer is structured to end at a certain time, though, the scarcity effect adds pressure. As we have all heard in a million ads on television, "this offer is for a limited time."

Another factor that causes scarcity is competition. When everyone else wants something, there is a tendency for us to want it more, too. We see this all over the commercial sectors of our world, particularly in marketing campaigns. Making it clear that everyone wants the item for sale can make even those with little use for it determined to buy it. Nobody wants to be left out. Watch what happens the next time you are in the supermarket, and notice that the big sale item of the week is almost gone, with just a few left on the shelf.

People seem to be hardwired to greatly fear loss. (Indeed, a number of experiments have shown that we tend to value a gain less than we dread an equivalent loss.) This often includes the loss of the deal being worked on or the danger that the other negotiator will just give up on us. Shell points to a tactic of walking out[2] as a powerful example. A take-it-or-leave-it tactic or an ultimatum in a negotiation can raise the scarcity effect to sky-high levels. Of course, such approaches pose great risks for the negotiator employing them. As is often the case, scarcity can work its pressure on all sides.

Overcommitment and loss aversion can be viewed as two sides of the same coin. When a negotiator has worked hard trying to get something, she is loath to quit or cut her losses, even if that means overpaying. Business students are taught to ignore *sunk costs*— money spent that is already gone—but find it very hard to do. We have a terribly strong urge to get back what we have put in. Time and again, we see warring nations refuse to withdraw or accept peace, even after their objectives are no longer attainable, because of the blood they have already spilled—even though, as their critics point out, continuing a conflict will bring only more deaths. This topic, escalation of commitment, is frequently studied by game theorists and is demonstrated in negotiation courses by dollar-bill auctions and other cases. Loss aversion, on the other hand, is the fear driving such escalating commitment. Once we have invested our time, money, effort, and self-esteem into a deal or enterprise, we are terribly reluctant to suffer the loss of it. This excessive fear of loss is subject to manipulation. Shell warns us about nibblers who demand a last-minute concession to keep the deal alive. He also points out that phrases like "we have come so far" and "let's not lose this after all this effort" are designed to heighten this effect.

Good negotiators use these human tendencies to their advantage. They also refuse to be bullied or manipulated by their use.

Thinking hard about issues related to closing the deal and planning carefully in this regard can reap great rewards. Of course, such careful preparation necessarily must be done in advance. When the pressure is on, it is frequently too late to do a good job.

Prepare to Be Patient

One of the best things you can do in the closing and commitment stage is to be patient. Try hard not to be in a hurry. The negotiator who is not rushed has a favorable position and is free to work for the best possible deal. She is much less vulnerable to the pressures that necessarily grind down someone who needs the agreement to happen right now. Some methods to help make this attitude possible include starting early, not procrastinating, and avoiding negotiating when you are in a needy state of mind. Just as you should avoid the grocery store when you are very hungry, you should not negotiate important deals when you are in a got-to-have-it state of mind. The best attitude in the world, where possible, is to be able to say, "I have all the time in the world to find the very best possible solution." Time is going to work to someone's advantage in most negotiation situations; work hard to make sure that the person is you.

The tools and techniques that advantage you in the final phase of a negotiation require thought and planning. Thus, the time when the best negotiators begin doing the work of the last phase of a negotiation is in the first phase. The preparation stage, discussed in Chapter 7, is when you should be plotting out the issues of gaining a lasting commitment and getting the other parties to closure. Once again, we see that the best way to begin the process of negotiation is by thinking about the end.

Chapter Summary

- You want an agreement they are likely to keep. This means that fulfilling their end of the bargain aligns well with their best interests. A deal that they are unlikely to live up to is of little value to you.
- The scarcity principle can be a useful tool in getting the other side over their last bits of hesitation.
- The best negotiators do everything they can to avoid being in a rush. They start preparing early, do not procrastinate,

and avoid negotiating when they feel vulnerable. Use time pressure to your advantage, and work hard to avoid having it used against you.

Notes

1. G. Richard Shell, *Bargaining for Advantage: Negotiation Strategies for Reasonable People*, 2nd ed. (New York: Penguin Books, 2006), 175.
2. Ibid., 181.

11

The Problem with Agents

I hope this book is building your confidence as a negotiator. With better skills and a stronger technique, you can be less reliant on others to bargain for you. Nevertheless, our lives frequently put us in a position where someone else is conducting a negotiation on our behalf. We turn to lawyers, brokers, managers, and dealers, among others, to act for us.

There are a number of reasons that might justify using an agent to negotiate in your stead. Among these are special expertise, emotional detachment, influence, and just the plain old ease of having someone else do it for us. Each of these has its proper time and place. On the other hand, it can be all too easy to simply assume that retaining an agent is a good idea.

Sometimes Employing an Agent Is Wise

Of course, sometimes the agent has so much specific knowledge about a subject that she is indispensable. Not only wouldn't you want to pursue a major lawsuit without a lawyer but also you probably couldn't do it. In other situations, the added knowledge is not indispensable but is very helpful. Consider, for example, how much more a skilled Realtor knows about the local real estate market than you do. Then there are agents whose special skill is not knowledge of subject but rather influence. Their expertise is not the *what* but the *who*. All those lobbyists on K Street in Washington command huge salaries because they know exactly the right person to talk with and can get access to those people.

Sometimes the special capability is procedural. Some people know precisely how certain special bargaining mechanisms work. For example, a labor negotiator may have so much experience in the stylized rituals of collective bargaining that it would be folly to pass up his guidance. You should be wary, though, of those who claim special expertise as negotiators. In my experience, very few of them have any significant talent or skill. Just because someone negotiates frequently does not mean he is good at it.

Another possible reason to engage agents is their detachment. There are situations where the emotional significance of a matter makes it very unwise for someone who cares deeply to negotiate for herself. Even those lawyers who, because of special negotiation training, are superstars know better than to handle their own divorces. What they could do brilliantly for someone else they simply cannot handle for themselves. A divorce advocate or mediator can be useful precisely because he does not care personally about the individual situation.

Often Employing an Agent Is Foolish

With all that said, however, there are some significant problems with agents. First of all, using them is expensive and adds to the overall cost of any deal you make. They also increase the complexity and communication challenges of a negotiation. Invariably, things go more slowly if agents are involved. Finally, there are a whole series of troubles related to conflicts of interest, asymmetries of information, and divided loyalties. Let's take a hard look at some of these difficulties.

As with any skilled work, agents of all types charge for their services. Sometimes they charge a great deal. This is particularly true in situations where either the value of their work or the exact amount of their fee is difficult to determine. Any charges and costs must, in the final analysis, be added to the overall price of the deal. Particularly concerning are those agents whose fee might be far higher than whatever value they are adding.

An accountant who charges $6,000 to take on the IRS may be worth a great deal to you. If at the end of the day, though, he is able to get the assessment of what you owe reduced by only $4,000, you may be very unhappy with him. To offer real usefulness, the agent must produce more value for you than he costs you.

Furthermore, the extra drag agents impose extends beyond money. There may also be reductions in speed, accuracy, and efficiency. It is almost inevitable that communications will be warped by having to pass through more people. This can be demonstrated by playing the kindergarten game of telephone, but it is just as true for a chain of adults: The more ears and mouths a secret must traverse, the more distorted it becomes. Furthermore, additional players mean time delays and a slower overall pace. Even if everyone is in town, at their phones or computers, and paying attention, things do not go as quickly as they would with one-on-one communication. When you add the difficulties of scheduling, double-booking, and distractions that seem to be the *sine qua non* of modern life, you are looking at a communications traffic jam.

Such a slowdown invariably means that it will take longer to reach an agreement. While this is not always bad, it can sometimes be a significant cost. If time is money, then we haven't got all day. When working on a time-sensitive deal, the careful negotiator may think twice about adding more bodies, opinions, and telephone numbers into the mix.

Are the Agent's Interests the Same as Yours?

The most disturbing problems in working with agents, though, have to do with conflicts of interest and divided loyalties. Does the person negotiating on our behalf have the same preferences, interests, and priorities as we do? The answer, of course, is sometimes yes and sometimes no. Where they differ, though, can be sources of real trouble.

Difficulties can arise over who really controls a negotiation. In theory, of course, the principal is the boss. The agent is charged with following instructions and advancing the agenda of her client. In reality, though, it is the agent who is on the ground and working with the other parties. It can be very easy for the one actually conducting the negotiation to manipulate situations and shade meanings to exercise excessive power. Where there are differences in agenda, incentives, constraints, or ethical norms, the risk increases that an agent may steer a negotiation in directions very different from the desires of the principal.

Are the agent's preferences the same as yours? For example, an agent may prefer a quick sale while the principal is willing to hold out for a higher price. Or the principal may be ready for a take-no-prisoners bargaining style that is opposed by an agent who must continue to work in the community. I witnessed an extreme example of this as a young attorney in New Hampshire. The rules there, at that time, did not prevent a district court judge from also being in the private practice of law. One Tuesday morning, a colleague of mine found herself on opposite sides with a lawyer before whom she would be appearing the very next day. Certainly, she must have had doubts about just how aggressive to be with this opponent today, judge tomorrow.

Agents often have interests and incentives that are not well aligned with those of their principal. Frequently, this conflict grows out of an agent's fee structure or way of getting paid. For many years, I have taught a real estate case designed to highlight the sharp divergence of interests between a real estate buyer and the Realtor she is working with. The aha! moment comes when the buyer realizes she wants the lowest achievable price but her agent will make the most money with a higher price.

As an aside, and a source of embarrassment to me, several years passed before I understood the full scope of the Realtor's incentives. I taught my students that the buyer's agent had strong financial reasons to want the sale to occur at the highest possible price. Levitt and Dubner take up this problem in *Freakonomics* and point to a stronger motivation that, in many cases, supersedes the preference for a higher price.[1] In Chapter 2 of their book, we are introduced to a real estate agent who is warm and caring and full of useful information. She appears to have our interests at heart. But does she? As Levitt proves, her strong incentive is to get us to close the deal quickly so that she can pocket her commission and go on to the next sales effort. Many real estate agents try to (subtly) pressure the seller into taking the first decent offer that comes along. So, too, the agent working with the buyer will try to get him to make a high enough offer to get the deal to close.

Like everyone else, agents are just human beings. In general, people have a strong tendency to respond to their own interests. Even those at the very highest levels of governmental, social, or commercial life usually take the actions they believe will further their own goals and objectives. Indeed, one way of looking at human relations is to start with the assumption that a person's sole motivation is to advance his own interests. Such a rational actor furthers the well-being of others only if he believes that to do so also somehow maximizes his own benefit. To put it simply, most agents facing a serious conflict of interest have a difficult time doing what is best for their principal at the expense of that which is better for themselves.

Where such conflicts of interest exist, a principal is left to question the wisdom of taking advice from the agent. Is the delegation of authority imprudent? How much should we trust this person? How strong does a conflict of interest have to be before it starts to affect her actions? How much temptation for personal gain will compromise the judgment of someone offering advice or acting on our behalf? At some point, the question shifts so that a prudent person must ask, "Would we be foolish to trust in this situation?"

Chapter Summary

- There are times when a negotiation can benefit from the involvement of a skilled agent. Such agents may bring to the table special expertise, emotional detachment, influence, or process knowledge. They are employed in the hope of gaining an advantage through their expertise or connections.
- There are significant reasons to resist the introduction of agents into a negotiation. They add expense, complexity, and communication difficulties.
- Agents frequently have interests that conflict with those of their principal. This can raise problems of trust, divided loyalties, and the potential for breaches of duty.
- Careful consideration of advantages and drawbacks are warranted before bringing agents into a negotiation. There may be some situations in which you are simply better off without them.

Note

1. Steven Levitt and Stephen Dubner, *Freakonomics: A Rogue Economist Explores the Hidden Side of Everything* (New York: Harper Collins, 2005), 215.

PART II

APPLYING NEGOTIATING
PRINCIPLES TO INVESTING

In Part I of this book, you learned about negotiating as it is taught at Wharton, Harvard, and other universities throughout the United States. In Part II, you will see that these methods can be applied directly to investing and, when you do so, they will help you achieve even better outcomes. Failing to comprehend that the investment decisions you make are part of a series of negotiations will cost you money. Not making the effort to improve your investment negotiating skills will cost you even more. Luckily, understanding investing as a series of negotiations and getting good at doing it is well within your reach. My goal in Part II is to guide you in applying the skills and techniques from Part I of this book to the activities we might call your "investing life."

It is important to note that I use "negotiating" in this context to cover the *entire* process described in Part I. Thus, a negotiation begins with preparation and research that commences long before anyone contemplates sitting down together at a bargaining table. It involves studying facts, circumstances, and historical records. It requires thinking about alternatives outside of this deal and working actively to strengthen ours and, perhaps, weaken theirs. You need to seriously examine your own interests and those of every other negotiator. You must put much thought into the nature of the relationship and the goals surrounding it. You must make great effort to ensure the likelihood that the other side will fulfill all promises. In other words, the concept of negotiating employed in this book is an intricate series of actions that work together toward ensuring good outcomes. It is neither easy nor quick; rather, it requires study, effort, planning, and patience.

Negotiation encompasses the entire process, from preparation through final implementation. Therefore an investment, such as purchasing common stock, is by my definition a negotiation, even though the investor-negotiator never has the opportunity to talk to or communicate with the seller of that security. Market transactions eliminate your ability to manipulate some parts of the negotiating process. Those that remain, however, offer ample opportunities for advantage and relative success.

Different negotiation situations may bring different parts of the process to the fore. For example, some investment negotiations are directly about the acquisition of securities, properties, or contracts. Others are between you and one or more intermediaries such as brokers, advisors, or middlemen. There are occasions when one cannot even tell the difference. In any of these circumstances, though, the skills this book offers will help you in critical ways. When purchasing shares in a liquid market, the most valuable of your negotiation skills might be preparation, research, and awareness of your best alternative. When discussing fees with a broker, greater advantage might come from information exchange, analysis of interests, and wise structuring of commitments. Even though different types of challenges will reap rewards in different parts of the process, your overall results will be dramatically improved by negotiating ably, skillfully, and thoughtfully.

As we did in Part I, we start Part II with the ending and with my favorite question: What is a good outcome? That is to say, what end result of your investing life will get you what you really, *really* want? Where will a successful journey take you and how will you know when you have arrived?

Chapter 13 will encourage you to think with care and self-awareness about whether your stated objectives are fully compatible with your truly "good outcome." Why are you investing and what do you hope to achieve? Are you being honest with yourself? Should you broaden or narrow your goals as an investor?

What distractions, impediments, or feints threaten your investment efforts? In particular, which specific systems and situations might interfere with attaining the best possible investment outcomes? In Chapters 14, 15, and 16, we examine some systematic challenges that are especially problematic for negotiators in the world of financial services. As you will see, the issues of conflict-of-interest, asymmetric information, and trustworthiness are critical to an investor-negotiator and cannot be ignored.

Those chapters lead directly to a discussion of professionalism. Which qualities are essential if you are to receive worthwhile guidance? The ideas expressed in Chapter 17, researched and explored for two decades, are the best answers I can offer for dealing with the challenges posed. They are also my contribution to solving one of our society's biggest problems: How shall we safeguard the wealth workers have saved up over years to ensure a comfortable retirement? As you will see, my solution to both your problem and that of the nation is the same: the creation, training, and socialization of true professionals whose skill, loyalty, and sense of caretaking is so great as to shrink the challenges from vast to minimal.

The solutions put forth in Chapter 17 are clearly aspirational and would require significant changes. Whether our society can embrace moving toward such professionalism as an answer remains to be seen. You, however, can use these ideas to distinct advantage. Finding a "true professional" who possesses all the qualities described in Chapter 17 is a powerful answer to the urgent difficulties that investor-negotiators face. Unfortunately, it presents a new quandary; you must be able to identify and engage such a professional. While the future holds promise for a great increase in the number of financial experts who are "true professionals," at present they are as hard to find as a needle in a haystack. The message to you as an intelligent investor-negotiator is that if you choose to seek expert guidance, the search for such a professional will be worth the effort.

Having examined the most significant systematic challenges facing you as an investor-negotiator, we proceed to applying the elements and stages described in Part I for negotiating your investment life. Focusing a sharp "negotiator's eye" on all that is occurring will make you a better investor and get you superior investment outcomes.

To the surprise of many people, it is you, the investor-negotiator, who holds most of the power. It is a "buyer's market" for people who have capital to invest. In addition, though, those who are trying to persuade, entice, or sell you investments face overwhelming competition. You are actually the one in the driver's seat.

Chapter 18, about the power of alternatives, will help you understand this fact and mobilize the power that comes with it.

After considering alternatives, we examine the importance of knowing and clarifying your genuine interests and those that drive the other side. Next we explore identifying the best of many possible options for structuring the deal. Chapter 21 is about the use of objective standards of fairness. Other elements of negotiation involve identifying the kind of relationship that is best for you and choosing the optimal communication tools to advance your effort. Then we look at commitment—deciding what to be bound to, how tightly, and when. Once you are prepared and ready, Chapter 25 walks you through the four stages of an investment negotiation.

Let's get started.

12

Why Is Investing Really Just Another Type of Negotiation?

The care and management of your financial life is best understood as a series of negotiations. An investor is seeking a deal in which she will exchange payment for some instrument that (she hopes) will appreciate in value. This may be a stock (an ownership interest in an enterprise), a bond (debt), or some sort of commodity (a thing that has value). Or the object of the deal may be some derivative or combination of those things. In any case, the terms of exchange are bargained for until a final agreement is reached. Both sides are looking for value from the deal, and each side hopes to claim as much value as possible.

You should remember that there is always someone on the other side of the negotiating table. The person you are buying that stock, bond, or gold coin from is just as interested in getting the best possible deal as you are. This is equally true whether you are interacting directly or through intermediaries such as brokers or advisors. They want the best possible price, and you want the best possible price. In that, your interests are in direct conflict.

Investing Is Similar to Other Big-Ticket Negotiations

For reasons explored later, though, most people do not comprehend financial transactions in this way. In particular, we are frequently blind to how similar making an investment is to buying any other kind of property—a strange thing considering the whole world seems to understand that buying a piece of real property, such as a house, is a negotiation. Everyone appreciates that the seller is trying to get the highest possible price from the buyer and that the buyer is seeking the lowest cost from the seller. They are instinctively on their guard around those elements of the negotiation that are "zero sum"; every dollar in one side's pocket is coming out of the purse of the other side. Such a real estate deal strikes everyone involved as a negotiation, and the participants are all aware that they are sitting on opposite sides of the bargaining table.

As with investing, a home buyer may be in several different negotiations at once. Not only is there bargaining between buyer and seller but, also, there is an ongoing negotiation between principals and agents. How much the real estate broker gets paid, and in exchange for what, forms another negotiation entirely. It can get complicated pretty quickly. For now, though, the thing to notice is that several negotiation processes are occurring simultaneously.

Rather than thinking about real estate deals, however, let's consider a classic tale of negotiation in America: going to the automobile dealer. This is a situation where virtually everyone in the country is aware that they are entering a negotiation. It is the stuff of Hollywood movies and family folklore. The preparation, the tire-kicking rituals, and the haggling are all familiar. Who hasn't had a good laugh over the idea of the car salesman going into the back to ask his manager? And what family doesn't have some myth concerning the hard bargain driven by a crusty old uncle or grandfather back in the day?

Everyone in the auto showroom is on notice that sitting across from you is a person, part of a team, who is trying to separate you from as much of your money as possible. You, on the other hand, are trying to pay the lowest feasible amount for the car. The salesman's living depends on the rewards he gets from selling autos at relatively high prices. The dealership's owners must sell cars dear to pay the overhead. At the very least, they cannot "give them away" at their true cost. The cash flow problems of the owners are not your concern, though, and you would be delighted to get the car for less than the wholesale price they paid for it. In most cases, neither side is any too concerned with the problems faced by the other, nor is anyone thinking all that much about what is "fair."

Do Not Be Fooled into Thinking It Is Something Other Than a Negotiation

What would happen, though, if you went to the car dealer thinking the experience was more akin to visiting your doctor? What might result if you simply determined to follow the guidance of the car salesman, believing that his efforts are motivated by concern for your well-being? If you viewed the car-buying process not as bargaining but rather as a time to do as you are told, what outcome would you expect?

Let's take this fantasy a step further. Imagine that when you arrive at the Toyota dealership, you are greeted by a man in a pinstriped suit. After sitting you down in a fancy and well-appointed office, he explains that they are no longer in the business of selling cars. "We are now 'car advisors,'" he announces, "and our job is to analyze your needs and future for the purpose of selecting exactly the right automobile for you." He promises that, after using a systematic scientific process that takes your entire life into account, his company will scour the universe of cars to identify just the right one for you and your family. The process that follows includes computer questionnaires, long discussions, question-and-answer sessions, and investigation into your past automotive history. It even incorporates a "dream book" designed by psychologists at a prestigious university to gather and interpret your nocturnal desires. A number of appointments are needed, and several outside experts enter the conversations. It would be rather exhausting, were the focus of the inquiry not you. Your interest in your own life holds your attention, so you are willing to see the thing through. Finally, after much talk, reams of paperwork, significant computer analysis, experts, reports, and conferences, an answer emerges. It is, you are told, highly scientific in its derivation and focused entirely on your needs. "It seems," announces the car advisor, "that the best car for you is a Toyota Camry."

Of course, in such a scenario you would likely be taken to the cleaners. The highest possible price would be charged for the car itself. Furthermore, all sorts of add-on items, options, and accessories would be included to drive up the final price substantially. You would end up paying a small fortune for the vehicle. Without the countervailing force of your haggling back, they would push and push until you could go no higher.

You weren't really fooled, though, were you? It is fairly clear that the whole "scientific process" in our fantasy scenario was ancillary to the dealership's real endeavor, which is selling you a Toyota. It was also quite apparent that all the scientific analysis was serving the purpose of diverting your eyes from what was truly going on. And, of course, that truth was simply a salesman trying to sell you something. What was it that, like a Las Vegas magic trick, you were being distracted from noticing? That a negotiation is taking place and you are the only one positioned to defend your interests and insist on fairness. Everyone knows that you go into the car dealership to negotiate the purchase of a new car.

You wouldn't be willing to buy a car in the manner described in that scenario. Setting aside all the special fees and charges extracted by the "car advisors," there are several reasons that this is a foolish idea. The conflicts of interest are as obvious as they are severe. There is a tremendous problem of asymmetric information; not only do they know far more about the cars, pricing, and industry standards but also they now know all about you, thanks to their car advisor process. Another problem is that you will be asked to foot the bill—directly or indirectly—for that elaborate car-advising procedure. Finally, you would refuse this whole business because it seems false and almost fraudulent. A great big system has been assembled to take advantage of you by diverting your gaze. When you realize this, you will decline to participate.

Buying a car is a negotiation. So are most other buy-and-sell deals and, indeed, most of the transactions in our lives. Our financial dealings are no exception. This part of the book is going to apply our newly learned negotiation skills to investments. The methods and techniques from Part I are completely applicable since all investments are made through a process of negotiation.

That many investors do not comprehend that these transactions are negotiations does not make them any less so.

Different Types of Investing Negotiations

While all investments can be considered negotiations, some are of a very different variety than others. In particular, investments made through properly functioning liquid markets (like the major stock exchanges) may seem dissimilar from investing through agents, middlemen, advisors, or brokers.

They are, indeed, different types of negotiations. Each presents special challenges and may well call for different items from your negotiating toolbox. But they are both negotiations, and the habits and practices of good negotiators presented in Part I of this book will improve your outcomes in each type.

You notice immediately that buying an investment on a stock market lacks some of the common attributes that make it *feel* like a negotiation. In particular, you cannot talk with the party on the other side of the trade. At first glance, it seems like a take-it-or-leave-it proposition. It appears that all you can do is buy at the ask price or walk away. Your gut may tell you that isn't a negotiation.

It really is a negotiation, though, and you can apply many of your negotiating skills to it. While true that you cannot talk with the other party, you do have a way of communicating with them. Financial markets use pricing as, among other things, a system of messages. Offering a bid price is a method to let the market know what you are willing to pay. It is really not so different from bargaining in the tourist bazaar where the crafty old trader starts out asking $20 for the cheap little trinket. You offer $3 and he drops his request to $16. You offer $4 and he comes down to $14—and so on until you end up buying the little piece for $6. Even if you could not talk to him directly, you could choreograph the dance. Imagine that he happens to be deaf. The two of you might not be speaking, but you are communicating.

Of course, in a highly liquid market, there may be many participants. It is always possible that when the man in the bazaar comes down to $16, someone standing near you in the crowd yells out, "I'll take it" and the little trinket is gone. (Don't worry, he probably has some more in the back.) So, too, in the stock market, there are many buyers and your bid may be too low to achieve an execution. That does not mean, however, that the whole process was take it or leave it.

Perhaps the highly structured configuration imposed by the exchange system and its government regulators leaves you feeling there is only one way for the process to happen. Without being able to manipulate it, you may conclude that it lacks the flexibility of a negotiation.

This is an illusion, though, and one that benefits those who have created and enforced the rigid structure. You are, theoretically at least, free to buy a share of Apple stock directly from your next-door neighbor at a mutually agreed-on price. The convenience and low transaction costs associated with the stock exchange system drives everyone to it, though, and usually it is the cheapest and easiest way for parties to connect and negotiate the best possible price. That is probably better for you and surely ideal for those making a huge volume business in the buying and selling of stocks. You may feel this is analogous to shopping in a supermarket; the "fixed price" structure would appear to allow no room for any alteration of terms. It really isn't so. Just as we teach that buying bread in the supermarket is actually a negotiation (they want your $2 more than the bread and you want the loaf of pumpernickel more than your $2), so, too, is the stock market transaction. The fact that other traders, and third parties structuring the marketplace, are trying hard to limit your flexibility does not eliminate the aspects of a negotiation. On the contrary, they are manipulating the process to maximize their advantage and minimize yours. Those parties are actually employing a negotiation tactic with you, and doing it rather well. As a good negotiator, your job is to figure out how to counter their move. This section of the book will help you do that.

In contrast to conducting negotiations in highly structured marketplaces, you may frequently invest by engaging brokers, advisors, and other types of middlemen. Those are situations in which the negotiation aspects are clear. Even if the other parties try hard to disguise the bargaining process, this book will help you see it clearly and react to it appropriately.

As discussed later at great length, a one-on-one interaction with a broker or advisor is clearly a negotiation. The more sharply you focus on that simple fact, the better you will do.

Sometimes you will encounter investment situations that are dressed up to disguise the plain fact that they are negotiations. For example, when the representative of an insurance company suggests that you invest in an annuity, he is trying to sell you a specific financial product offered by his company. The proposed deal is that you hand over money and they enter into a contract with you. That contract makes certain promises. The salesman may argue mightily that no changes or alternative terms could ever be possible. He may insist on the take-it-or-leave-it nature of the contract on offer. But this is not an investment instrument that trades in a liquid marketplace like a stock or a bond. This is just an agreement between you and the company. The only reason they won't discuss changing the terms is that they don't want to. The situation is as pure a negotiation as you are likely to find. And, like other situations discussed in this book, your failure to act like a strong negotiator in such a situation will cost you dearly.

Whether an investment situation looks like a "classic" bargaining opportunity or exactly the opposite, you are facing what this book and any good college course on the subject would consider a negotiation. Start your preparation with that understanding. Take it on faith, if you must. But follow the outline laid out in Part I and applied in Part II. In most cases, it will be worth a great deal of money for you to do so.

Chapter Summary

- Investing is a negotiation like any other.
- You are already practiced at negotiating over other big-ticket items.
- Those who would fool you want you to think it is something other than a negotiation.
- It is a terrible mistake to think that investing is a place where you do what you are told.
- Apply the negotiation lessons to your investing and you will do dramatically better.
- Different investing situations call for different negotiating tools.
- While buying investments on a stock market may not *feel* like a negotiation, it really is.
- Investing through an advisor, broker or intermediary is clearly a negotiation.
- Financial firms benefit when customers think negotiation is inappropriate, so they sometimes encourage that misapprehension.

CHAPTER

13

What Is a Good Outcome Regarding Your Investments?

The best negotiators begin by thinking about what would constitute a good outcome of the negotiation they are working on. Once clear on that, they begin envisioning improvement. What would an even better outcome look like?

In Part I of this book, we explored many different kinds of good outcomes. Some involved maximizing money or financial well-being. Others did not. There was an emphasis on good outcomes reaching far beyond gaining economic advantage. Indeed, Part I stressed that sometimes achieving financial gain is a Pyrrhic victory while the path of less money leads to the truly better result.

The first step in successfully negotiating your investments involves some fruitful thinking about what a good outcome looks like for you. What are you really trying to achieve? What would be the attributes of true success in this area of your life? Let yourself imagine where you are trying to go with your investments. In your own mind, try to move beyond simple phrases to get at the deeper meanings of accomplishment and satisfaction in this regard. What is your financial good outcome truly all about?

You will recall that two big obstacles to achieving best outcomes are failing to pursue the path that leads to the real good outcome and getting distracted by irrelevant (or worse) detours that lead away from—rather than toward—the deeper and true goals. Essential to actually attaining good outcomes is a process of sifting through those things that are actually irrelevant to your genuine success. These are distractions that must be eliminated or, at least, put out of mind. The world generally, and the financial services industry in particular, is forever suggesting paths that lead somewhere other than to your maximum success. As any good negotiator must, you have got to find ways to sidestep these diversions.

A good outcome is about the authentic attainment of what you are actually trying to do. It requires taking the actions necessary to *really* get where you want to go. That, in turn, can be very different for different people.

The One Investment Goal That Almost Everyone Shares

Investing involves at least one goal that is shared by almost everyone: capturing the best possible returns. In other words, most people invest to make money. This shared objective is a key theme of Parts II and III of this book. Before delving into that topic, though, let's examine other reasons you may be investing and how they might influence your actions and shape your notion of good outcomes.

Over many years of working with families, I have found something distinctive in each person's investment ambitions. This surprised me as, early in my career, I believed that almost everyone was single-mindedly trying to make as much money as possible. Over time, though, I have found that people invest for varied reasons.

Your Investment Good Outcome Is Uniquely Your Own

Over years of practice and study, I have learned that people invest for many different reasons. Their fondest hopes and ultimate goals reflect a multitude of potential results. Of course, there is a shared element of wanting to achieve financial gains and we will talk about that further. For the moment, though, let's focus on some of the goals that people bring to their investment lives.

People invest for many different reasons and their goals reflect this. Most of the motivations driving investor behavior can be divided into the following categories: to be safe, to be clever, to be wise, and to feel connected to a peer group, as well as to make money. These different kinds of goals can be useful in examining your own desired outcomes. Consider which of these groupings may play a part in your own goals, hopes, and targets.

Investing to Be Safe

Many people feel insecure about their money. For some, this manifests itself as a strong aversion to risk. Lots of folks are terrified of losing money.[1] It may seem a paradox that one who is scared of financial loss would seek to invest what they desperately wish to keep safe. There is, however, a method to that madness. Some readily available investments are considered extremely safe. Indeed, lending money to the United States is presumably far safer than "noninvestment" alternatives such as keeping money in the mattress. Sometimes a program of investment is designed less to gain wealth than to avoid losing it.

Not all who seek safety are risk averse, however, and the desire for safety doesn't always lead to a conservative investment program. Sometimes an aggressive portfolio, aimed at achieving high returns, can help you feel that you are advancing the overall level of security in your life. Whether it is to advance a particular goal, such as a comfortable retirement, or for a more generalized sense of well-being, investing can produce a feeling of taking action to create a safer future.

Needless to say, some types of investments may actually make you safer while others only create an illusion. In finance, as in other areas of life, increased security may be real or a chimera. Either way, though, trying to satisfy the need can be a powerful driving force behind investment decisions.

Investing to Be Clever

Many investors seek to somehow get ahead. They want to gain advantage through their investments. People who view life as a kind of contest are often obsessed with winning it. This attitude is often playfully summed up as "the one with the most toys at death is the winner." If you are open to such a view, the investment markets make for an almost perfect game within the game. Hence the television commercial for a brokerage house in which an investor declares that he is in the markets "to win." Actually, making money can take a back seat to a feeling of "emerging triumphant."

Although it can be minimized through science or prudence, there is always some part of investing that is akin to gambling. For those who find games of chance to their liking, or are addicted to them, the investment markets are a perfect match. Furthermore, most gamblers don't see it as "chance" at all. Rather, they are almost obsessed with gaining an advantage in the game. If you are clever enough, the belief goes, you will win. Thus an imagined meritocracy can grow out of even games of pure randomness.[2]

There is much in our social structure to suggest that those who invest successfully are the ultimate winners. When high-profile mutual fund managers are treated as rock stars and hedge fund guys live better than kings, it is hard to escape the message that investing well is among the highest of human achievements. Heck, the United States even has a *special tax break* to reward such endeavors.[3]

If you are someone who invests, at least in part, either to "win the game" or gain an advantage over other people, great caution is appropriate. As suggested in later chapters, these motivations leave an investor extremely vulnerable to several types of manipulation. A great deal of care, study, and insight is necessary for you to emerge as a "winner" in the world of competitive investing. Furthermore, as this book will argue in Part III, even diligent study will not suffice. As much as you may not want to hear it, economic science suggests that you will also need luck.

Investing to Be Wise

Many people invest out of a desire to do "the right thing." They seek to act sagaciously and responsibly both to achieve life's legitimate rewards and as an end in itself.

The history of financial markets in the twentieth century shows that investing is not only an industrious act but a prudent one, as well. It is sensible to save some of your money. The smartest thing to do with those savings is investing in the various stock and bond markets made readily available by the financial services industry. There is every reason for you to participate.

A concern with stewardship can also be viewed as an attempt to act wisely. Some seek to continue caring for loved ones after their own death. Others want to shepherd certain people or causes into the future as, for example, when a grandparent finances her grandchildren's college educations. Many investors are trying to further their estate planning goals; they wish to leave something and are concerned not only with who will receive it, but also with how much it will be worth.

People who have successfully delegated authority in other areas of their lives often find wisdom in selecting just the right person for the job. A gerontologist whom I admire has long cared for his elderly patients by identifying medical problems and then selecting the perfect specialist to deal with each one. He views his role as an investor the same way: find the right man or woman and put the matter into those capable hands. For this good doctor, taking care and selecting wisely are essentially the same thing.

Almost everyone wants to feel that they have made the right choices, or at least that they have avoided the most egregious mistakes. To the extent that investing represents steering the ship of your financial life, you may find ultimate success in having avoided the jagged rocks and navigating to the safe harbor.

If you sleep better at night knowing that you have acted judiciously in looking after your financial assets, you are in good company. Many investors place great importance on having done the very best they could with what they have. Both comfort and satisfaction can come from knowing that you have done the wise, smart, or prudent thing regarding those elements of life that have great monetary value.

Investing to Feel Connected to Your Group

Almost everyone wants to belong. For some, that means feeling attachment to the groups we naturally fit into. For others, the desire is to be part of not just *any* group but, rather, to connect with a group that we admire or look up to. Groucho Marx famously said that he would not want to join any club that would have someone like himself for a member. Investing can play a significant role in how you see yourself and your place in the community.

The particulars of an investment program can be a way to feel that you are doing as well as others. Many of us want to keep up with the Joneses, or at least not to feel we are somehow inferior. We want to be able to hold our head up in the group. A sense of successful investing can play a significant role in this desire to fit in with our chosen group.

In a similar vein, some people fear being left out or excluded from the social group to which they seek to belong. The ability to hold your own at a cocktail party or in the water cooler discussion has significant value. Sometimes the details of your investments are useful in gaining that place. Ideally, they may win you admiration. At the least, you will be seen as a solid member of the group.

For a small but significant number of people, it is not their natural peer group but a more desirable one to which they wish acceptance. Some seek to do what the cleverest or most in-the-know people are doing; they are forever trying to emulate "the smart money." Others want to fit in with what used to be called "the beautiful people." They are interested in investing with, and like, those whom society elevates. Still others seek influence through their proximity and imitation of power people. One may think of Jay Gatsby throwing grand parties for all those upper-class New Yorkers.[4]

Of course, seeking acceptance or social advantage through investments can leave you very vulnerable. A virtual army of financial folks stands ready to take advantage of such behavior. To mention only the most egregious example, why did all those people hand their money over to Bernie Madoff when even a little deliberation would suggest that his deal was too good to be true?[5] Those who want their money to mingle with that of elite people must take great care that they are not sheared like sheep in the process.

It is easy to understand, though, that investors may seek to join with those they see as most clever, able, connected, or even fashionable. We are human beings, and seeking to emulate and be in the company of leaders comes naturally to us.

Should You Narrow Your Investment Goals?

In light of the many motivations that drive investors, there are numerous ways to think about best possible investing outcomes. My own preference, though, is to keep investing goals narrow and focus tightly on those related to making money.

The entire range of motivations driving investments, discussed earlier, are worthy of respect. There is a danger, though, that some may prove to be distractions or lead to unfruitful paths. The vision of a good outcome I bring to my own investing is straightforward. I seek to make the maximum amount of money while avoiding excessive or undue risk. Avoiding the headaches that come from human or technological errors is desirable and I generally seek ease of use. While willing to pay a fair price for services that are useful to me, I do not care for excessive fees. Furthermore, I demand transparency of such fees—hidden costs strike me as dishonest trickery. Like most people, I do not wish to pay even a cent for anything that economic science can show is actually worthless. I will not pay any-one to gamble for me (it is much cheaper to do that for myself). I never want to feel that I am being cheated, lied to, or played for a fool. Finally, as discussed in Chapter 17, I want to be treated as the client of a "true professional."

It is a rather short list compared to the many things considered in Chapter 1. When negotiating investments, I omit many interests that would play a big role in some other negotiating situations. Among these are building strong relationships, living up to my code in life, making the world a better place, improving how I am seen by others, and boosting my self-esteem. Moreover, I have con-cluded that the investment world is not a place to look for solid new friendships.

This contraction reflects my concern about distractions and diversions in the investment world. As discussed in later chapters, the financial services industry and various intermediaries have developed sophisticated ways of manipulating human desires to reduce financial returns. Of great importance in pursuing best out-comes is avoiding actions that may look inviting but actually lead in other directions. An investor-negotiator should constantly ask her-self whether a given move really leads to her ultimate goals.

In the end, it is for you to decide whether to follow me in thin-ning out the components of your investing good outcome. Such a decision is not required to make good use of this section of the book. It is best, though, that you consider the issue fully informed about the hazards and the stakes. You will find the chapters that fol-low very useful in thinking that through.

Chapter Summary

- Think hard about what would constitute a good outcome in light of what you are trying to achieve through investing.
- Avoid distractions and detours.
- Almost everyone invests, in part, to make money.
- Beyond increasing wealth, people invest for many different reasons.
- Be honest with yourself about your investing goals and motivations.
- Consider whether you should narrow your investing goals.

Notes

1. Amos Tversky and Daniel Kahneman, "Judgment Under Uncertainty: Heuristics and Biases," *Science* 185, no. 4157 (September 27, 1974): 1124–1131.
2. Nassim Nicholas Taleb, *Fooled by Randomness: The Hidden Role of Chance in Life and in the Markets* (New York: Random House, 2005).
3. Lynn Forester de Rothschild, "A Costly and Unjust Perk for Financiers," *New York Times*, February 24, 2013.
4. F. Scott Fitzgerald, *The Great Gatsby*, reissue (New York: Scribner, 2004).
5. Robert Lenzner, "Bernie Madoff's $50 Billion Ponzi Scheme," *Forbes*, December 12, 2008.

CHAPTER 14

The Problem of Conflicts of Interest

Whenever we ask someone to act for us, place our trust in another, or fundamentally rely on anyone else, we must contend with the problem of conflicts of interest. Economists have long studied this simple truth: People have a strong tendency to respond to their own interests. Even those at the very highest levels of governmental, social, or commercial life usually take actions they believe will further their own goals and objectives. Indeed, one way of looking at human interactions is to start with the assumption that a person's sole motivation is to advance his own interests. Such a rational actor will further the well-being of others only if he believes that to do so also somehow maximizes his own benefit.

The challenges posed by this problem are particularly acute when negotiating your investments.

For one thing, the stakes are very high. Where large amounts of money are involved, people's tendency to advance their own interests above others' is increased. With its long history, culture, and track record of placing its own interests above those of its clients, the financial services industry is particularly prone to this effect. Common sense tells us that extra caution is required when placing big money in the hands of people who covet it.

Furthermore, the financial world leaves us little recourse but to rely heavily on others and there are limits to how much an investor can become a do-it-yourselfer. A great deal of the process is necessarily not in your direct control. You must depend on others to identify, connect, execute, deliver, and record. With such reliance comes vulnerability. Will the other people involved in the transaction do what is best for you, or will they act according to their own motivations?

You have more choice, however, when deciding on investment strategies or choosing individual investments. It may be possible to minimize your reliance on the knowledge, judgment, and skill of others. Obviously, though, this comes with a big downside: You cannot know everything yourself, and eliminating others' insights will leave you with few resources. One way or another, you end up looking for wisdom and guidance from other people. In doing so, there are steps you should take to minimize the dangers posed by the conflicting interests of the folks you seek help from.

Incentives Matter

In thinking about human behavior, economists say that incentives matter a great deal in deciphering how people act. As an investor-negotiator, you must think hard about what incentives are influencing those you are dealing with. How do they get paid? What pressures are being placed on them? What actions will bring them success? And, of course, which paths lead to their failure? Remember that this analysis must focus on how *they* understand their incentives. You might think that serving clients loyally is the highest measure of a job well done, but they may see it as a road to the unemployment line.

To put it plainly, most financial advisors labor under terrible conflicts of interest. The history of the financial services industry is a system of commission-based compensation, and most of these folks still make their living from some variant of that arrangement. The conflicts are stark; the advisor wants to make as much money as possible, while the client seeks the best (which often correlates, at least in part, with least expensive) method of solving financial challenges. This problem is exacerbated by expensive multilayered organizations that often incentivize advisors to recommend actions contrary to what is best for their clients.

In the worst cases, they are but salespeople trying to place an expensive product. Why else would anyone recommend a mutual fund with a 5.75 percent sales charge when an equally good one exists with no such charge? The answer, of course, is that a significant part of their income flows from that charge. Similarly, why recommend a mutual fund with a 1 percent internal operating fee when a superior choice has an operating fee a tenth of that level?

While the financial services industry has a long history of commission-based sales, some financial advisors do not currently work that way. So-called fee-only advisors are compensated based on an agreed-upon rate and thus may avoid some of the conflict problems that commissions generate. This is a step in the right direction, but it by no means eliminates the problem. Consider, for example, what happens when the client asks a fee-only advisor about the wisdom of paying off a mortgage early. He may be loath to recommend a payoff when the funds used to reduce that debt will mean less money available to invest. That, in turn, would mean less revenue for him. Once again, the advisor may find the source of his own income to be the most compelling rationale for action.

Some Conflicts Other Than Money

Commissions and fees are among the most obvious sources of conflict, but they are by no means the only ones. Various indirect payments, soft money arrangements, sales quotas, inventory arrangements, and pay-to-play schemes are likely to influence the behavior of anyone in a position to route your money.

Consider this sobering thought: While claiming to scour the world on your behalf in search of the best investments, a big Wall Street firm is actually competing with you in that pursuit. When an advisor who is a registered representative of such a company suggests you buy stock in XYZ, his firm has decided to bet against the XYZ Company. If XYZ was really a great investment poised to go up, your advisor's company would choose to hold its shares and buy as many more as it could *for the firm itself.* Even worse, it may be selling you shares from its own inventory. They are selling while urging you to buy. Not only are their interests not aligned with yours, but they are actually your competitor in the same marketplace.

Beyond money, time is an interest that is often in conflict. Financial workers are under great pressure, both external and self-imposed, to get new prospects. Every minute spent serving the needs of current clients is time not used searching for new ones. From your point of view, though, appropriate client service is as important as it is time-consuming. Doing competent work takes care and attention and cannot always be achieved quickly. Even the basic matter of doing a thorough job can raise serious conflict-of-interest issues.

Remember, too, that the overwhelming majority of financial advisors work for someone else. As with most other people who labor for a living, pleasing one's boss is a compelling personal interest. Financial advisors of all sorts are under tremendous pressure to increase revenues. Thus, the heart, soul, and character of the person sitting across the table from you are not the only things determining how he may behave with your wealth.

Over the years, I have had the chance to teach many advisors, stockbrokers, and financial practitioners. On occasion, I have tried to focus their attention on the overwhelming challenges posed by ongoing conflicts of interest. Those attempts have not always been successful. It is not something that people in the industry wish to examine closely. Perhaps the difficulty is best summed up by this famous quote attributed to Upton Sinclair:

It is difficult to get a man to understand something, when his salary depends on his not understanding it.[1]

The problem of conflicts of interest is neither easily solved nor likely to go away. Careful attention to it, though, can give rise to dramatically better results. You are going to be negotiating with people who have such conflicts. Ignoring them is a mistake. Simply accepting their ill effects will make you poorer. On the other hand, minimizing their impact on your investments and demanding that those you work with do the same can make a tremendous difference in your outcomes.

Chapter Summary

- Economists know that people usually act to advance their own interests.
- You are vulnerable when the stakes are high and when you must rely heavily on others.
- Incentive structures play a huge role in just how conflicted someone will be.
- The financial world is full of conflicts of interest over money.
- Watch out for conflicts that are not about money, too.

- Don't try to teach someone about the conflicts problem if his understanding will cost him his livelihood—he won't get it.
- Pay attention and work to minimize the negative impact of conflicts of interest on your investing.

Note

1. Upton Sinclair and James Gregory, *I, Candidate for Governor: And How I Got Licked* (1935; reprint, Berkeley: University of California Press, 1994), 109.

CHAPTER 15

The Problem of Asymmetric Information

Along with conflicts of interest, an investor-negotiator faces a second set of challenges related to what economists call asymmetric information. This is a fancy-sounding name for a very common-sense problem. Basically, you must negotiate with people who know a lot more than you do about the subject at hand.

Just as the car dealer recognizes which one is a lemon, and the home seller is aware of the secret damage to the roof, so, too, the financial worker knows a great deal more than you about the investments you are negotiating over.

They Know Much More Than You Do about the Tricks of the Trade

Most advisors have command of a great many practices, mores, and tricks of the trade that are far beyond the knowledge of even very smart regular people. This is even more relevant in fields where special jargon, routines, and techniques make common sense an almost irrelevant attribute. The result is an uneven playing field between the advisor and the client. The person receiving advice is badly disadvantaged and very vulnerable to being manipulated.

This is particularly true of investment advisors in light of the complexity and counterintuitive nature of financial markets. The advisor knows far more than you do about the investment arena. Regardless of intelligence or life experience, you possess only a sliver of the necessary information about the system, players, norms, jargon, and customs of the financial services industry. The fellow across the table, on the other hand, knows the system, the techniques, the players, and the secrets. Indeed, the advisor even knows the client in ways that can be used for gain.

A historical example may illuminate the point. Although it is quite illegal now, in the bad old days many stockbrokers engaged in a practice called front running. When a customer was about to buy a significant amount of a certain stock, that purchase would have the effect of raising the price. If the broker knew in advance, she could buy it for her own account before entering the client's order. This ensured a profit for the broker, essentially at the client's expense. While no one is making accusations of front running today in light of legal, ethical, and regulatory prohibitions, it nicely illustrates a large and troubling problem. Financial intermediaries know all sorts of things that you do not. They are in the business of using what they know to make money *for them.* You are left to wonder if they will use that knowledge to advance your interest in making money. Or, even worse, whether they will use it to make money at your expense.

Knowing More Creates Tremendous Opportunity to Take Advantage of Others

The opportunities to take advantage of such situations are many and vast. Among these are overcharging, underserving, moving bad merchandise, guiding business to friends (or reciprocators), hiding fees, selling things that have no value, misleading, stealing, taking credit unfairly, and claiming random chance as skill. This list goes on and on. In reality, absent some sort of strong professional or moral code, those who guide us in areas we know little about can do just about whatever they wish. To use an extreme example, Bernie Madoff did not just mislead people about their investment returns—he made them up.

One answer to the problem of such information asymmetry is to learn more. It is a wonderful response, and I endorse it heartily— after all, isn't that what this book is all about? That course of action has significant limitations, though. We cannot all become experts in the many areas of our lives. In the case of your investments and financial decisions, even dedicated study is unlikely to level the information playing field with those who work in that field every day.

To make matters worse, some portion of the financial industry's profits are specifically based on taking advantage of the relative ignorance of other people. The markets are, to some extent, viewed as a contest, with the spoils going to the fittest players. That may be all well and good in transactions between giant investment banks, but it is immoral and unacceptable when the losers are working folks who foolishly place their trust in the wrong people or institutions. Giant firms loaded up with PhDs, former treasury secretaries, banks of computers, and all of my brightest Wharton students are always going to win. No society can long endure if it lets such behemoths vacuum up the life savings of everyone else.

Consider the case in which the Securities and Exchange Commission charged and then settled with Goldman Sachs over the sale of a financial product called Abacus.[1] Goldman was accused, in essence, of working with Client A to create a financial instrument likely to blow up so that Client A could short it (bet that it would lose value) and then turning around and selling that same instrument to Client B, whose expectation was that it would retain its value. Goldman's defense was that it owed no duty to Client B that was violated. The inference is that Client B's losses were its own fault—it failed to discover that its trusted advisor was deliberately rolling up excrement and selling it to them. This is an extreme example of *caveat emptor*; not only must the buyer beware but also he should be on notice that those who have inside knowledge of the situation are going to use it to take unlimited advantage.

How can one possibly thrive in such a situation? It may remind you of those games where, in the end, the only way to win was not to play. That cannot be the right message, though, since we know that the financial markets offer the best opportunities to deploy your capital effectively. Economists speak with great confidence when they state that, over the very long term, diversified stock investments offer the best risk-reward ratio of any major class of investments.[2] Stock investments cannot be avoided, and yet they leave you very vulnerable to the abuses that accompany information asymmetries.

What are you, as an investor-negotiator, to do? The answer, of course, is the same thing you would do in any other negotiation. Investing is by no means unique in its vulnerability to the hazards of information asymmetries. To the contrary, the problem exists whenever you negotiate with experts. You must focus your learning not only on the subject matter of investments but also on the people and companies you work with in pursuing them.

Many solutions to this difficulty can be found in Part I of this book. You will also find direct help in the upcoming chapters on "Whom Can You Trust?" and "Who Is a True Professional?" For now, though, remember that you cannot trust blindly but, rather, must negotiate wisely. As for the very specific challenges of investing in a world of knowledgeable sharks, there is no single answer. The best advice is not a simple prescription but a set of cautions and admonitions. You must stay vigilant. You cannot trust imprudently. You must be keenly aware of the problem of asymmetric information and be constantly on guard to avoid being its victim.

Chapter Summary

- The people you are negotiating with know more than you do about the subject at hand.
- High levels of complexity make matters worse.
- This asymmetry leaves you quite vulnerable.
- Learn more to minimize the problem.
- Don't trust blindly, but rather negotiate rigorously.
- Stay vigilant, don't trust blindly, and remain on your guard.

Notes

1. Stephen Grocer, "'Fabulous Fab,' Goldman and Abacus—a Timeline," WallStreetJournal.com, July 15, 2013.
2. Jeremy J. Siegel, *Stocks for the Long Run: The Definitive Guide to Financial Market Returns and Long-Term Investment Strategies*, 2nd ed. (New York: McGraw-Hill, 1998).

16

Whom Can You Trust? And Why?

The combination of conflicting interests and asymmetric information creates a situation in which it is unwise to trust most advisors. They may be decent people with good intentions and a warm heart, but, in reality, they are not likely to put their client's interests ahead of their own. It would be imprudent even to expect that level of unselfishness, and experience shows us that extreme caution is called for in light of typical practices. The incentives are stacked against an advisor being highly trustworthy and, since advisors are human, most of them act on their own interests. This creates a huge difficulty for the client in need of the best possible advice.

For historical and legal reasons, this dilemma is particularly difficult when dealing with our financial lives. The problems of conflicting interests and asymmetric information, however, are not unique to investment advice. Indeed, they arise whenever we pay someone to give us highly skilled guidance about subjects on which they have much greater knowledge, which could include anyone from an auto mechanic to a hairstylist to a financial advisor. What is to be done about this predicament? How can we get the guidance, care, and help we need in an area outside our own expertise without being preyed upon by someone who has the requisite skills?

Be Extremely Careful about Whom You Trust—and How Much

The first step is to trust carefully and only when appropriate. It is tempting to extend our trust to warm people who seem eager to help us. In this busy and overburdened modern world, it is also very convenient. But, of course, it is a big mistake. You don't offer unearned trust to the car salesman or the other side's real estate broker. Neither can you give unguarded trust to the financial salesperson. This is a situation that cries out for caution and skepticism.

It is worth examining, though, why we are often less than appropriately skeptical when dealing with financial advisors. Part of the problem, I believe, is that we have a bias toward trusting members of our own team. We are brought up to think in terms of us and them. Our socialization includes rooting for our side and learning to boo (and even hate) the other.

If you think back, this training started at the beginning of your schooling. Most of us went to elementary school and competed against the kids from the other elementary schools in the city. When we got to junior high, our teammates were those kids who had been adversaries at the other elementary schools. In my town, the new enemy was the other junior high. Those two junior high schools dumped into a single high school, and now the adversaries were high schools in surrounding towns. Most of my peers went off to the state university, where their teammates were from all the other high schools. The new enemies were the surrounding state universities. Of course, when bowl games came around, we rooted for our division champion—the very neighboring state U that we hated two months earlier.

So who is really your teammate, and who is your adversary? In light of the constant shifting and rearranging, there is plenty of room for confusion. Somehow, though, we have automatic good feelings about whoever is currently declared to be our teammate. Those good feelings and the blind trust that can grow from them leave us vulnerable to being taken advantage of.

Sophisticated financial firms, aided by top behavioral scientists, make every effort to win your confidence, allay your suspicions, and sit at your table as a trusted member of your negotiating team. I am reminded of the television commercial featuring an older man in a tux making a toast at a young woman's wedding. "We worked and strived 24 years for this moment. Seeing our beautiful girl walk down that aisle makes all the effort worthwhile." And then the punch line: "But hey, I'm only the financial advisor, let's hear from the Dad."

The effort to win his way onto your team is easy to understand. Whether he intends to serve you or cheat you (or doesn't know the difference), sitting on your side of the table will bring the advisor great advantage. It is incumbent upon you to see the situation clearly. He is not really on your team in that his interests are not well aligned with yours. The incentives driving his behavior are likely to steer him away from the very best solutions for you. By the very nature of the system he works in, he has remarkably strong motivations to sell you things and ideas for his own advantage. His company wants to use your capital for its own benefit. To all this must be added the lopsided division of applicable knowledge; he knows all about the subject at hand, and you know far less. You are at a sharp disadvantage in dealing with this advisor. That disadvantage will be many times greater if you are mistakenly lulled into complacency by warm assurances of a team effort.

You Can Work Well with People without Trusting Them

As a skilled and confident investor-negotiator, though, you need not fear working with such an adversary. It is not even necessary to think of him as an opponent. You can work fruitfully with such people to create win-win solutions where everyone comes out ahead. What you cannot do, however, is stop being vigilant about who is fully on your side and whom you should fix with your sharpest negotiator's eye. These folks may be part of your team, but you must use all your negotiating skills to deal with them carefully, negotiate with them actively, and afford them only the amount of trust that prudence will allow.

To put it bluntly, these are not people you should trust.

You Can Trust Those Whose Best Interests Make Them Trustworthy

Whom can you trust, then, to do what is best for you and put your interests first? Skilled negotiators know that the way to get someone to do what you want is to make it be in their best interest to do so. The folks you can trust are those whose interests will be best served by acting for your well-being and keeping your trust.

In light of the human tendency to act in one's own best interest, the actions of others can be influenced by changing their incentives. In other words, if you can make it be in your partner's best interest to do the thing you want him to, he probably will. Even people with greater knowledge, power, authority, and strength can be influenced through a change in their incentives. You can get others to be trustworthy by making it clearly in their best interest to do so.

We trust people all the time because we are confident that their best interests will keep them from betraying that trust. For example, we never worry that drivers will seek advantage by traveling on the wrong side of the road. The negative consequences of the likely crash are simply too great for them to risk it. So, too, we put our lives in the hands of airline pilots without a worry. It is in their best interest to use all their skills to bring the plane in for a safe landing. We trust the tellers at the local bank not to take our money and run off to the casino. It would little profit them to lose their job and end up in jail. The local restaurateur will not deliberately serve us rancid food because word would get around town and his enterprise would be ruined.

I play a game with many of my students in which I ask them to give me a hundred-dollar bill. After they hand it to me, I suggest that I might keep it. They have little worry, though, because they realize my authority and influence as a professor would be deeply harmed if I were to keep the money. Since they know I treasure the teacher-student relationship above most things, there is little doubt that I will jeopardize it for a hundred dollars. (I usually caution them, though, that the result might not be the same for a million dollars.)

In short, we can trust people whose best interests require that they remain trustworthy. By the same token, those whose interests do not require keeping faith are probably poor candidates for our unmitigated trust. Be extremely careful, though, in the educated guesses you make about their underlying interests. If you guess wrong, you may place too much reliance on someone unworthy of it. As a result, you will want to do a whole lot of checking.

Placing trust only in those whose interests and incentives point strongly toward their trustworthiness in a given situation is only a partial solution. It does not solve the problem posed at the beginning of this chapter. How can you get the guidance, care, and help you need in areas requiring expertise you do not have? What are you to do about the danger of being victimized by those who possess the necessary skills? The next chapter offers answers to those very big questions.

Chapter Summary

- Be careful with trust, and do not have undue confidence in people because they are nice.
- Do not trust anyone simply because they are on your team.
- You can negotiate and work well together with people you do not trust.
- Place more trust in those whose best interests strongly suggest their trustworthiness.
- The problem of trust when investing is never fully solved.

CHAPTER 17

Professionalism: Who Is a True Professional and Why?

It turns out that society, having long struggled with the problem that people must trust certain experts, has come up with a pretty good answer. Individuals have always needed help, guidance, and care in dealing with their greatest treasures. In particular, our health, wealth, rights, and relationship with the Almighty are areas of great vulnerability. We need assistance but are terribly at risk of being abused by those who would help us. The societal answer is that in these areas our care is entrusted to professionals.

The Traditional Professions' Struggle with Society's Need for Trustworthy Help

The traditional professions of medicine, law, and the clergy have unique histories and cultures that developed over very long periods of time. What they have in common, however, is an understanding that service, care, and safeguarding are an intrinsic part of professional work. With this shared knowledge, each of the traditional professions trains and socializes its members (novices and elders alike) in these core attributes that are simultaneously skills and values. To be a member of one of these professions requires mastery of a body of knowledge, some sort of certification or passing of a test or assessment, and an apprenticeship of one kind or another. I propose, however, that what they ask for is far greater than that. The traditional professions seek from their practitioners, not only skill, but also adherence to a code that has at its core an understanding that professionals must not violate the complex trusts placed in them by those they serve. It is this focus on faithfulness that is the essence of what separates professionals from others possessing skill and knowledge.

To be a professional, historically, was to be a member of one of these traditional professions. To gain such a place was not easy; it required long, hard work, intense study, and passing various tests. It also required undergoing a powerful socialization; the professions went to great lengths to get their members to think and act as prescribed. Included in this socialization was some variation of the idea of keeping trust. Furthermore, once a person had attained this status, the profession itself was always looking over her shoulder and seeking to encourage, maintain, and enforce the agreed-upon codes and expectations.

The Traditional Professions Don't Always Succeed—but They Must Always Try

My purpose here is not to idealize the historical professions. It would be naïve in the extreme to suggest that they have always been effective in training and socializing their members to serve and safeguard with the highest levels of faithfulness. The professional bodies, as well, were often as interested in self-protection and promotion as in loftier goals. Sometimes they function more like guilds than as protectors of the highest societal needs. The point, though, is that when they have failed to uphold their self-articulated highest ideals, they have badly fallen short of their avowed professionalism. The professions, and their members, are far from perfect. In their unattained perfect form, however, they are the answer to the great societal problem of who will fairly and faithfully help people protect that which is most precious and important.

Of course, it is neither practical nor reasonable to suggest that an answer lies in always getting a highly ethical physician, lawyer, or member of the clergy to help us with all our problems. We are a society served by a great many groups, vocations, and practitioners. How can we pull together the highest levels of knowledge, skill, training, certification, and apprenticeship and effectively blend them with the concepts of keeper of trusts and safeguarding agent who will never violate or betray the precious things placed in their care?

Reclaiming Professionalism

The answer proposed here is to reclaim the notion of professional and restore to it a precise meaning and high purpose. Our modern society has allowed it to evolve into a word for anyone who has a strong set of skills. This has led to confusion and a loss of usefulness. We have left out the most important part.

After many years of thought and study, I have concluded that the most useful definition of what makes someone a professional is this:

> A true professional uses his or her ability and power solely to advance the best and truest interests of the client. When the professional's interests diverge from those of the client, the professional always follows only the client's interests.

By decoupling professionalism from particular groups and, instead, defining it by its special attributes, we can broaden our understanding of who may legitimately be viewed as a true professional. Such a definition, however, stays faithful to the teaching of the traditional professions found in their codes, training, and socialization. The professional uses her skills, knowledge, experience, and training solely in the service of the client. Indeed, whatever power of any kind she possesses is to be brought to the exclusive task of advancing the client's interests. Although the professional makes a very good and fair living, she is never permitted, under any circumstances, to enrich herself at the expense of that client.

This notion of what makes for a true professional, with its attendant strengthening of expectations and duties, can guide practitioners and providers to a higher level of service and responsibility. By restoring the concept of professionalism to the level of responsibility and trustworthiness prescribed by the traditional professions, a new set of obligations will be assumed by those who would hold themselves out as professionals. This will lead to greater openness, conscientiousness, and reliability on the part of those who wish to be viewed in a professional light. This, in turn, will drive a commercial imperative; few people will seek guidance from less than a true professional. Thus, the choice to embrace this new understanding of professionalism simultaneously helps the practitioner and the client she serves.

Chapter Summary

- The need to trust experts is a very long-standing problem.
- The traditional professions understand that care and safe-guarding are an intrinsic part of professional work.
- True professionals go through a great deal of training and a lot of socialization.
- Members of the traditional professions sometimes disappoint, but, when they do, they are in violation of the basic tenets of their professional aspirations.
- Society makes a mistake when it lets anyone with high levels of skill call himself a professional.
- A true professional uses her skills, knowledge, experience, and training solely in the service of the client.
- Asking for such high levels of responsibility and trustworthiness from all who would call themselves professionals would greatly benefit everyone.

CHAPTER 18

Use the Power of Your Alternatives

As discussed in Part I, power in negotiation comes from having a strong alternative—your best alternative to a negotiated agreement (BATNA). What will you do if the deal being discussed does not come to pass? The negotiator with the stronger BATNA has great power over the counterpart with the weaker one.

Those trying to persuade you to make a particular investment have a big problem. They are faced with overwhelming competition for your attention and your money. Never forget that you have the choice to walk away from any investment proposal. At any given time, there is a vast array of investment choices that are seeking your consideration. In almost every situation you will encounter, those choices include some that are just as good, if not better, than the investment you were originally contemplating.

What this means, of course, is that you hold the greater power in your investment negotiations. You are the one with the money in your pocket and an entire world of attractive alternatives for where you will invest it. It is a buyer's market for those seeking to invest their capital.

You may be surprised by the preceding paragraph. Very few investors feel that they have the upper hand when dealing with the financial services industry and its representatives. It's true though; they need you to make their living and you don't need them very much in light of all the other avenues you can pursue. That is one of the overarching themes of this book and one of the most valuable things I have to teach you. Don't lose sight of it.

Alternatives When Making Direct Investments in Actively Traded Securities

As discussed earlier, investing directly by purchasing a stock on "the market" may not seem like negotiating. I have argued strenuously that it really is a negotiation and, indeed, it is exactly the kind of deal that this book was written to help you with. Nevertheless, I need to acknowledge the different kinds of investment negotiations.

All right, I agree that buying a hundred shares of XYZ doesn't really *feel* like a negotiation. It is certainly quite different from bargaining with a broker, advisor, or "rep" as to whether you will pay for her services or follow her advice.

We can separate investment negotiations into two categories. The first is direct purchase of individual securities or other investment vehicles from the company or organization selling it. The second is investing through some broker, dealer, advisor, or other intermediary.

When directly buying investments that trade on a properly functioning market, the invisible hand actually does the work of creating alternatives for you. The basic idea is easy to grasp. As economists know, properly functioning markets raise the price of bargains and pull down overpriced goods until every item is priced correctly in relationship to all others. As a result, every stock, bond, or other traded investment is priced *appropriately* by the market at any given time.[1]

Why is this important? Because it means that all the investments you are considering are already at "the right price." The stock of one company is not a bargain relative to that of other companies, absent unexpected or unknowable future events. Effectively, this means you have many equally valuable alternatives from which to choose.

For example, if you feel a strong desire to invest in a large U.S.-based pharmaceutical company, there is no reason to believe that the stock of one large multinational drug company is better than another. Merck stock is not expected to be a better investment than stock in Pfizer, or vice versa. Of course, one of those two stocks is going to be better than the other over any given period in the future. But the market has priced them so that only events unknowable in advance will influence which appreciates more. And there is nothing that anyone can do to effectively predict unknowable future events. Anyone who tries to convince you otherwise is flying in the face of economic science and, mostly likely, trying to sell you something you are better off not buying.

In a market full of appropriately priced alternatives, an investor need never be stampeded into a hyped or mispriced investment. When Facebook went public in 2012, to choose a recent example, many factors pushed the stock price high above a proper valuation. Wise investors knew two things that could help them avoid the trap. First, there were plenty of alternative investments to make in lieu of that young company's brand-new shares. Second, Facebook would soon trade on a very liquid market that would eventually result in more realistic market-based pricing of its shares.

Turning back to the example of stock in Merck and Pfizer, there is no way of knowing which will appreciate more in the future. (Keep in mind that at the current moment there are millions of investors making a bet on each of them.) Indeed, absent transaction costs, the better move may be to buy some shares of each. In any category or asset class, you will find many alternative possibilities. This means that there is no overwhelming imperative to invest in any particular one. Even better, you are free to bypass all those investment vehicles that are excessively difficult or expensive due to complexity or added costs. You don't need any one particular investment. This ability to go down a different road with minimum harm to your own situation is the very definition of power.

Alternatives When Investing Through Intermediaries

Investing through financial intermediaries is more easily recognized as a process of negotiation. A person or company seeks to guide your investments in exchange for fees, charges, commissions, or some other combination of payments. You are dealing directly with someone and the terms and conditions of the financial relationship are subject to change (whether they wish to admit it or not). You are in a position to bargain in pursuit of the best possible outcomes.

These intermediaries are middlemen. They necessarily add an extra level of complexity to the negotiation. You may find yourself involved in more than one negotiation simultaneously. For example, when a broker suggests buying something on which she earns a commission, both the matter of the investment and the terms of the commission can be subjects of negotiation. Furthermore, the very existence of intermediaries increases the cost of investing. They must contribute *real* value to be worth anything at all. Making sure they contribute such value, and holding its cost down to a minimum, is part of your job as an investor-negotiator.

Consider investing with a large, multiservice investment company. These are the giant multinational financial services companies you read about in the press and advertisements. They offer one-stop shopping and internationally known brand names. If you wanted to work with one of these firms, you would apply the entire negotiation process from Part I in this book to shopping and coming to terms with them. Your pursuit of best outcomes requires bargaining with them. (Of course, these companies desperately want you to see the process as anything but a negotiation.)

What is your alternative if you don't like what one of these companies is offering you? As you probably realize, it is to do business with large investment company number two, which has an office across the street. These firms are in competition with each other for your business, and they offer pretty much the same services. The investor-negotiator has strong alternatives and, therefore, the greater leverage.

Furthermore, these financial companies are in a business that has long been extraordinarily profitable. Such extreme profitability has resulted in many players trying to poach some of this business. Insurance companies, banks, credit unions, mutual fund companies, and others have all moved into the investment advisor space. They all offer more or less the same things to investors. Negotiate with them to your heart's content, secure in the knowledge that if they won't give you the deal you want, you can always move across the street to the next one. You have a multitude of alternatives, and so you have tremendous negotiating power. (The critical question about whether you want what they are selling is handled elsewhere in this book.)

Among these competing industries, insurance companies merit special caution. For the most part, they sell various types of insurance dressed up as investments. This has proven to be extremely lucrative for them and usually a terrible deal for the investor. Their complicated, sleight-of-hand products significantly raise costs. Your best choice in this case is to just cross the street in pursuit of better ways to invest.

Mutual fund firms have a long history of offering their original product. A mutual fund is an individual company whose purpose is for investors to gather their money and invest together. The benefits of this include significant diversification and economies of scale. They also claim advantages of "professional management," although that claim is probably unsupportable in light of economic knowledge.

Recently, traditional mutual fund companies have started offering other services to compete and capture more of the consumer wallet. Many now offer checking, cash management, and credit cards much like banks do. Some want to sell you "financial advice," presumably about which of their ever-growing stable of financial products is best for you. A few will even try to sell you insurance, mortgages, and other lucrative financial products. As a result, the lines are becoming blurred between these firms and other financial services companies.

Mutual funds themselves have much to recommend them. As previously mentioned, they can bring you the benefits of very broad diversification at low cost. There are measurable savings when thousands of investors work together. And the people running a fund are "insiders" who can avoid some of the costs extracted from outsiders and rookies. While shares of many mutual funds can now be bought from all sorts of firms, costs are often minimized by getting them directly from the company running the fund. Typically, though, mutual funds run the gamut from reasonably priced to obscenely expensive. Exploring your alternatives and knowing your BATNA will be critical to dealing successfully with any mutual fund company.

Another alternative is to work with an independent investment advisor. These practitioners go by many names, with different identities, business models, and ways of getting paid. They are regulated by different governmental entities and don't even all have the same level of duties to their client. As a result, it can be difficult to compare them in an apples-to-apples manner. To put it bluntly, the whole thing is a big mess. Furthermore, many of them are so tied into the large financial companies that it can be hard to determine with which category you are dealing. (If the answer is both, you are likely to incur far too much intermediary cost drag.) The Dodd-Frank law passed in 2010 was, among other things, supposed to make this situation better.[2] So far, though, it has failed miserably in that respect.

To the extent that investment advisors are independent actors, though, they are ripe for negotiation. You can be very assertive with them in shopping, questioning, requesting, demanding, and reviewing. You can often bargain directly with the owners or decision makers. They have real discretion. They need you because their business can make money only through clients with capital. And frankly, many of these firms have such high profit margins that they can easily grant you a discount without threatening their ability to pay the rent. Of course, these folks tend to be very savvy businesspeople and extremely money focused. While some are hungry, many are not desperate. Successful people in this field make so much that they can afford the luxury of turning away some new business. Just because they *can* offer you a better deal does not mean they will wish to. There are few things as unpleasant to a small businessperson as cutting prices or watching margins shrink.

With regard to independent financial advisors, you may find that you are a good negotiator and she is a good negotiator. Such a circumstance can be very positive and holds out the promise of reaching an excellent deal that maximizes value for everyone. Your job though, as an investor-negotiator, will be to employ all the tools and methods suggested herein. Of particular importance will be your skill at analyzing alternatives and using your BATNA. Remember that negotiating strength does not come from wealth or connections. It is derived from having stronger alternatives. You are the one with the power to move yourself and your cash on to another advisor down the block.

With So Many to Choose from, You Can Demand What You Want with Confidence

When negotiating with investment advisors, or any service provider, it is critical to fully understand what you will get from them, what that is worth, and what you are actually paying for it. Providers have a great deal of opportunity to manipulate exactly what the client receives. It is all too easy for them to grant a discount and then reduce the service or product to pay for it. As always, caveat emptor.

One of the things well-prepared negotiators have is self-confidence. That is a big piece of what this chapter is all about. If you have solid alternatives and a relatively strong BATNA, there is no reason for you to have less than complete self-confidence. You are the one in charge, and I want you to feel that, understand it, and act on it. A large part of the financial services industry's *modus operandi* involves making you feel weak, unsure, and afraid. What this chapter points out, though, is that you are the one who has alternatives. You are the one in the negotiating power position. You are actually the one who can easily say no. You should do so without hesitation if you are not getting exactly what you want. And what you want, of course, is exactly what your preparation (including this book) indicates will lead to the best outcomes for you.

Chapter Summary

- You are the one with the greater negotiating power.
- For direct investments, the market automatically provides you with many strong alternatives.
- For investing through intermediaries, the very competitive nature of the industry gives you access to strong alternatives.
- The big "name brand" financial companies have many competitors offering essentially the same things.
- Insurance companies are not a wise choice for investment guidance.
- Mutual funds have many favorable attributes, but beware of fund companies trying to sell you other investments and services.
- The pricing on mutual funds ranges from bargain to absurd rip-off, so be careful.
- For a number of reasons, independent registered investment advisors are ripe for negotiation.
- When you have strong alternatives, you can demand what you want.
- When your best alternative is strong, you should negotiate with confidence.

Notes

1. Eugene Fama, "Efficient Capital Markets: A Review of Theory and Empirical Work," *Journal of Finance* 25, no. 2 (1970): 383–417.
2. www.sec.gov/about/laws/wallstreetreform-cpa.pdf.

CHAPTER 19

Knowing Your Interests and Theirs

Interests can be thought of as what someone really, *really* wants. They are the deep truths that lie below positions and issues and they are comprised of every preference, want, concern, need, and fear that a negotiator brings to the table. Good negotiators concentrate very hard on interests, for they are ultimately of greater importance than the positions staked out by the parties. You should work hard to examine and understand the interests of all the parties involved as you negotiate your investments.

Understanding Your Own Interests

Start by understanding your own underlying goals and interests. Take a deep look. What lies below the surface of what you think you want from your investments? Be careful; we often try to fool ourselves about our deeper motivations.

Think back, for a moment, to what constitutes a good outcome for an investor. The focus there was on your broad objectives and the things that might get in the way of achieving them. It had a particular emphasis on avoiding distractions and wrong turns that could lead away from where you really want to go.

Now we are shifting attention to the specifics of exactly the things you seek to achieve. What do you really want from the process and acts of investing? In the final analysis, these answers must come from you. The next few paragraphs offer a partial list that you can use as a starting point. These are underlying interests that resonate for most investor-negotiators. In particular, these items relate to a negotiation with financial service providers.

1. Low Costs

The desire shared by almost all investors, to maximize returns, makes it important to hold down the costs of investing. You will soon learn that every dollar lost to excessive costs is one dollar of reduced investment return. Avoiding inflated or hidden costs will directly advance your pursuit of higher returns.

2. Clear and Complete Explanation of Costs and Fees

In order to effectively negotiate about costs, you will need to know what they are. This is not always as easy as it sounds. Therefore, one of your interests is to be honestly, clearly, and completely informed as to how much it is all costing you.

3. Honest Dealings

This follows directly upon your need to know the truth about all costs and fees, whether direct or indirect. (I would add that payments made by third parties also need to be disclosed as part of understanding costs.) It may seem so obvious as to be unworthy of mention, but reality dictates that you should list and emphasize complete honesty.

Regretfully, transparency may be the most important thing you are seeking and the hardest one to get. The financial services industry is not a straightforward business.

4. Comprehensive Explanations of What Is Being Done on Your Behalf

You need to understand what is being done for you. Furthermore, you need it explained in plain language that you can easily understand. A bunch of jargon that is meaningless to you cannot suffice.

In addition, good faith efforts should be made to estimate the value of the services you are receiving. Do the things being done for you have value? Are they worth a great deal, a little bit, or nothing at all? Can their value be quantified? Financial service providers are better situated than you are to offer an educated guess on how much their work actually puts into your pocket. Of course, they may be reluctant to offer you this estimate if they are claiming more than a fair portion of the value. An honest provider, however, should be more than willing to have this discussion with you.

5. Expertise, Knowledge, Skill, and Care

If you are to take guidance from anyone, that person must have the necessary expertise. Is she knowledgeable? Does she have all the essential education and training? Do her skills rise to the level of excellent? To put it plainly, does this practitioner really know all that is needed to do the job properly?

Beyond questions of training and expertise, you want someone who will always use good sense, utmost care, and best effort. An advisor who has all the necessary traits but fails to use them consistently on your behalf is not worth having. He must not be overwhelmed or distracted by other things (such as recruiting new clients or making other sales).

To this list, you should add scientific knowledge. It goes without saying that those who hold themselves out as experts in this area must have a very strong understanding of the science of investing. A surgeon who has never gone to medical school, or who studied only psychiatry, would not be an acceptable choice to operate on you. A lawyer who has studied nothing but the tax code in law school would have no business defending you in a criminal matter. So, too, an investment advisor who knows little about economics or finance is not the right person for the job.

You have the strongest possible interest in making sure that all who would guide you possess the knowledge, education, experience, and skill necessary to do the job correctly. One must genuinely "know what he is doing" before you should work with him.

6. Loyalty

In light of the challenges illuminated earlier in this section, you need to work with people and firms who will put your interests ahead of their own. You are looking for providers who not only have the requisite knowledge, but will also use it for your benefit. Will they subordinate their own goals to advance yours?

Other strong interests follow directly from those previously listed, and I urge you to give them full consideration. Look for solid understanding of the problems of conflict-of-interest and asymmetric information, along with evidence of a practitioner's hard work to address those problems in her business or practice. A business model that is plainly about using expertise on the client's behalf and clearly rejects making money off your money. You want truth and integrity from those you allow to place their hands on your money. You have a tremendous interest in their truthfulness.

Thinking about Their Interests

Skilled negotiators are also keenly aware of the interests and goals of those sitting across from them at the bargaining table. You deal with many people, directly and indirectly, when you invest. Their aspirations and intentions are often far less straightforward than your simple desire for a fair and generous return on capital.

Start by acknowledging that some investment situations are a zero-sum game. When you buy a share of stock from someone, the more you pay, the more they receive. Pure market transactions are usually this way; you are locked in a contest to get the most favorable terms possible.

When dealing with people and companies, though, the situation can be very different. As we did previously, let's narrow our focus to negotiations with brokers, advisors, and other financial service providers. Coming to terms with them, and using their guidance, is the kind of easily recognizable negotiation in which you can use the full range of your developing skills. To further clarify the task, let us break the providers into two groups: companies and individuals.

The Interests of Financial Services Firms

The interests of financial services firms include the following concerns.

1. Getting Customers

    As is true with any business, financial firms must be concerned with obtaining customers. This can be an advantage when they are pursuing you, in that they want your business. It may be to your disadvantage when their search for other clients competes with their efforts to serve your interests. In any case, though, most financial firms are constantly attempting to win new clients.

While some companies seek any customer who might come through the door with money, many firms are looking for new clients who fit certain profiles. Different providers have different ideas of "the ideal client" but it is safe to say that everyone in financial services is looking for folks with a great deal of money. Well-endowed customers tend to be more profitable, whereas less affluent people may cost just as much to serve yet often pay less.

2. Making as Much as Possible from the Clients They Have

Almost all financial service firms seek to increase profitability. Beyond getting new clients, the way to do this is to make more money from the clients they have. High level strategists may speak of "getting more of the customer's wallet," while retail salespeople may be thinking about meeting a quota, but in the end it is about getting more money from folks with whom they are already doing business.

Not all financial firms have the same business model and, as a result, the ways they increase revenues can differ. Some seek greater commission revenue by selling more or better "financial products." Others may wish to increase the number of transactions to capture more fees or to profit from the "bid-ask" spread. Still others seek to increase distribution of their own "proprietary" products at the expense of other investment vehicles. One way or the other, though, almost all of these companies are seeking to increase their profits. And that goal is a very significant motivator behind the actions they take.

Take note, as well, that some of the ways a company makes money from its customers are very indirect. For example, there are "soft money" arrangements wherein payments are made by third parties, often not in cash, to compensate for influencing or directing client business. A very typical example is a mutual fund company that offers free computers and software to those brokers who will promote their funds.

3. Controlling Your Capital

Many firms make a great deal of money by being in control of your money. The fewer strings attached to your capital, the more they can use to advance their own needs.

Just a few examples can help to illuminate this point. When banks or other companies engage in underwriting, they must sell newly created shares. Having a built-in clientele for such new shares is very valuable for them. Or, consider any situation in which there is a spread between what they must pay to use your money and what they can then bring in by deploying it. For instance, if a bank borrows your money at 1 percent but can lend it to a mortgagor at 3 percent, it stands to profit handsomely. Finally, think about a life insurance company that is definitely going to pay out everything you put in at the time of your death, but gets the free use of the capital for (on average) many decades.

4. Keeping You as a Client

In most cases, it is significantly more profitable to keep a current client than to obtain a new one. Financial services companies have a strong interest in retaining the clients they already have. Thus, it is strongly in their interest to keep you as a customer. It may be worth their while to keep you satisfied and happy as a way to pursue this goal.

The Interests of Individual Financial Practitioners

Individual brokers, advisors, and salespeople can have very different motivations from those of financial companies. Their career and personal goals can result in some interests that are contrary to those of their employer. Or, to be more precise, some of their interests are aligned and some are in conflict. You want to always be cognizant of this when dealing with individual providers. The interests of individuals who earn their living offering financial services include the following.

1. Getting New Clients and Retaining Current Ones

Like their bosses and companies, investment advisors seek to gain new clients while retaining their old ones. They are trying to increase their income by building up what the industry calls their "book of business." As a general rule, they want to hang onto you.

2. Building Referral Networks

One of the primary ways that such brokers and advisors get new business is through their current clients. It is well known that the single best way to grow is through referrals. You have a potential role to play in their future success and you should bring that prominently into your negotiations.

3. Meeting Quotas and Keeping Their Bosses Satisfied

Almost everyone has a boss. And everyone who does has a strong interest in keeping the boss happy. Many financial firms set quotas, directions, and sales goals. They also push particular products for their employees to sell based on internal criteria. Even if cloaked in very fancy industry jargon, they must "move the merchandise" to please their superiors. This is obviously a significant interest that tends to motivate behavior.

4. Winning

The financial services industry tends to draw some very competitive people. Many of the men and woman in this field are naturally inclined to see their work as a kind of game. Such folks are determined to win. When dealing with such a competitor, it is helpful to learn what they understand winning to be. Then you can exchange your help with it for the fulfillment of some of the things you need.

5. Making Money

Over the years, I have often said that not many people go into the field of money for altruistic reasons. Most individuals working in these financial fields have chosen to do so because they want to make a lot of money. They are often the type of people who are never satisfied that they have made enough. Making more money is a huge motivation for many of the folks in this industry.

6. Time

You have heard the expression "time is money." That is particularly true for anyone whose job includes searching for more business. As previously mentioned, brokers and financial advisors spend a significant part of their working days searching for leads, introductions, and new clients. As a result, they have a huge interest in freeing up time to pursue those endeavors. They tend to want things that are quick and easy and are put off by situations that are time consuming or require significant attention.

They are usually looking to get the deal done, have the papers signed, complete the trade, or quickly finish whatever the matter is. For myriad reasons, they would like to be granted as much discretion as possible. And they are unlikely to be pleased with spending too much time on your problems.

Interests That Can Lead You Astray

In discussing good outcomes, I invoked King Pyrrhus to urge against seemingly desirable actions that actually lead us away from the results we seek. There are many such dangers as you pursue positive investment aims. Be on your guard for interests that are ostensibly positive but have great potential for steering you wrong or taking your eyes off the real prize.

The relative weight and importance of various interests is deeply subjective. In the end, only you can decide what is too essential to put aside. Years of experience, though, have led me to believe that some things are better off left out of your investment activities. I offer them to you now.

When investing, I omit my usual interests in building strong relationships with the other negotiators, living up to my code, making the world a better place, and improving how I am seen by others. These wonderful human activities leave an investor vulnerable to manipulation.

The world of investments is not a place to look for solid friendships. Jane's story may illuminate the point. She got an exciting new job in a new city. It was all-consuming, though, and Jane had little time for friendships or leisure activities. Her substantial salary and stock options compelled her to make time to search for a financial advisor, and she quickly found a female broker who made her very comfortable. They quickly became friends and occasionally got together for social outings. The broker was very involved in several wonderful local charities and Jane began joining her in those activities. Many years passed before, one day, Jane's nephew Matthew inquired as to what her friends' services actually cost. She had never bothered trying to figure that out and always assumed that the broker was held to some sort of industry standard. The bold nephew was studying economics and finance in graduate school and was motivated to really explore the question. It turned out that the broker was extracting fees, commissions, and charges of more than 3 percent per year. By the time Matthew finished crunching all the numbers, he concluded that the friendly broker had cost Jane over $6 million.

I have also found that when making investment decisions, leaving my self-esteem at the door keeps me from making poor choices. While issues of ego, self-esteem, pride, and place in the community pecking order come up for me regarding personal finances, I try hard to disregard those impulses. At the very least, I don't want them influencing investment judgment. Seeking to feel better about oneself through investment practices is a ticket to losing a great deal of money. As mentioned earlier, some people invested with Bernie Madoff in an effort to be part of a very desirable crowd. Similar examples can be found throughout history.

A great deal of investment marketing is aimed at your ego and actually ignores your pocketbook. Here is a list of things that, in my opinion, you don't really want:

- Superior research: It isn't going to help you make more money.
- Ease of trading: The easier it is, the more of it you may do. Few things are worse for your investment returns than frequent trading.
- An advisor who "cares deeply" about your individual situation: You are not likely to find one who cares more about you than about money.
- Online services: This is primarily about lowering costs for the investment company.

Beware of the images that advertising tries to establish as somehow real. Slogans and heroic music, helicopters and private jets, and the visual trappings of outstanding service—elegant lobbies, crisp suits, warm handshakes, personalized letters, and snazzy online tools—will not enrich you. They don't take you one step closer to your good outcome. In fact, these marketing ploys are attempting to deflect your focus away from strong returns, low costs, and solid economics. You don't want bells, whistles, tools, levels, or lists unless they *actually* improve your financial return. Glitzy images and minor services are worthless, and you should decline to pay even a penny for any of them.

Chapter Summary

- Figuring out underlying interests in an investment negotiation will help you create better deals.
- Ultimately, it is you who must determine your true interests.
- Some typical interests are low costs, clarity on fees, honest dealings, and full explanations.
- Indispensable characteristics of worthwhile advisors are expertise, knowledge, skill, care, and loyalty.
- Investment companies and their representatives have some interests in common, but also some that conflict.
- Investment companies typically want new customers, maximized profits, control of capital, and client retention.
- Individual advisors really want to retain old clients and get new ones, build networks, get referrals, keep bosses satisfied, win, have free time, and make money.
- Beware of seemingly important interests that only lead you away from your good outcomes.
- Consider sharply narrowing some human interests when making investment decisions.
- Be cautious about friendships that are linked to investing arrangements.
- Marketing for financial services is often about distracting you from what is really important. Keep your eyes on the prize.

CHAPTER 20

Many Different Possible Options for How to Structure the Deal

As you recall from Chapter 2, *option* means something very special to a negotiator. Unlike alternatives, which are all the things you can do outside of the deal you are working on, options are all the different ways you can structure this deal. In most cases, there are a great many different ways to structure any deal.

Trade Their Interests for Yours

How can you, as an investor-negotiator, engineer the best possible agreement from among the many possible options? By trading things that you want and need for items of great importance to the other guys. By making use of "if–then" statements and conditional proposals, you can offer them greater value in exchange for what you really want.

As you realize, the lists of underlying interests that you began putting together in Chapter 19 are the raw materials to be used in crafting good deals. You are looking to trade things that they really, *really* want for those items most important to you. Thus, the process of finding out what they truly care about is one of the most important things you can do. In the case of brokers, dealers, and other types of financial advisors, separating their true motivations from what they say is critical. After all, you will only be able to meet some of their true interests if you can learn what they are.

You have a pretty good idea about some of their interests and you already know how important it is to continue learning more. Together, we surmised that financial services firms tend to want new customers while simultaneously keeping you and other current clients. They also want to make as much money as possible from each customer, maximize their control over capital, and, perhaps, weed out the least profitable accounts. Meanwhile, individual brokers, advisors, and salespeople share most of those interests but many have some individual wants and needs that differ from their employers'. Among these are strengthening their network, meeting quotas and sales numbers, and making more money for their families. Some of them care an awful lot about winning. And, like almost everyone, they seek to keep their bosses happy and impress those who can help them climb the ladder of success in their field.

Work Together to Create Packages of Interests

The task becomes working together to create packages that meet everyone's interests well. For example, you might propose a deal that helps them keep you as a client and get referrals for new clients in exchange for your desire for low fees, full disclosure, and all the attention you need regardless of how long it takes. Tying the fulfillment of their interests to making sure your own get met is the key to success. As with most businesspeople selling something, they will be glad to make you promises; the critical next step is to link together the completion of your requirements with beginning to meet theirs.

When it becomes clear that more than one satisfactory agreement could be reached, the next step is working together toward choosing the best agreement. The word "best" here refers to the agreement that meets everyone's interests to the fullest possible degree. The way you work from any acceptable agreement toward the best one available is through a series of proposed trades aimed at bettering what is on the table. Suppose you learned that the advisor you are negotiating with highly values your ability to recommend him to your social circle. In that case, you could suggest improving the deal by cutting the annual fee in half once you have introduced him to a certain number of your friends.

Find the Best Investment Deal among Many

As you can imagine, the number of potential agreements is almost endless. To make this point concretely, take the previous example of deal improvement. Why stop at an agreement that cuts the fee in half? It could be reduced to a quarter of the original proposal if you make a sufficient number of quality introductions. How about no fee at all; is that possible? Might he start paying you? (Careful here, as there are lots of legal constraints.) The point is that any one potential trade of interests could be arranged many different ways. When you multiply that by the numerous interests that each party holds, you find there are hundreds of possible ways to structure the deal. To some extent, you are searching for the ones that meet your interests best while doing the same with regard to their interests. The ability to trade, though, and have one side meeting the other's interests in exchange for reciprocation is the road to great progress.

Debbie Clay did exactly that.

Working as a teacher was so important to Debbie Clay that, for many years, she could not find the time to learn more about her investments. She had turned the whole matter over to her advisor, Katrina Pulos, a decade ago. Katrina, in turn, was a representative for one of the largest financial companies in the world. In recent months, though, Debbie had started to learn more about dealing with a financial company. A friend suggested paying closer attention and, as a result, she began to study the matter in earnest. She read this book, as well as others by Bogle, Malkiel, and Tobias. When Katrina called to suggest investing in a variable annuity-based retirement product, Debbie knew it was time to have "the talk."

The meeting started out with Katrina falling back on various sales and reinforcement techniques her company had trained her in. When Debbie made it clear that this was going to be about finding fairer terms, Katrina got defensive. Debbie was able to turn things around, though, by steering the conversation to what Katrina wanted most from their working relationship. While making sure to emphasize that serving Debbie was Katrina's greatest concern, Katrina was able to say that she wanted to keep Debbie as a client, maximize the money she made, and get help in bringing in new clients. Debbie, in turn, stressed her desire to pay fair (and, in this case, much lower) fees, never be guided toward commission-paying investment choices, and better understand the rationale behind each investment recommendation.

From there, the two women explored a new deal that would be based on meeting more of the interests of each. There were a great many questions to be answered. Did Katrina's company grant her authority to lower fees? How much leeway did she have concerning which investments to recommend? Was she willing to be more forthright and truthful with her old client than the company guidelines suggested? As for Debbie, what did she consider a fair fee to be? Would she promise to remain a client for a certain length of time? Would she be willing to recommend Katrina and/or to personally introduce her to friends? How much money did her friends tend to have?

They used the if–then structure to investigate the possibilities. If Katrina could reduce the annual fee by 20 percent and promise no commissions, Debbie would recommend her to three best friends. Although Debbie had concerns about her own reputation, she might be able to accompany two of the friends to a first meeting if Katrina would level with her about how much the firm actually makes off each client. And, if all of Debbie's requests could be met in full, she felt sure that a promise to remain Katrina's client for at least five years would not be excessive.

After sharing information as fully as possible, they found that some of their interests were in direct conflict, some were aligned, and some were neither aligned nor in conflict. Thus, there were areas in which Katrina could not make more money unless Debbie paid higher fees. There were things that left both of them better off, such as Debbie recommending Katrina to her financially disorganized mother. And there were areas where one's indifference, and the other's deep need, made a trade obvious. Two examples of the latter were Katrina's willingness to spend an extra hour each month explaining recommendations to Debbie, and Debbie's promise to continue working with Katrina for at least another year (since she felt unable to do the necessary research on other choices in less than 12 months). These two nonconflicting interests could be traded and each woman was better off.

The deal the two finally worked out was their very best effort to meet each one's most important interests as fully as possible. Debbie got lower annual fees, no more commission-based products, more explanation, and some semblance of the truth. Katrina got to keep her client for at least another year, and the opportunity to win her for the longer term. She also got a definite referral of Debbie's mom and the possibility of at least two more recommendations. And, of course, they each now have the opportunity to prepare fully for the meeting they will have 12 months from now. Such preparation will include taking actions over the coming year that make it far more likely that the other woman will say yes to future proposals.

The story of Debbie and Katrina, with its happy ending, probably means that I owe you a few more cautions.

A Few Cautions

Financial people want your money. They tend to be rather sharply focused in that direction; it is the nature of the beast. You need to be aware of that, cautious of its implications, and at least slightly skeptical. What this chapter helps you remember, though, is that you are not to hand your money over to them until you have structured a deal that meets most of your underlying interests regarding investing. They very much want a client who is "signed, sealed, and delivered." You will not sign until the agreement meets your needs.

Two more cautions: Pay attention to where you get information, and to the timing of that information. Most of the financial people you deal with are highly skilled at "closing the deal." Many have had extensive training in sales, persuasion, and influence. You should expect them to be quite selective about what facts and "proprietary information" (company secrets) they will share. Some may even "shade the truth" from time to time. It is very important that you use outside sources to verify what you are being told. Furthermore, they probably know the value of getting their interests met before acting to fulfill yours.

Be careful to structure agreements so that you get what you need before, or at least simultaneously with, fulfilling their interests. In short, craft the deal so that the rewards they seek come only after you have received all that was agreed upon. This method of keeping them honest is very important. Just as you would not pay now for a vague promise to deliver a share of stock next year, you also must not hand over your wealth without forcing them to meet your legitimate financial needs.

With those concerns in mind, try to work with them to put together the best possible deal for all. They want something from you and you want a number of things from them. The stage is set to make the trades and put together the deal that will leave everyone much better off than they started.

Chapter Summary

- Use if–then statements to explore trading packages of interests.
- Find the best deals among many potential ones.
- They want to close the deal, but you should not sign until your most significant interests are met.
- They might not always be totally truthful.
- Make sure that the deal implements your important needs before theirs.

CHAPTER 21

Insist on Using Objective Standards of Fairness

Along with seeking to fulfill various interests, you should insist on fairness. Nobody wants to be treated unfairly, and those with negotiating power should always be adamant about it. "Fair terms or no deal" is a very appropriate motto for the investor-negotiator.

Gather Your Measures of Fairness

Good negotiators look to objective criteria, such as authoritative standards and norms, to guide them. These outside measures of fairness can help you in two ways: guiding you as to the general range of what is fair, and making your proposals more persuasive to the other side.

I once had a client who wanted to pay me an hourly fee. Unused to working that way, I had little idea what a truly fair hourly rate would be. The situation called for a little time to collect relevant data, inquire of others, and generally pull together some object criteria on which to base a proposal. She was in a hurry, though, and asked if I could set a fee right then and there. To accommodate her, I decided to come up with something quickly. I realized she had been referred to me by a man I greatly admired. Leigh Bauer was a lawyer and teacher known for his kindness, intelligence, and playfulness. He was also widely regarded as a thoughtful, caring, honorable, and, above all, fair professional. I had my response: "I will charge you whatever hourly fee Leigh charges," a seemingly gutsy move on my part, since I had no idea how much Leigh charged. Actually, I felt totally comfortable relying on the basic fairness of it.

Fair is not the only consideration in getting really good outcomes, but it is a tremendously important part. If you can get to fair, you and the people you are working with can all leave the negotiation table feeling good about the deal and each other. It cements the present and brightens prospects for future dealings.

Beware of What They Call Fair

It is to be expected that negotiators appeal to different standards, customs, and practices and then try to convince the other side to accept their own formulations and definitions of "fairness."

A big challenge facing you as an investor-negotiator is that those sitting across the table have a huge head start in creating a one-sided idea of what is fair. The financial services industry has been doing this for a long time and is aided by the best marketers, psychologists, and human behavior specialists in the world. Theirs is a business full of jargon, perceived wisdom, and tautological definitions designed to confuse. It is important that you negotiate using your own language. The jargon of the industry is going to make it very hard to achieve understanding and then work toward fairness.

Just because a practice is "customary" doesn't make it fair. This industry has long stood virtually unchallenged in setting terms, pricing, and industry standards. One deeply troubling practice is the industry-wide use of a one-sided contractual agreement. One of its provisions makes it almost impossible to work with any broker-dealer without first signing away your right to sue them in a court of law. Such "contracts of adhesion" are usually forced on a weaker party by a stronger one. Any attempt to confront it may be met with an indignant declaration that everyone in the business uses that contract and it is a firmly established industry standard. There will be similar resistance if you challenge pricing, lack of transparency, incomprehensible prospectuses, or conflicts of interest. These are all Wall Street norms and will be presented as inherently fair.

As an investor-negotiator, you must counter the standards and norms put forward by industry representatives and answer with more appropriate ones. To gather these, you should look to standards from other industries, academic research, philosophical ideas on fairness in the commercial arena, or the judgment of consumer advocacy professionals.

As good negotiators do in all fields, propose objective criteria that meet outside ideas about justice and be adamant about a fair deal. It can help to present fairness measures that have achieved a kind of social consensus. A practitioner who gets a fee but is also receiving hidden payments will have little success in claiming that to be a fair practice. Even if it doesn't rise to a legal definition of fraud, it is generally understood to be outside the bounds of legitimacy. And defending the practice based on its "disclosure" in a long and virtually unreadable document does not change the palpable unfairness.

Keep Your Eyes on Profitability and Transparency

Complete transparency of fees and costs is another objective standard that should be beyond doubt in the court of ethics, good sense, and wise practice. How can you discuss fair pricing, fees, and compensation without knowing what is actually being paid? Imagine going to the grocery store to buy apples and, upon reaching the cash register, finding out that various charges and fees were added to the price displayed in the aisle. To make the image even more troubling, imagine that some of those charges were displayed in code, in an ancient dead language, or in invisible ink. The very idea of hiring an advisor who will not reveal to you her financial incentives and income streams is absurd.

Following closely behind issues of visibility and obscurity, you should think about what a given action or service is really worth. In questioning the level of fees or costs, do not hesitate to inquire about their basis. You should frequently ask, "How did you arrive at that figure? Why is it fair?"

Some years ago, a new client came to us just after having sold a large number of shares of Dell Computer stock. We noticed that the trading fee for that single transaction was over $500. The firm we employ to trade for clients would have charged $12. Why the huge discrepancy? Was there something special or advantageous to the method they used to execute the trade? What is a fair price for that service?

Then there is the issue of how an advisor is paid for her services. Many brokers, representatives, and financial advisors cite industry standards in charging some percentage of a client's assets. Again, it is worth posing the question about why that particular percentage is the fairest one. Would an hourly or task-based fee be more or less fair than that? What factors influence the cost of the service? Are there historical issues controlling this pricing, and, if so, are they fair to all parties or only to one?

Consider ways to ask how profitable a service is to its provider. You should not begrudge a fair profit to those you work with, but price gouging is unacceptable. To argue that airfares were too high during the past decade requires reconciling the fact that none of the major airlines was profitable. If they were not even charging what it cost to provide the service, there is a strong argument that they were not overcharging. On the other hand, if a provider or industry is consistently making more money than comparable work in other sectors, it is possible that they are charging too darned much. And if they are taking too much, strong arguments can be made that lower fees are not only appropriate, but also necessary to meet common definitions of fairness.

Excessive costs, fees, and charges necessarily reduce the actual return on your investments. There eventually comes a point at which unwarranted fees cut so far into the return on your capital that they defeat the very purpose of investing.

Demand a Fair Division of All the Value That the Deal Creates

As an investor-negotiator, you must claim a large chunk of the value created by the deployment of your capital. Lax and Sebenius[1] warned that we must not only work to create value, but also claim our fair share of it. John Bogle argues the absurdity of a split in which the manipulator of the capital claims more of the value than its owner.[2] Justice requires an equitable split of a deal's value, but reality reminds us that we had better see to it.

What portion of the deal is it fair for advisors, brokers, dealers, traders, and other intermediaries to take in light of the work they do? This turns out to be a complicated question, but one we dare not ignore. Big money is at stake here, and the math is not always straightforward or intuitive.

Do the Math on Fees and Costs

Remember, this is a search for fairness. Nobody should be expected to work for nothing, and skilled assistance is worth paying for. However, excessive fees, even those that seem "reasonable," can be extremely costly over time.

As you negotiate over fees and costs, you will surely encounter the argument that 2 percent of your capital is just a tiny amount to pay for good help. Be careful here, for it is a mistake to examine fees in relation to the amount of your capital. Rather, you should compare fees to your expected return on the capital. Thus, if your investment portfolio is expected to return 8 percent next year and they propose to take 2 percent, it would appear that they are expropriating a quarter of the return for themselves. That is more or less correct for one year. But let us not concern ourselves with one year. The numbers, and the seeming injustice, change drastically over long periods of time.

One dollar, earning a return of 8 percent over 30 years, will grow to $10.93. Reduced by costs of 2 percent, though, an after-fee return of 6 percent will be achieved. And a dollar growing at 6 percent for 30 years will become $6.02. In this example, a "mere" 2 percent fee reduces the return by almost 45 percent. When we put it that way, does it seem fair?

John Bogle gives an even more dramatic example. He looked at an investor in a tax-deferred retirement account whose return averaged 5 percent annually. Compounding year after year at that rate, $1 becomes $7.04 over 40 years, or a $100,000 input becomes $704,000. When you subtract fees and charges of 2 percent, however, the result is striking. Just like long-term gains, the bite of fees also has a compounding effect. As Bogle figures it, the projected gain from $1 to $7.04 over 40 years gets cut way down by the cost bite—down to $3.26.[3]

"Where did the nearly $4 difference go?" Bogle asks. "It went to the fund or to Wall Street in fees. So you the investor put up 100 percent of the capital. You take 100 percent of the risk. And you capture about 37 percent of the return. The fund or Wall Street puts up none of the capital, takes none of the risk and takes out 63 percent of the return." In these very dramatic long-term examples, we know intuitively that the share being claimed by the industry is wildly unfair.[4]

Pay Only for Services That Provide You with Value

If legitimate investment services that carry excessive costs are bad, services that add no value to you are a terrible deal at any price. As mentioned before and explained in detail in a later chapter, economists can show that most stock-picking strategies perform no better than throwing darts at the *Wall Street Journal*. This means that a great deal of the investment advice and services being offered are actually worth nothing to you. Essentially, they seek payment for the playing out of random chance. Even if such firms spend millions of dollars on salaries, computer programs, and high-priced New York rents, their services are overpriced at a nickel.

One is reminded of the children's story "Stone Soup." As you recall, the hungry soldiers offered to make a delicious soup for the townsfolk out of nothing but water and stones. Slowly but surely, as they won over people's confidence, they persuaded local folks to add meat, vegetables, milk, and spices. Eventually, the soup was delicious because the townspeople added the appetizing ingredients. The hungry soldiers' rightful reward for their cleverness was to share the soup with everyone else. It is a heartwarming story that leaves us with a good feeling. Imagine how we might feel, however, if the soldiers demanded a high fee for the stones that were the initial soup base. The twist in the tale is that those stones are worthless—they add neither flavor nor nutrition. In fairness, nobody should be paying anything for them.

Chapter Summary

- "Fair terms or no deal."
- Your idea of fair may differ from theirs.
- Just because they have always done it that way does not make it fair.
- Transparency is necessary to even talk about fairness.
- Demand a fair share of the value being created by the deal.
- Do the math on costs and fees.
- Costs compound over long periods, so amounts that seem fair for one year may not be over the long term.
- Don't pay for anything that has no real value to you.

Notes

1. David Lax and James Sebenius, *Manager as Negotiator: Bargaining for Cooperation and Competitive Gain* (New York: The Free Press, 1986), 29.
2. John Bogle, "The Retirement Gamble," *Frontline*, PBS, April 23, 2013.
3. Kerry Hannon, "The Three Surprises in 401(k)s," *Forbes*, January 13, 2013.
4. Ibid.

CHAPTER 22

Plan the Type and Tone of Communication You Want

Communicating successfully is important in any investment situation. It is going to be critical, though, as you negotiate your working relationship with any sort of financial advisor. Because it is likely to be unfamiliar territory, you will want to control how you communicate with other parties and make sure you receive clear, valid, and complete information in return. You never want to negotiate about your investments in a state of confusion or misunderstanding.

Communication to Enhance Your Understanding

Start by promising yourself that you will not be shy or intimidated.

You need to insist on clear explanations in understandable English. Financial service providers habitually use jargon and vague terms both to obfuscate and intimidate. Persist until you have a full understanding and stand firm against any suggestion that you should be able to "read it in the prospectus." Those documents cannot be understood by humans, or even lawyers, and you can quote me on that. Every assertion and every promise must be made in plain English that a high school student would understand.

Furthermore, be adamant that all such statements must be supplied to you in writing. While some parts of the financial industry are more slippery than others, you must insist on having everything in a complete written document in all your dealings. In this area of your life, if you don't have it in writing, you don't really have any deal at all.

Communication to Make Things Clear to Them

How can you let them know of your requirements, interests, and inviolate standards in the clearest way possible? You are telling them explicitly that any agreement must be better than your best alternative, meet your interests well, and be demonstrably fair. It will also have to be stated clearly in writing with all its terms verifiable. It cannot in any way "lock you in" but, rather, must give you the right to step away whenever you wish. How can you best communicate all this and more in a manner that keeps the door open for fair and honest dealing?

One suggestion is to be warm and friendly in person, yet firm and unyielding in writing. You will want to follow up all conversations with letters that summarize and confirm what was discussed. Those letters are an opportunity to make clear the firmness with which you are insisting on your needs. Be explicit in your written communications about your expectations, requirements, deal-breakers, and understandings. Choose language carefully, leaving no room for interpretation or discretion by those whose interests may differ from your own. For example, use the phrase "This is a letter of instruction" at the start of any message in which you are telling them to do something.

Create the Tone and Atmosphere You Want

Of course, being firm and unyielding is not a style that comes easily to everyone. Although some people are comfortable taking that tone, others find it nearly impossible. Even though it may be the theoretically ideal posture for dealing with a shrewd and crafty industry, it is not a viable choice for everybody. After identifying the quality of interaction that is right for you, it will be important to work hard to create that atmosphere for the negotiation process.

A truth about negotiating is that success tends to flow from being yourself. It is almost never a prudent strategy to pretend to be someone you are not. Be sure to create an atmosphere in which you are comfortable and centered. Prepare this carefully with an eye toward nonverbal cues, body language, setting, speech patterns, and physical comfort. Plan to play on your own ball field, and then make it happen.

Regardless of mood and tone, though, you will need to make clear those things on which you intend to hold firm. Being friendly, warm, and considerate is not incompatible with being determined, strong, and resolute. To the contrary, that is exactly what Fisher and his colleagues meant when they instructed us to be "soft on the people and hard on the problem."[1]

Chapter Summary

- Insist on clear and complete explanations in plain English.
- Everything must be explained clearly to you in writing.
- You need to let them know in writing all of your requirements.
- Think about and then create the negotiating atmosphere that is best for you.
- Set a tone that allows you to be yourself.

Note

1. Roger Fisher, William Ury, and Bruce Patton, *Getting to Yes: Negotiating Agreement Without Giving In*, 3rd ed. (New York: Penguin Books, 2011).

23

Think about Relationship Goals

Good negotiators know that the process will benefit from an appropriate and helpful relationship between the parties. Thinking through the kind of relationship you want can help guide the interactions in the proper direction. In particular, you seek an affiliation that will best lead to fulfillment of your investment goals.

Your earliest interactions with a financial advisor are likely to set the foundations and rhythms of the working relationship that will follow. You have an excellent opportunity to craft the kind of relationship you want. You should seize it.

A Good Working Relationship Need Not Be Personal

Your interests as an investor-negotiator are best served by a professional relationship that advances your financial goals. While friendships are always nice, they are not always appropriate.

One of the messages of this book is that the investor-negotiator faces a lack of clarity about who is an adversary and who is a partner. The most frequent answer is that the people you are working with are at least a little bit of both. It is often the case that those guiding you with investments are also competing with you on the other side of the deal. As a result, you probably want to build a relationship that does not depend on trust. You don't want to be in a position where blind faith is required in place of substantiation. Not only is it bad for you, but it also probably puts too much strain on the relationship. It is best avoided.

Along the same lines, your investment life is probably not a good place for making new friends. Friendship often leads to a slow increase in trust and gradual lowering of caution. Many of us have a strong desire to build trust in our friendships. Unfortunately, this tendency can be used against you. Television ads about financial advisors making toasts at the wedding of a client's daughter are part of a campaign to lull you to sleep. Investment relationships require a consistent level of vigilance that may be incompatible with close and loving friendships.

That is not to say, however, that a warm, friendly attitude is not possible. A "businesslike approach" need not be cold or standoffish. Everyone around the investment table can be kind, helpful, and gracious with each other. You must remember, though, that they should not be confused with teammates, family members, dear friends, or others who are "on your side." The conflicts-of-interest are simply too numerous and the dangers too great to permit the level of unguarded interaction that can happen with those we hold dear.

Pay Attention to Power Dynamics

While seeking to build the most appropriate working relationship, an investor-negotiator must be alert to managing the power dynamics that develop. It is typical that financial intermediaries position themselves as authority figures and expect a kind of deference. You do not want to let them seize the mantle of decision maker or wise elder.

Rather, be sure they understand you are equals. Even better, they should appreciate that they are (or potentially will be) in your employ. You need not behave like an absolute boss, but legitimate control over content and outcome lies with you. And you get the final word. Do not allow yourself to be seen as the sheep willing to follow. At the very least, display enough authority that your decision making will not be taken for granted. Make it clear that nothing happens without your explicit consent and that such consent is given only for actions that are fully explained and make complete sense to you.

Here is one way to envision the process of negotiating with those who advise you on investments. You are the CEO of your family's investment company. The people working with you are consultants brought in to assist with your family company and to make suggestions. It should always be clear that you are the boss and that you sign all the checks. They are advisors and you are the decision maker.

Special Concerns about Financial Advisors

A strong word of caution is appropriate regarding relationships with financial advisors. Most work for companies that have long studied how to manipulate this interaction. They have concluded that there is advantage to being seen as your friend, confidant, or loyal ally. Sophisticated and powerful marketing campaigns prop up efforts to "befriend" clients. While pleasant to experience, it is one more factor encouraging clients to take their eyes off the ball.

Representatives of investment companies often seek unquestioning trust without truly earning it. Such blind trust will work tremendously to their advantage, not yours. Nor will they offer to return it in kind.[1]

Again, avoid overly friendly relationships with such advisors; they are simply not suitable. Former President Reagan liked to quote the Russian proverb that translates "trust but verify." It is very good advice for the investor-negotiator.[2]

Chapter Summary

- The people you invest with are usually part teammate and part adversary.
- Friendship is probably not appropriate.
- A good working relationship can be kind, helpful, and gracious.
- Know your power and make it clear to everyone involved.
- Blind trust is out of the question; verify everything.

Notes

1. Andrew Tobias, *The Only Investment Guide You'll Ever Need* (New York: Houghton Mifflin Harcourt, 2011), 65.
2. Ronald Reagan speech at the signing of the U.S.–Soviet INF Treaty, December 8, 1987, available at www.youtube.com/watch?v=As6y5eI01XE.

24

When to Commit—and to What

In Chapter 5, we considered how snugly or loosely we wish to be bound to the agreements, obligations, and requirements of our lives. These questions are tremendously relevant when thinking about your investments. And what of your negotiating partners? How tightly can you bind them to promises they have made? Good negotiators pay a great deal of attention to these questions and are careful to consider when such binding takes place.

In most situations, an investor-negotiator is looking to lock in the other side but preserve as much personal wiggle room as possible. At the very least, you are trying to keep an escape hatch open in the event that an investment situation turns bad.

Avoid Getting Locked In

It is very important for you to avoid situations or deals that tie you into investments for long periods. Indeed, the shorter the better. You would prefer a contract that permits you to quit without reason with five days' notice to a contract requiring three months' notice. A firm billing for services six months in advance locks in the client to a greater degree than does their competitor charging only after the work is completed. An agreement that can be terminated without penalty, whenever the client wishes, is superior to one that imposes an exit fee. That, in turn, is less onerous than one requiring significant notice as well as imposing a price to get out.

Many investment vehicles impose significant exit fees, which are really penalties, for trying to get your money back. For example, "back-loaded" mutual funds sometimes charge 6 percent to get your money back in the first year, 5 percent in the second year, and so on. The right to your own money without penalty will not be granted until six years after the fund was purchased. Most variable annuity products have a similar "early exit" penalty. A man recently came to our office seeking help with an "equity indexed annuity" product. To my amazement, he had been swindled into a contract that had a penalty schedule stretching 14 years from the date of purchase.

Although there are many situations in which the investment merchant wants to lock you in but you are better off with a less binding deal, sometimes things work the other way around. A great example is a debt investment known as a "callable bond." A typical bond pays a fixed rate of interest throughout the life of the instrument. That life is defined as ending on the "maturity date," when the investor's principal is paid back. A callable bond has an added feature, though; the issuer may "call" the bond by choosing to pay back the principal at certain defined times. This is wonderful for the borrowing company; if interest rates fall, they can terminate this bond and, presumably, borrow at lower rates. In such circumstances, of course, the investor would like to be able to keep the bond for the full length of time until its maturity. I refer to callable bonds as "heads they win, tails you lose."

Who decides how much each party is to be bound? It is a negotiated matter. If you lack the power and will to impose fairness, though, or are not paying attention, there is the potential for abuse. Josh Brown came to us recently holding an investment in a private equity partnership put together and sold to him by one of the nation's most prominent investment houses. This brand-name firm had, of course, drafted the contracts and made all the rules to maximize its advantage. The client wanted to get out of the investment, and we agreed to help him. To our amazement, the representative of the sponsoring firm explained that he "cannot get out." Although it seems incredible, the contract and agreements specified that investors could get their money back only at such times as the general partner determined, in its sole discretion, or upon the termination of the partnership. In plain English, he would get his money back when they decided and not any sooner.

As an investor-negotiator, you must examine carefully how any proposed commitments will actually work. It is your job to determine what will be advantageous and what might lead to disaster. If the terms of a deal under discussion are to your disadvantage, you should bargain hard to change them. Where change is not possible, or the other side declines to be flexible, you should walk away. Refuse to be bound in ways that work against you or make a good outcome unlikely.

Pay Attention to the "When" of Commitments

In addition to how much each party is bound, a careful investor pays close attention to when the various obligations, contracts, and binding events take place. The key thing is not to get tied up until you are completely ready. Since one of a salesperson's primary goals is to close the deal, trickery might be used to create a binding situation.

This sad story is typical. A senior citizen approached me after one of my classes to ask for guidance. The previous year, a "financial advisor" had been trying to persuade him to invest in a variable annuity product. It went by another name and, like almost all of them, was incredibly complex. The man indicated that he would probably go ahead and do as he was being told. First, though, he wanted to bring the complicated document to his long-time personal lawyer. The advisor put tremendous pressure on him to sign the documents first and then take copies to the attorney for review. As you can guess, by the time the lawyer raised concerns about the product, it was effectively too late. The gentleman was stuck with a terrible investment.

Many complex investment schemes become compulsory upon signing or when payment is made. Others require some formality, such as a notarized signature or guarantee. Great care should be taken before signing, giving over money, or otherwise entering into a deal. You should absolutely refuse to be rushed. Prudence dictates you should "sleep on it" in any case. Beyond that, though, it is good practice to require review by an expert you trust to exercise strong judgment in just such matters. A great deal of money can be lost in the time it takes to sign a document.

Chapter Summary

- Try not to be tied in and avoid exit fees, penalties, back-end loads, or anything else that makes it harder for you to walk away whenever you wish.
- Investments that can be "called away" from you aren't so good, either.
- It is up to you to examine carefully because some deals can bind you in tricky ways.
- Pay attention to *when* the agreement binds you, and for how long.
- Don't agree until you are good and ready.
- Consider having the investment deal reviewed by an expert you trust.

CHAPTER 25

The Four Phases of an Investment Negotiation

As you recall, there are four phases to any negotiation. The process of investing is no different. As an investor-negotiator, you should seek to stay focused on these four stages and what each one requires of you.

There is a great deal going on simultaneously when you are negotiating over your investments and, ideally, you will try to anticipate and stay on top of it all. Pay attention to the who, what, when, where, why, and how of the entire process. You want to do the necessary research and planning before engaging with the other parties and then continue to observe and adjust throughout the entire negotiation. There can be a lot to do. As you will soon see, a gigantic amount of your money is at stake. It is worth making the effort.

The Preparation Phase of Investing

Being well-prepared pays off in better negotiation outcomes. Many experts consider this the single best piece of advice they can give. This first phase of the negotiation is tremendously important.

The preceding chapters of this book create something of a checklist for your preparation:

- Determining your good outcome—where you want to end up
- Identifying everyone's interests

- Finding strong alternatives—strengthening your BATNA, and maybe weakening theirs
- Reviewing which options create the best deal for you
- Articulating your standards of fairness
- Setting the tone and managing the power dynamics of relationships
- Deciding what communication modes best suit your purposes
- Thinking through what commitments you are willing to make, and when, what commitments you must have from them, and how you can ensure their promises are carried out

Not only should you work through this checklist from your point of view, but you should also anticipate the other side's approach to each of these areas.

Break down your planning into substance, relationship, and process issues. For substance, go back and review your interests and theirs. For relationship issues, consider how you want to work with and feel about those who will have access to your money. Remember that you should never ignore matters of substance for the purpose of relationship building. Rather, use relationship tools to strengthen the relationship and substantive tools for finding fair solutions for the specific terms of a deal. Relationships can be strengthened with honesty, small gifts, acts of kindness, and friendly gestures. The specific terms of a deal should be hammered out using outside measures of fairness, balanced trades of important interests, and appropriate compromises.

An old law school classmate of mine had a problem. His child-hood pal had become a stockbroker and, over the years, invested more and more of the lawyer's money as a representative of one of the nation's giant financial firms. After long calling himself a "financial advisor," he was now a self-styled "wealth advisor." This year, he left his longtime financial company to join a different one that was also a household name. Now he was pressuring the lawyer to transfer his account to the new firm. My classmate wondered if this was good idea.

He worried about the new company's reputation (it had recently paid a huge fine to the SEC) and was awakened to the possibility that his investments were not well-managed. His great concern, though, was that the friendship hung in the balance. "If I don't switch my account to the new firm, I fear he will stop being my friend," he confided. After he reviewed much of the material that is in Part III of this book, my classmate became more apprehensive. He wondered aloud why his old friend had switched firms. "Probably for a large check," I told him. We spent some time on the Internet and were able to hazard a guess that his friend had probably received in excess of $1 million to switch firms. The lawyer's concern gradually changed to disgust. "He should have told me. I was ready to do it for him out of friendship, while his motivation was money." The stockbroker's failure to use the relationship tools of honesty and straightforward dealing were as critical as his failure to offer a financial incentive as fairness would seem to dictate.

As far as the negotiating process, there is a good deal of advance planning that can help you succeed as the negotiation unfolds. Much of the thinking and research you want to do needs to happen before you start talking to the other side. Where should the negotiation take place? How will the seating affect the assumptions, flow, and power dynamics? Are there physical changes to the room that can alter the process to your advantage? What role might food or beverages play in a constructive discussion? What nonverbal messages do you want to send?

Consider the sequence you'd like the discussion to follow. What information will you reveal up front? Later on? Never? What trades might you make? What partial deals might help set up the approach to reaching final goals? What promises will they need to make, and how can you ensure that those will be honored in full?

Gather New Data Continuously

As you work through the details and sequencing of the anticipated negotiation, it will become clear that you need more information to succeed. Negotiators must constantly gather data as they proceed. Here are five things your preparation should cover:

1. Notice what information you are missing. What do you need to learn from them? Write down your questions and work them into the conversation in ways that will encourage the other side to answer honestly.
2. What math are you going to need to understand? Have you taken compound interest into account?

3. What industry terms and jargon are likely to be used in discussions? Do you know what they mean?
4. Are there typical selling points, industry practices, illustrations, or deceptive claims for which you need to be prepared?
5. What can you find out about the individuals with whom you will be negotiating? How about their firm? Matters of their style, reputation, experience, needs and wants would be helpful to know.

Speak with others who have gone down this path before. What are useful questions to ask? Prepare, prepare, prepare, and you will be ready for the negotiation to come.

Keep in mind that the preparation phase is both a concrete time and a state of mind. You should do a great deal of preparation *before* the rest of the process begins. In addition, though, you can always go back and do more of what might be called "preparation work" once the negotiation process has begun. As you talk, listen, and bargain, you will see that there are gaps in your initial preparation. Go back at that point and fill them in. There is no point in the process at which learning more is without profit.

There is an ancient story of a wise man and a king preparing to play chess. If the king won, he wanted the wise man to tell him all the secrets of science and mathematics. When asked what he desired if he should prevail, the wise man requested the following. The king should put one grain of rice on the first square of the chess board. On the second square, he would double that (two grains of rice). On the third square, he would double that (four grains). On the fourth square, double that (eight grains), and so on, until the proper amount of rice for the entire board was gathered up. All this rice should be the wise man's prize for winning the game. The king readily agreed and even worried aloud that it might not be a sufficient prize for besting the sovereign. They played chess, and it came to pass that the wise man won.

The lesson of this story, as perhaps you can guess, is that the king failed to prepare. After listening to the wise man's request, he should have insisted on some time to do a little research.

You should do the same. Never hesitate to continue your data gathering at any point. Do not allow yourself to be pressured, manipulated, or coerced into deciding something on the fly that really calls for further study. Failing to take the time necessary for planning, analyzing, and researching can be dangerous. In this case, the wise man knew the arithmetic of compounding. The king did not, which is why the kingdom had to import rice for many years to accumulate the 461 billion metric tons necessary to pay off the bet.

The Exchanging Information Phase of Investing

Your goal in this second stage of the negotiation process is to learn as much as you can. Not only should you fill in any gaps and confirm information that you have gathered, but you can also learn a great deal more. The people you are talking with have access to almost everything you want to know. Your job is to create a conversation that encourages honesty, creates openness, and doesn't reveal your weak points. You want to get them talking. Of course, they will seek to gather information from you as well. You should try to be genuine but careful—don't reveal things that you shouldn't, but allow for open conversation that encourages sharing.

The best negotiators do a lot more listening than talking. The same is true for the best investors. Once you sit down with the other side (even if communicating electronically over thousands of miles), the door opens on an opportunity for gathering valuable knowledge.

Among the most important subjects you seek to learn about are all the particulars concerning the people with whom you are negotiating. As mentioned earlier, the good news is that you are now conversing with the world's biggest experts on that subject. The very best way to learn all about them is from them. You want to find out about the individual you are talking with, the firm as a whole, and their business.

You seek straightforward information about what they are offering, what systems they use, their business model, and all the ways they make money. You would also like to learn how they address the issues of conflicts of interest, asymmetric information, trustworthiness, and professionalism. Ideally, you will also glean information about their honesty, character, and business practices. Can you get some insights into what they think their BATNA is?

Here are some questions you might explore: How do they see themselves and their business? What do they like and dislike about it? What is important to them as individuals and as a company? What kind of relationship do they want? What are their goals, interests, and underlying objectives? What do they see as fair and why? What are their usual methods of working together?

Plan to Put Them at Ease

Plan how you will ask these questions. Consider writing them out in advance and working to improve how you ask them. Set an open and friendly tone; you don't want them to feel that you are interrogating them. By conversing in an open and friendly manner, you can help them relax and reveal far more of their true selves. You want your partner to be at ease and not on guard. Not only will truth flow more easily, but also you will be laying some groundwork for building a solid relationship.

An open and warm approach worked well for my old friend Mary.

Mary came to see me with several investment questions. When I asked if she had ever thought of working with a "financial advisor" she told me this story. Everyone in her social circle used Karen Smith, an admired senior investment advisor with the biggest financial firm in the country. Why didn't Mary and her husband follow their friends' lead in light of how highly regarded Karen was?

When Karen came to their home for an initial appointment, she was well dressed, drove a nice car, and looked very polished. She had studied the documents that Mary sent her in advance and spoke knowledgably about their investment assets. She inquired about any potential inheritances. She answered questions about investing for education and recommended a 529 college savings plan.

Karen talked authoritatively about the mechanics of how she worked with clients, her fee of 1 percent of assets, and how her clients had lost only about 20 percent in the recent market catastrophe that sent averages down by over 40 percent. In light of the strong recommendation of their friends, Mary and her husband decided in their heads that they would hire this sharp and professional-sounding woman. They also found her friendly and the conversation turned personal and informal. Karen seemed to sense that she had "made the sale."

Small talk followed. Karen spoke of how good her business was and proudly explained that most of her clients came from referrals.

Then the subject turned to family. Mary held forth for a while about her children's accomplishments. The two women began to speak about their men. With her guard down, Karen laughed and said that her husband regularly teases her about the fact that she knows almost nothing about finance or investing and yet is paid handsomely to advise others.

By creating an open and friendly tone for conversation, Mary was able to learn the essential fact. Karen, unguarded and no longer "negotiating" or selling, had offered up the true answer about her qualifications. As her husband put it, she knew almost nothing about the subject for which she was offering expertise. Without really trying, Mary had implemented the second stage of the negotiation to great effect. She got the information needed most to make a wise decision.

Here are some of the things you will want to find out from a financial advisor who seeks your business:

- How does he understand his duty to his clients? Is he willing to put it in writing in a clear letter to you? You are looking to see if he really understands fiduciary duty and acts like a fiduciary at all times.
- Who does he see as his competitors? With whom does he compare himself?
- Does he see himself as costing clients more, less, or the same as others who provide similar services?
- What are his costs and fees? You are looking for a thorough and complete answer. (Thereafter, if you ever catch him making money in a way he didn't tell you about, you should quit on the spot.)
- What exactly will he be doing for you? You want to ask about each type of action, each investment, each service, and his estimate of its true financial value to you.
- Ask him to explain the company's business model. How does it encourage him to use his expertise on his client's behalf? (And make sure he provides compelling evidence to go with his answer.)
- How does he make money from your money? (Your hoped-for answer is "not at all.")
- What conflicts-of-interest does he have with fully advancing what is best for his clients, and how does the firm deal with those conflicts?

Obviously, one possibility is the person may lie to you. Or, he may stretch the truth and omit information to make his proposals seem more attractive. Although you must always verify critical information and cannot assume the veracity of what someone is saying, the answers will be of great use to you. In any event, the advisor is revealing a whole lot about his style, attitudes, methods, and ways of doing business.

One of the things you want to know most is how honest this person or firm is. As I see it, there are many situations in which an outright lie will be all the information you need. My own preference is to minimize working with liars and, if my BATNA is strong, I might well walk away at that point. In life, though, you cannot always afford the luxury of never working with people who lie. Under any circumstances, however, you are going to want to know all you can about just how honest and forthcoming they tend to be.

Be careful, though, not to assume deceit where it may not exist. In my experience, great numbers of people working in financial services truly believe things that are simply not so. Daniel Patrick Moynihan famously said, "Everyone is entitled to his own opinion but everyone is not entitled to his own facts."[1] The person trying to win your business by telling you untrue things may not be lying. Then again, do you really want to put your money in the hands of someone who is seriously misinformed about her own field?

The Bargaining Phase of Investing

At some point, the discussion will shift away from learning about each other. Talk of prices, terms, and conditions will begin. At that point, you will have moved into the bargaining stage of the process. This is when exploration of trades, offers, and counteroffers occurs.

You are seeking to make investments on the most favorable terms possible, while the other side is also looking to maximize their advantage. Although some compromise may eventually be called for, the best way to proceed is by seeking trades that increase the overall value on the table. Look to offer them something they value highly that you are willing to trade for those things having great value for you.

Propose Ways for Them to Meet Their Most Important Interests

How can you persuade the other side to meet your primary interests? By offering them much of what they want in exchange. There are numerous ways you can put the deal together to move in the direction of your good outcome. What packages can you propose that will meet some of their important interests in exchange for most of what you need? What sequence should you follow? What compromises are you willing to make?

Remember to word these trades as if–then statements. Always pair offers with your requests. For example, you could suggest a lower annual fee like this: "If you could bring the fee down to match your lowest cost competitor, then I could increase the amount in my account from a quarter of my total assets to half."

Another thing you can offer them in trade is the promise of referrals. Of course, you will make this contingent on their fulfilling their end of the bargain for a certain length of time. A good investor-negotiator may trade referrals, introductions, and testimonies of satisfaction, but only for long-term and verifiable performance. In short, let them know what you will do to help them succeed if they do all that they have promised. And, of course, be sure to follow through on your offer and keep your word.

You are presenting possibilities, not demanding that they concede. Start with proposals that are very good for you, yet demonstrably based on some fair standard that you can show them. From there, make small concessions on the things that are most important to you. Make more generous concessions on those matters that have less value to you. Take care not to move beyond demonstrably fair. And when you move in their direction, don't just give in but rather offer a legitimate reason for each change.

Thus, for example, if you seek a promise that the advisor will receive no commissions, explain why that is fair. You might offer them a calculation of how much higher the operating costs of those funds tend to be in comparison with alternatives. Whether articulated or not, they will be concerned about the amount that such a promise would cost them. You could propose to pay them a fixed fee to make up some of their lost revenue. Couch that idea in conditional language such as "*If* we can agree on no-load funds with internal operating fees under 30 basis points, *then* I could consider paying you a greater fixed fee to make up for some of the lost revenue."

Let Them Know the Things on Which You Cannot Compromise

There are going to be areas where you have little room for compromise. For example, when you demand a fiduciary pledge, defining that term in writing, some firms are going to want vague language. This might look conditional on their part, but it is probably more of a dodge or a play for time. You can still use the if–then structure, but with less flexibility. *If* they can put their fiduciary pledges in an acceptable written form, *then* you can consider entering into a deal.

A special note about complexity: It is not your friend. At best, it adds costs that result in you paying a higher price for whatever it touches. At worst, it is a window that lets thieves in the door. Bargain for simple and straightforward approaches. Resist structures that are too complex to easily comprehend. Finally, crucially, if you do not understand something completely, do not allow it to remain in the agreement.

Keep in mind that a good deal creates value for everyone involved. Or, to state it more accurately, it definitely creates value for them—this is their business and they will not agree to unprofitable terms. Whether there will be value for you may depend on how well you assert your claim to a fair and substantial share of the value created by the deal.

Be Aware of Their Salesmanship Skills

Achieving this is not necessarily easy. The people you are negotiating with are experienced and trained; they are experts at deflecting requests for deals more favorable to the investor. During this bargaining stage, remind yourself of some of the things you have learned. Most important is the strength of your BATNA; they need you a great deal more than you need them. Also remember that this is not the equivalent of dealing with your doctor or lawyer, situations in which you tend to do as you are told. Rather, it is a negotiation in which a great deal of the authority at the table is yours. Finally, keep in mind that you have no intention of accepting something that is fundamentally unfair. Show them how you measure fair, and make them respond.

Warren Buffett is often quoted as follows:

> There is always a patsy at the poker table. And you can almost
> always identify who it is. If you have been playing for a while,
> and you still don't know who the patsy is, you're the patsy.[2]

You will not be played for a patsy, nor will you be fooled. All
that preparation and learning and gathering information was for
the purpose of holding your own in the bargaining phase. Be pleasant, be friendly, be nice, but above all, hold your ground. And if
you find that a bargaining session is not going your way, take a
break. Decline to sign anything, but promise to return at a certain
date. Then go home, take a deep breath, review your alternatives,
and reread the relevant parts of this book.

The Closing and Commitment Phase of Investing

As you continue bargaining, an acceptable deal will eventually
come into view. This is the time to review what you are *really* trying
to accomplish. Think about the interests you wrote down and make
sure the proposed deal truly leads toward your good outcome.

Build In Your Ability to Check on Them and to Get Out

Make sure the emerging deal includes two essential things: (1)
enough transparency that you can continue to monitor that your
interests are being met, and (2) your right to easily get out of the
arrangement if that proves not to be the case. This is particularly
important in the investment context because changing market conditions can alter your situation rather suddenly.

You also want to increase the likelihood that all the promises
made by the other side will be fulfilled. How can you structure the
deal to make that as likely as possible? Try to work into the agreement incentives that reward them upon successful completion. At
the same time, penalties for failing to follow through will increase
their motivation. Remember, they will perform on those promises
that they see as being in their best interest to keep.

Watch out for terms or situations that will limit your ability to
walk away whenever you want. Are there penalties, charges, or other
structures that lock you in? Will your ability to alter or terminate the
deal be hampered by complex requirements or paperwork? Are you

promising something unconditionally that you might later wish had caveats or escape clauses?

A client came to us recently with a partnership interest that required him to meet capital calls whenever they might occur. In other words, the people running the investment vehicle could demand more of his money as they deemed necessary. As you can imagine, he soon came to regret that.

Your ability to end the deal or walk away with ease serves more than one purpose. Not only can it potentially free you from an arrangement you later consider unfavorable, but it also increases your power. If someday a disagreement occurs or something promised is not carried out satisfactorily, your leverage will be greater if you can credibly threaten to take your business—and your capital—elsewhere. Getting locked in necessarily weakens your BATNA. Being able to walk away will strengthen it.

You can also put the scarcity principle to good use.[3] Throughout the bargaining and as closure comes into view, let the other side know that you have an alternative. Without sharing its details, help them understand that its terms are almost as good as the ones you are discussing. Since what you offer—client, capital, or both—is relatively scarce, the threat of losing you will garner some attention.

As you work toward closing the deal, take your time and get it right. Patience is a quality that rewards the well-prepared investor-negotiator. In light of your strong alternatives, you should have no reason to be in a hurry. Let them know that you have all the time in the world to craft a very good deal.

Of course, effectively conveying a patient attitude is easiest when it is true. Use time to your advantage by being prepared, starting early, refusing to be rushed, and avoiding deadline squeezes. Furthermore, reject any attempts to stampede you or coerce you into urgency. That is someone else trying to use the scarcity principle against you, and it is almost always based on false pretenses. You are investing for the long haul—much of your thinking should be in decades—and there is no reason to rush.

Get Everything in Writing

Deals of this sort are often closed with a handshake, and there is nothing wrong with a hearty grip to indicate concurrence. It bears repeating, though, that you want to get every agreed upon detail in writing. There should be no exceptions to this rule. Not only will this improve communication, but it will also make error-free implementation far more likely and will create a path to follow if a dispute should later arise.

Over the years, we have seen many examples of "forgetfulness" on the part of financial people. One advisor could not remember the exact percentage that formed a client's annual fee. Another was not sure of the precise terms of an investment product that he sold day in and day out for decades. Many forget the promises they make during pre-deal negotiations. Memorialize it all in writing. Good, clear, concise memos, agreed to by everyone, make for better working partnerships.

Because industry and government have tried their best to hopelessly cloud the meaning of "fiduciary," your agreement should define it in writing. You should ask anyone who will have power over your investments to sign a document acknowledging that they owe you the same duty that a trustee owes. Although a bit of a long-shot, getting this in writing might have the added benefit of weakening contractual clauses that force you into an industry-run arbitration system, since fraud in the inducement of the agreement could render it void.

This book argues that very few investments are uniquely valuable and most compete with very good alternatives. It is in the nature of financial markets that underpriced bargains and exclusive opportunities tend to get driven out. It follows that very few advisors, brokers, managers, or investment experts have something truly extraordinary to offer you.

Of course, if an advisor did have something uniquely valuable to offer, he would be in a position to charge mightily for it.

There is an apocryphal story about a uniquely talented expert that goes like this:

A company developed an amazing monster widget-making machine. They had sent out invitations for a great demonstration and celebration. Government, press, and business leaders were all in attendance. A few minutes before the start of the event, with the grandstands full, television cameras trained on the dignitaries, and the place in a frenzy of excitement, the widget-making machine shut down. No amount of cajoling by the operators could get it to fire up. In a panic, the company president suddenly remembered that their most experienced old engineer had just recently retired. The president got him on the phone and pleaded with him to come in and get the machine working. The engineer finally agreed to come in and fix it but said that he expected to be paid as a consultant for doing so. The president, his terror subsiding, readily agreed.

The engineer arrived quickly. He looked over the machine, taking special note of several tiny rivets on its surface. He then took a small hammer out of his bag and delicately hit one of the spots. The machine immediately sprang to life. The day was saved. The engineer put the hammer back in his bag and started out for home. The grateful president reminded him to submit his bill.

When the bill arrived several days later, it read:

> For Services Rendered: $10,000

The president called the engineer to express dismay. He protested that all the engineer had done was hit the machine with a small hammer. He sarcastically asked the engineer to submit a "more detailed itemized bill." That second bill arrived the next day. It read:

> For Hitting Machine with Hammer: $1
> For Knowing Where to Hit: $9,999

It's a wonderful story with several lessons to teach us. Let us start, though, by pointing out that the tale supposes a unique and desperately needed skill. That is what many investment salespeople would have you believe about their wares. With the aid of hindsight and cold, hard, scientific facts, we know they cannot offer any such thing. If they succeed in persuading you, they will have turned the scarcity principle against you. Don't fall for it.

The engineer's story also reminds us that it is critically important to "put it in writing," avoid assumptions, and not wait until the last minute to get the help we need.

The final phase of your investment negotiation concludes with an agreement that is reduced to writing in plain English. It includes terms that increase the likelihood of full compliance. You have gotten most of what you want and made sure all the others get enough to ensure their satisfaction. Furthermore, the deal is structured so that if, at any point, it is no longer good for you, there will be no trouble getting out of it. You obtained at least your fair share of the value created and made sure that nobody else is walking away with an excessive slice of the pie. Your patience and preparation have paid off. Well done.

Chapter Summary

- The first stage of an investment negotiation is about getting fully prepared.
- The earlier chapters of this book create a checklist from which you can work.
- Continue gathering useful new data throughout the whole process.
- Take advantage of the second stage to learn all you can.
- Listen more than you talk and encourage them to be open with you.
- You are now in conversation with the biggest expert on the subject of "them," so take full advantage of it.
- In the third stage, propose possible deals without getting locked into anything before you are ready.
- Trade what you need in exchange for what they want most.
- Be straightforward with them but cautious to check what they tell you.
- Be careful in the final stage to close a deal that the others will keep but that you can escape from if necessary.
- Prepare so that you won't be hurried, and then be patient.
- Get everything in writing.

Notes

1. George Will, "The Wisdom of Pat Moynihan," *Washington Post*, October 3, 2010.
2. Robert G. Hagstrom, *The Warren Buffett Way* (Hoboken, NJ: John Wiley & Sons, 2013), 212.
3. Robert B. Cialdini, *Influence: The Psychology of Persuasion* (New York: HarperBusiness, 2006), 237.

III

THE ECONOMIC TRUTHS YOU NEED TO KNOW TO BE AN EFFECTIVE INVESTOR-NEGOTIATOR

Economists know a great deal. Study, observation, and compilation of data reveal new understanding on an ongoing basis. The knowledge that economic science has accumulated is worth a fortune to the investor-negotiator. For reasons only touched on in this book, however, most Americans invest as if this body of scientific knowledge did not exist.

As made clear in Parts I and II of this book, there are a number of steps necessary to consider yourself a good investor-negotiator. Among these are thorough preparation, a great deal of learning, careful planning, and familiarization with the vocabulary, customs, and standards of those with whom you will be dealing. To this partial list we can add taking full notice of scientific teachings.

For our current purposes, the knowledge accumulated by economists can be broken into three categories: (1) the things they know, (2) the things they are aware that they don't know, and (3) the things they are certain that nobody can ever know. Each of these has value to you as an investor-negotiator.

This portion of the book will teach you, with a minimum of technical language or math, a number of these things that economists know. They are things that you need to know, too.

CHAPTER 26

Nobody Can Consistently Beat the Market

Most people think there is some magic skill that, although vaguely defined, will lead to the best investors making tons of money by exploiting underpriced investments. In other words, they are thought to possess a special talent for finding bargains, buying them, and then selling them for a huge profit. People go to great lengths to develop this skill. Furthermore, they spend astonishing amounts of money hiring advisors they believe possess this ability. Unfortunately, there are really no such bargains to be had. Let me explain why.

The Markets Are, for the Most Part, Rational

An individual investor will have great difficulty doing better than the overall market by selecting individual stocks or bonds. Economists have long known that financial markets are rational; that is, such markets price assets based on all information known at the time. This is widely known as the rational market theory or, sometimes, the efficient market hypothesis. Burton Malkiel articulates this important idea with great clarity in *A Random Walk Down Wall Street*.[1] In essence, the theory states that stock prices accurately reflect all the information that is known about a company at any given moment.[2] This means that future price changes can be the result only of surprises or unexpected events. Since, by definition, surprises or unexpected events cannot be predicted, nobody can successfully know in advance about the future performance of a given stock.

Taken to its logical extreme, a monkey throwing darts at the stock market page of the newspaper should be able to perform as well as anyone else. Consistent with that idea, in 2013 a cat named Orlando bested professionals by throwing toy mice at a stock grid.[3] (I was introduced to the theory by my college Economics 101 professor,[4] who allowed us to choose five stocks any way we wished, including asking anyone we knew, while he threw darts at the *Wall Street Journal.* He beat most of us.)

This theory is very counterintuitive, however, so it is easy for those with a motive to cast doubt on it. Indeed, not only do thousands of companies and individuals who make their living from stock picking dismiss the theory but so do many economists. There is a huge difference, however, between those two groups. Economists write PhD dissertations arguing between strong, semi-strong, and weak forms of rational market theory, but virtually every serious economist acknowledges its validity. Folks whose livelihoods depend on choosing stocks, on the other hand, simply throw stones at the whole idea, completely rejecting it.

Most of us have our own doubts as well. We may tell ourselves that every year lots of stock-picking newsletters, brokerage companies, and mutual funds beat the market averages. "My own neighbor, Charlie, is way ahead of the markets this year." How can the experts do no better than a bunch of amateurs? "I have based my whole life on the idea that doing research and working harder pays off in better results. . . . I just know that to be true." The concept of a market that cannot be beaten through some sort of hard work is counterintuitive, and we just don't quite believe it.

Don't Confuse Random Chance with Skill

It is true that lots of stock pickers beat the market every year. That fact just confirms rational market theory, though, rather than refuting it. If nobody can successfully pick investments better than anyone else, it stands to reason that about half the pickers do better than the average at any one time and half do worse. The folks doing the picking hold this out as a demonstration of a special skill but, upon examination, it is easy to understand that this is merely mathematical probability working itself out.

Andrew Tobias[5] helps us see this clearly: Line up 100 stock pickers (or children), give them each a penny, and ask them to try as

hard as they can to flip heads. About half of them can do it successfully. "That is pure luck," we say. Ask the successful ones to
do it again, and about 25 of them flip heads a second time. Try
again, and about 12 get heads for the third time in a row. Once
more and about six flip heads for a fourth straight time. Flip again,
we demand, and about three of them get heads for a fifth consec-
utive time. A sixth flip probably produces a single champion who
was able to get heads in each of the six tries. We all know, however,
that this does not represent any special talent for flipping heads.
Rather, it is simply the law of chance. Our champion's odds of getting heads on the next flip remain 50-50.

Random chance suggests that some stock pickers will beat the
markets in any given short period of time. An interesting experiment, though, is to compare the records of actively managed
(stock-picking) mutual funds with the market averages not over
one or two years, but over 10, 20, 30 years, or longer. Despite what
major fund managers may claim, the longer the time period, the
fewer funds remain ahead of the market. In the meantime, we see
huge ads trumpeting the successes without any mention of the failures, self-produced statistics that cannot be proven or replicated,
and the tendency of the industry to close down or merge losing
funds and obliterate them from their records. These and other
tricks are used by fund companies to improve the appearance of
their stock-picking records.

Everyone who goes to cocktail parties (or barbecues or fish
fries) knows people who play the market. A remarkable number
of those folks report that they are doing extremely well. Indeed, if
you ask specifically, they will tell you that they are handily beating
the market. Better take that with a grain of salt. In my professional
career, I have never found a nonprofessional investor who keeps
accurate records and is willing to share them. The acquaintances
who are beating the market are doing so because they are not keeping accurate track. Human nature predisposes them to remember
their winners and forget about their losers. (Ironically, the current
level of regulation of hedge funds allows for a similar trick—they
report their returns only when things are going well for them.)

Perhaps you recall the story of the Beardstown Ladies? This
group of elderly investors was reported to have consistently beaten
the market from 1983 to 1994, earning an average 23.4 percent per
year. Their investing prowess was widely discussed across the nation.

They were awarded a lucrative contract to write a book explaining how they were able to consistently achieve above-average returns. Notwithstanding what their book said, it turned out that the secret of their success was very simple. Their record-keeping system was flawed and, when examined properly, the actual return on their investments was very different from what they reported. In fact, the Beardstown Ladies had not beaten the market. From 1983 to 1994, they had earned an annual average of 9.1 percent,[6] while the Standard & Poor's 500-stock index returned 14.9 percent.[7]

But even if we give our neighbors the benefit of the doubt about their reports of success, none of them is beating the market over significant periods of time. The pros can't even beat the market over many years. Care to guess the number of mutual fund managers who beat the benchmark Standard & Poor's index every year between 1990 and 2005? One.[8] Bill Miller became a household name because of that feat and earned more money than you could count in all your days.[9] (Although subsequent years were not so kind to Mr. Miller, and by 2011 he was removed as full-time manager of the fund that he had made famous.) So the next time some Little League dad or storefront stockbroker tells you he regularly beats the market, ask to see his records—that will end the conversation.

Still, there is something deeply troubling about this efficient markets theory. It suggests that those who work hard, do their homework, put in the time and study, and really devote themselves will not do any better than those who throw darts. Even more disturbing, many of those hardworking investors will lag behind their neighbors who invest in index funds and know from the start that their performance will be just average. It is simply not the way we were brought up. It feels so Un-American (or Un-British, or Un-Moravian, or un-whatever your hardworking background). Surely there are rewards for working hard. These feelings of doubt and skepticism are played on by marketing campaigns that tell us we must get better stock research tools, and we should actively trade, and we ought to purchase the compilations of recent mutual fund performance records. In life, though, our gut intuition is not always correct, (try flying an airplane in a cloud or playing Three Card Monte with a street hustler), and the ads urging stock research are just trying to take advantage of us.

Stock Research Offers Little Value

It turns out that, despite what we are often told, research into individual companies cannot help you much in getting better investment returns. All the information you can turn up is already known by the experts on Wall Street,[10] and they have already figured it into the price of the stock. Let me give you an example. Suppose you have done a great deal of research into Boeing (stock symbol BA) and find out that its commercial airliner business is booming. In mid-2013, Boeing stock had reached its all-time high of $103 per share and had generally been rising since 2007.[11] Despite some technical teething pains with their Dreamliner jet, an impending union strike earlier in the year, and the impact of sequestration on its government sales, Boeing had an order backlog of $392 billion. This is a company with a solid future.

The thing to notice, though, is that Boeing stock currently sells at 19.4 times last year's earnings precisely *because* its future looks good. The pros on Wall Street who have bid up the price to that level know every single thing that you know about the company. And they know more than that; they know the expected profit margin per plane, the number of new planes the airlines are expected to need, and the current thinking on Boeing's prospects of winning that next order away from rival Airbus (EADS). In other words, they know everything that you could possibly learn through your research (after all, whose reports do you think you are reading?), and they have already caused that information to be worked into the current value of the stock.

What does that mean: "worked into the current value of the stock"? How does that happen? Let's try another example. Say that XYZ Company makes widgets and has 1 million shares of stock outstanding. Until today, everyone who pays attention to XYZ expected the company to make a profit of about $1 million a year (about $1.00 per share) this year and for the several years to come. Based on those projections, the stock has traded steadily at about $12 per share for a long time. At 11:00 A.M. this morning, you saw a news story on the internet saying that XYZ just got a huge government contract and the expectation is that the firm's profits will double to $2 million a year for each of the next several years. You think to yourself, "Wow, XYZ is a real bargain in light of this good news."

When you click to the stock market quotes, however, you see that the stock is already selling for $24 per share. What happened? The folks on Wall Street saw the same news and started buying the stock. They bought up all the shares that were offered at $13 and $14 and $15. They kept buying. The shares kept rising. More and more people read the news. The stock hit $16, $18, $20, but the pros kept buying because the stock was still a bargain even at $23 per share. However, at $24 per share, the stock was no longer a bargain because that is the price at which the profits from the new contract are fully factored in. And that is when Wall Street stopped buying. The stock stopped rising at $24, and that is where it remained by the time you went to the stock quotes page. The whole process may have taken less than a minute.

Research cannot help you with that. "But wait," you say, "what if vigorous research allowed me to see that they were likely to get the contract before it was actually awarded?" Here is the difficulty: Let's say you found out from public sources that XYZ might get that contract. More research told you that the odds of their winning the contract were 50-50. The problem is that all other investors, including very sophisticated Wall Street types, had access to that same information, and they, too, believed that XYZ had a 50-50 chance of getting that contract. If XYZ wins it, the stock is worth $24 per share; if they don't get the contract, it is worth $12. By the time you turn away from your research and look at the stock quotes, you will find that the stock is trading for $18 per share (reflecting the 50-50 chance that the company will go from being worth $12 to being worth $24).

"Well," you may ask, "what if I can gather information that nobody else has?" For example, let's imagine that you are a world-famous domestic design and fashion maven. One day, while flying to a vacation on your private jet, your stockbroker calls to say that he just got off the phone with one of his other clients who is CEO of a company you have invested in. This other client let slip that some very important negative news about the company will be made public tomorrow morning. You have the opportunity to sell your shares before the stock falls the next day. Yes, that will work to give you the advantage you seek regarding this particular company. There are only two problems with this scenario: (1) You are not a world-famous domestic design and fashion maven for whom some broker is going to risk everything by sharing inside information;

and (2) if you were the famous domestic design and fashion maven in our example, then you might be sent to jail for trading on inside information. It has been known to happen.

In general, you cannot get information that is unavailable to anyone else unless you have insider sources (you know, people within the company who know its secrets, etc.), and use of that insider information is quite illegal.

An example of the relative futility of this kind of research can be found by examining the recent history of automakers Ford (F) and Toyota (TM). Let's say that in 2006, you set out to learn all you could about these two companies. You would have found that Toyota was the dominant player in the industry and was continuing a string of earnings increases. Ford, on the other hand, was having one of its worst years ever. In 2006, the company recorded a loss of $17 billion. Ford was in trouble and in danger of going under. Given these facts, it is very likely you would have deemed Toyota by far the stronger of the two companies. Given the opportunity, you undoubtedly would have preferred to invest in Toyota stock.

In the years that followed, however, Toyota's stock stayed about even while the value of Ford nearly doubled. How can that be? It is as simple as the efficient markets theory.

Yes, Toyota was a better company. The stock price had already factored that in, though; Toyota had a market capitalization (the value Wall Street assigns to the company by multiplying all its shares by its price per share) 12 times greater than Ford's. So the question you needed to ask in 2006 was not "Which is the better company?" but, rather, "Is Toyota worth more or less than 12 times the value of Ford?" Even that question is of limited utility since a lot of smart people who think a lot about the matter had determined that, at that time, Toyota was worth almost exactly 12 times what Ford was worth.

The answer to the overall question of which stock would perform better would be answered by unexpected and unpredictable future events. By their very definition, unexpected and unpredictable future events cannot be known in advance.

Earlier in this chapter, I wrote that economists disagree about rational market theory in that some argue for a strong version, some believe in a semi-strong variant, and others claim that a weak version is the correct way to understand the theory. If you are itching to do some research, you can look up the differences.

For our purposes here, however, all you need to know is that none of these variations of the theory leads to the conclusion that average investors, or even experienced folks with millions of dollars, are going to be able to beat the market. Rather, this is an argument among academics as to whether inconsistencies exist in stock pricing that might be taken advantage of by, say, a huge Wall Street firm with hundreds of computers and the finest Ivy League minds to run them. Yes, there may be a few holes in the rational markets theory, but, no, you aren't going to be able to make any money out of them.

Once you understand how markets work, you can see that no amount of research or historical study is going to make you rich. Most of the results you are observing are the reflection of random chance. Neither you nor anyone you can hire is going to be able to beat appropriate market benchmarks. One thing you get to do, once you realize these economic truths, is relax. There are now a dozen things you can just ignore. In turn, you can focus your efforts more robustly on those remaining things that will actually make a difference in getting you good investment outcomes.

Chapter Summary

- Economists know that stock picking cannot consistently beat relevant benchmarks.
- Nobody knows what a given investment will do in the coming weeks or months or one-year period.
- There are no secret ways to beat the market that are legal.
- Distinguish between what can be known and what is a reflection of random chance. Save your efforts for the former, and spend no energy on the latter.

Notes

1. Burton Malkiel, *A Random Walk Down Wall Street* (New York: W. W. Norton, 2007).
2. For simplicity, I may at times refer only to stocks but the theory holds for other investments, such as bonds, as well.
3. Mark Gongloff, "Stock-Picking Cat Named Orlando Trounces 'Professionals,'" HuffingtonPost.com, January 15, 2013.
4. Professor Peter Kilby at Wesleyan University.
5. Andrew Tobias, *The Only Investment Guide You Will Ever Need*, 4th ed. (Orlando, FL: Harcourt, 2005).

6. Mark Gongloff, "Where Are They Now: The Beardstown Ladies," *Wall Street Journal*, May 1, 2006.

7. http://money.cnn.com/data/markets/sandp.

8. William H. Miller III of Legg Mason.

9. Joe Light and Tom Lauricella, "A Star Exits After Value Falls," *Wall Street Journal*, November 18, 2001.

10. The world is growing more mobile and connected by the day. People I refer to as "on Wall Street" are all sophisticated about investing, but they can be located in New York, Omaha, Bangalore, or anywhere else on earth.

11. Daniel Ferry, "Will Boeing Stock Fall Back to Earth?" *The Motley Fool*, May 24, 2013.

27

Past Performance Does Not Guarantee Future Results

Past performance does not guarantee future results. We all know this to be true. After all, it is a requirement that this fact be stated in financial ads and prospectuses. We have read it a thousand times and memorized the words, the same way a smoker is familiar with health warning labels. Trouble is, we don't quite believe it. Our instinct tells us that some people are more skilled at picking investments than others. Furthermore, we believe in the hot hand or the lucky streak. Sure, our statistics teacher told us that the champion coin flipper in the previous chapter was just a lucky recipient of the gift of random probability, but, deep in our hearts, we think he is more likely to flip heads again. Our gut and our brain are in conflict.

Well, it turns out that our brain is right, our gut is wrong, and past performance offers no guarantee at all. Not only does it provide no assurances but, in fact, past performance is not even a useful predictor most of the time. It is, more or less, worthless in picking stock investments that will appreciate in value. Future results and past performance have little to do with each other.

No One Can Predict the Future

To understand this, we need to think hard about random chance. There are many thousands of people making their living picking stocks, in one way or another, and trying to get you to buy what they sell. It stands to reason that a few of them would be doing extremely well at any one time. A smaller number still would logically have a pretty long string of winnings. And those doing well have very strong incentives to make sure the investing public knows how well they are doing. This small group of winners, though, sits among a vast pool of folks who are having less success. Take a look at the mutual fund page of the *Wall Street Journal*. If I told you that one of those mutual funds was going to have a truly extraordinary year but didn't identify which one, the information would be essentially useless to you—there are thousands of them. And last year's big winner is no more likely to be next year's champion than any of the others.

It is foolish to invest in a stock or mutual fund because it did well recently. Funds that claim to be among the top performers in a given category want you to assume such success is likely to be repeated. That assumption would be mistaken. If the fund is among the top performers once again, it will be primarily the result of random chance. There is little or no causal effect.

Past performance is not a useful indicator of where investments like stocks, bonds, and mutual funds will go in the future. Knowing what they did yesterday will not help you guess where they will be tomorrow. And there are no bargains to be found. The market already knows what you know and what your financial advisor knows and has taken that information into account.

Economists can show that past performance offers us very little useful information about what is to come. Our most admired scholars have no more insight into next year's big winners than anyone else—because nobody can know based on past performance.

Chapter Summary

- For the most part, past performance is of little use to investors.
- A great deal of performance is a reflection of random chance.
- Even the most brilliant economists don't know which investments will do well in the coming year and, thus, it is a certainty that no stockbroker or TV guy does either.

CHAPTER 28

The Concept of Present Value

A dollar today is worth more than a dollar one year from now. That probably sounds like a recitation of common sense rather than an important concept in understanding finance. It turns out, though, that it is a big deal when we seek to understand many of the investment choices we are faced with.

In its simplest form, we understand present value by thinking of putting $100 into a savings account at the bank. Let us suppose that the bank pays 1 percent interest on such accounts. If you put $100 in today, one year from now you will have $101. If you will permit some rounding to keep the math simple, in our example $100 next year is worth only $99 today. So if someone asked you how much you would be willing to pay for $100 a year from now, you would reply, "No more than $99."

As you may have intuited, the present value of a future amount is dependent on what interest rate is applied. Indeed, over long periods, different interest rates make huge differences in present-value calculations.

Here is the math, which I give you full permission to skip:

Calculating Present Value

$$PV = C/(1 + r)^n$$

where:

C = The amount of money you want to have at the end of the period
r = The interest rate
n = The number of periods

So to determine how much money you need to deposit today to have $1,000 in the bank a year from now at 5 percent interest, you calculate:

$$\$1,000/(1 + 0.05)\ 1 = \$952.40$$

A deposit of $952.40 today, earning 5 percent annual interest, will yield $1,000 at the end of the one-year period. At that interest rate, $1,000 a year from now is worth $952.40 today.

I encouraged you to skip the equation for three reasons. The first is that I know you really wanted me to exempt you from your old high school math. The second is that we all have access to present-value calculators that will do this math for us. The third and most important reason is that what is important to understand is the *concept* of present value.

Understanding what present value is all about can help us unravel some of the confusing puzzles in our investing lives. Here are some examples.

What Is Tax Deferral Worth?

Why is an Individual Retirement Account (IRA) so valuable? (Or any other tax-deferred retirement account, such as a 401(k) or 403(b) plan.) These plans are an incredibly good deal because they let you keep and invest money that would otherwise be paid to the IRS today. The future value of that money is far greater, and the tax deferral allows you to claim that future value. In other words, the government is making you an interest-free loan of the money you would ordinarily owe in tax today. You get to use that money (as investment capital) until the funds are removed from the retirement plan.

The same principle is at play with a 529 College Savings Plan. Be careful to note, though, that the greatest benefit of tax deferral comes from putting off paying taxes for long periods of time. If the time frame is shorter, such as the difference between today and when your elementary-schooler is in college, the future value is less. While the tax deferral is still valuable, it may not be so great as to offset any fees or added costs of the more expensive 529 programs.

Present Value and Life Insurance

Present value also helps us understand how life insurance works. How can the insurance company afford to insure a 25-year-old man for $1 million for 40 years if he pays premiums of $3,000 per year? If you simply add up $3,000 times 40 years you get $120,000. Won't the poor insurance company go broke? Nope. If the man dies at age 65, the insurance company must pay his beneficiaries in *future dollars*, but each year it is collecting far more valuable *present dollars*. The insurance company invests all the money it takes in and is able to pay claims with plenty to spare. And if the man lives past 65, the insurance company does even better.

Present Value and Money-Back Guarantees

Variable annuity products (and their cousins that are sold by insurance and investment companies under a hundred different names) offer a seemingly irresistible guarantee. If the investment choices within the product fail to grow your money, you are guaranteed your original investment back. You get the better of (1) investment growth or (2) your original money back. It would seem you cannot lose. Perhaps that explains why these terrible investments sell like hotcakes in the present economic climate.

How can the insurance companies do it? The answer, of course, can be understood using the concept of present value. Like insurance, the annuity product is being funded with valuable *present dollars*, and the guarantee will be paid off with less valuable *future dollars*. For example, let's suppose the insurance company is able to achieve a 10 percent annual return on the money they receive under the contract. Let us further assume that it must pay off on the guarantee 15 years after receiving the investment dollars. In this instance, the company would have been able to quadruple the money paid in. Thus, its guarantee would cost it only about a quarter of the value it received. To view it from the annuity buyer's perspective, the money-back dollars received 15 years later, in a 10 percent interest rate environment, are worth only about a quarter of what the original pay-in dollars were worth. (Pardon me for rounding numbers.) In this example, what was billed as a full money-back guarantee starts to look more like getting a quarter of your money back.

Present Value and Comparing Investments

Comparing two investments can be hazardous if some of the dollars are in the present and some are counted at future value.

An example of this is my neighbor Irving. This good man will not sell his house at a loss. Rather, he insists on holding onto it until "the market comes back" and he can sell for more than he paid for it. The problem, you may realize, is that he is comparing present dollars with future dollars. So far, he has let the house sit empty for 10 years. Never mind the decay and slow breakdown of parts of the home, let's just look at the financial numbers.

Let's assume that Irving sells his house tomorrow for the same amount he paid for it 10 years ago. In his mind, he has broken even. With an understanding of present value, though, we can see he has not done nearly that well. Rather, he bought the place with 10-years-ago dollars and is being paid back in today's dollars. If the interest rate applied is 7.2 percent (chosen, in part, because the "rule of 72" makes the calculation so easy), the value of his house has doubled in that time. Accordingly, if he sells it today for what he paid for it 10 years ago, we can say that he has gotten back only half of what he paid for the house.

Whenever the returns on two investments are compared, accuracy requires that you account for the time value of money. A dollar today is always worth more than a dollar in the future. Unless you figure out just how much more, comparisons across different time periods will be very misleading. Beware of those people who use deceptive comparisons deliberately because they do not want you to clearly understand what they may be selling.

Chapter Summary

- The value of money in the future is less than what that same amount of money is worth today.
- Calculating present value can help you compare different investments.
- This concept is especially helpful in thinking about tax deferral, insurance products, annuity products, and any sort of financial guarantees.
- Beware of sharpsters offering misleading comparisons.

CHAPTER 29

There Is Really Only One Interest Rate

The statement "there is really only one interest rate" sounds absurd on its face. How can economists say that when we can look in the paper and see dozens of different interest rates listed? Here is what they mean.

Higher Rates Reflect Higher Levels of Risk

At any given time, there is only one rate of interest for lending your money with total safety. All the other rates are different levels of risk premium. In other words, lenders charge a higher rate to borrowers that are less safe to compensate for the increased risk. If we think about it in the context of the previous chapters, this makes perfect sense. If there was more than one interest rate for totally safe debt, I could easily borrow money at the lower rate and then lend it out at the higher one—as could lots of other clever folks. Eventually, the borrowing of the one and the lending to the other would force rates to converge. Thus, it is the rational market that is causing rates to be the same for an equivalent level of risk.

When an investor buys a bond (which is to say, lends her money to the bond issuer), there are two kinds of risks. The first is default risk and the second is interest rate risk. Let's examine each one in turn.

Default risk is the danger that the borrower will go bankrupt or in some other way not pay back the loan. Clearly, this is of huge concern to a lender. If you buy bonds, either directly or through a mutual fund or pension plan, you are such a lender, and the concerns are yours, too. Some borrowers are considered extremely unlikely to default. As a powerful example, the United States is thought to be incapable of doing so. Some companies and countries, though, could default. Indeed, many companies go into bankruptcy every year. Some countries decide not to pay their debts every once in a while. And Mom's old Uncle Willy hasn't made a payment on his loan from Grandma in over 30 years. The financial world has rating services that try to assess the relative risk of different companies' bonds and other debt instruments. Moody's and Standard & Poor's are among the best known. As you can guess, bonds that are judged more likely to default, and thus have lower ratings, must pay higher interest rates to convince anyone to invest in them.

The second risk with a bond is called *interest rate risk*. It is the danger that if interest rates rise, an older bond will be worth less. This is because the same money that bought the bond yielding, say, 5 percent last year could now buy the equivalent bond yielding 6 percent. Thus, it stands to reason that the bond bought last year yielding 5 percent now has a lower market value. (Of course, interest rates could also fall. The converse of interest rate risk is the potential for gains when rates drop.) The longer the duration (how long until you get your money back) of the bond, the greater this effect. Thus, longer bonds carry more interest rate risk than shorter bonds. (Indeed, longer bonds usually have greater default risk as well, since the longer period of borrowing means there is more danger that it will not be paid back in full.) It follows that if longer bonds carry greater risks, investors will demand a greater return for buying them.

Occasionally, the likelihood of falling interest rates seems so great that longer bonds have lower interest rates than shorter bonds. This is referred to as an *inverted yield curve*. It doesn't occur all that often, though; after all, economists know that nobody can reliably predict future interest rates.

There is also currency risk with bonds that are denominated in a monetary system other than your own (for instance, a U.S. investor buying Japanese bonds denominated in yen). To redeem your investment, you must sell the bond and then convert the yen back into dollars. If the dollar rises or the yen falls, your investment will have lost money. Of course, the dollar may fall or the yen rise, in which case you will make extra profit on the currency appreciation.

In any case, though, purchasing bonds using currency other than your own involves taking on an additional risk beyond that of the bond alone.

Money lent to the United States (by buying Treasury bonds, notes, and bills) is considered to be the safest debt in the world with regard to default risk. The United States is one country, the financial world unanimously agrees, that will always pay its debts. (One of the biggest reasons for this belief is that the United States figuratively owns printing presses. It can print U.S. dollars, the strongest currency in the world.) Thus, we might say that the interest rate for lending money to the United States for one day is the world's true interest rate.

The practical consequence is this: You cannot get a higher yield than the one true interest rate without taking on more risk. Savers and investors who don't understand this are in danger of holding far more risk in their portfolios than is appropriate or that they would be comfortable with if they were aware of it. Parts of the financial services industry seek to take advantage of people's misunderstanding by doing a hard sell on junk bonds, long-term bonds, and even emerging market bonds. Many clients, over the years, have complained about the return on short-term Treasury bonds and money market funds. On occasion, they propose exchanging into a higher yielding debt instrument by stating that "such and such bond fund is paying twice as much." Then we have a long talk. . . .

Risky Investments Involve a Danger of Losing Much of Your Principal

A bond with an effective interest rate far higher than what other bonds are paying reflects a much greater level of risk. Those high-yield bond funds are invested primarily in junk bonds, which come by that name honestly. Junk bonds are debt securities that have very low ratings—in other words, bonds that have a very significant risk of default. Emerging market bonds are the debt of countries (and companies in them) with very weak or unstable economies—they are very risky! Even long-term U.S. Treasury bonds have a great deal of interest rate risk, particularly in a time of inflation or when interest rate increases are expected.

The risks are real. One client came to us after working with a stockbroker (although he called himself a financial consultant) with a portfolio full of junk. One bond, though, bore the name of a county in Pennsylvania. At first glance, it appeared to be municipal debt. On closer inspection, it turned out to be an industrial revenue bond that raised money for, and bore the risk of, a steel company in the county. That company is now bankrupt, and those bonds are worthless. The lesson is clear: You can lose a great deal of your principal investing in high-risk bonds.

An investor must understand that bonds, like stocks, carry with them different levels of risk. The higher the interest rate offered, the higher the risk. Interest rates are a function of the one true interest rate—what you would receive to lend money to the U.S. government for a very short period.

Financial markets do not afford possibilities for receiving a higher interest rate from one borrower to the next without taking on greater risk. Any appearance of such opportunity is an illusion. Furthermore, the additional danger can be difficult to analyze. While the various rating agencies work hard to assess the risks of various bonds, their conclusions are often wrong. Nobody can ever know with certainty about the future of interest rates, currencies, or inflation. Anybody who thinks that stocks are risky and bonds are safe is laboring under a mistaken impression: There is plenty of risk in bonds, and various bonds have dramatically different risk profiles.

Chapter Summary

- At any given time, there is only one interest rate for lending your money in total safety.
- Higher interest rates reflect increased risk.
- Investments in bonds that pay higher than expected dividends entail substantial danger that you could lose a great deal of your principal.
- Bonds are not *per se* safer. Risky bonds can be just as perilous as risky stocks.

30

There Is No Such Thing as a Free Lunch—Except Diversification

Most people know the expression "there is no such thing as a free lunch." An economist named Leonard P. Ayres uttered those words in 1946. Every benefit must be paid for in one way or another, directly or indirectly. With one big exception: It turns out that diversification is the only free lunch in all of economics.

By diversification we mean the strategy of combining a variety of investments of different kinds, which are specifically chosen because they are unlikely to move in the same direction at the same time. Diversification is an attempt to reduce the level of risk of an overall portfolio. The concept is as simple as the old admonition not to put all your eggs in one basket. The mathematics, on the other hand, can be mind-numbing.

The good news is that we need not do any math to use the concept. Here is an extremely simple example. If you invest in a company that makes sunscreen, you will do well in years with lots of sunshine and poorly in rainy years. Now if you make a second investment in a company that sells raincoats, you will do better when rain predominates. This is the essence of diversification. When one company does well, the other does poorly, and vice versa. You reduce your risk by investing in both companies so that in either weather you will have some success.

Why You Want to Diversify

Portfolio theory posits that proper diversification can lower the risk of a portfolio without reducing its expected return. It follows that by increasing risk, we can expect a higher return at the original risk level. In other words, we can either reduce risk and expect the same return or hold risk steady and raise return. A free lunch! Well, not totally free, since it will cost more to buy lots of investments than to purchase just a few. Luckily, there are some pretty good answers to that problem, which we will discuss later in the book.

Consider this example to illustrate the principle of the value of diversification. Two investors in the year 1999 each sought capital appreciation by buying stock in large-capitalization American companies. One asked a stockbroker for the name of a highly recommended, fast-growing, can't-miss, large company to invest in. The broker suggested a company called Enron. The second investor, wary of risk, sought broad diversification among large U.S. companies and bought shares in an S&P 500 fund. In essence, the first investor bought shares in Enron and the second investor bought an interest in each of the 500 largest U.S. firms. As history teaches us, Enron was a fraud and eventually went under. Both investors lost money. The first investor lost all his money. The second investor, though, had perhaps 2 percent of his capital in Enron, and that is the proportion of her investment that was lost. The second investor had diversified away the risk that a particular company might fail.

Across what parameters are we seeking to diversify? We can spread risk across companies, industries, and countries. Beyond that, we can look to diversify with respect to regions of the world, types of economies, currencies, and sources of information. I will argue later that it is wise to diversify over time, as well, to avoid putting all of the eggs into, or out of, the basket all at once.

Chapter Summary

- Diversification of investments can lower risk without reducing expected return.
- Diversify within an asset class and also across asset classes.
- When diversification can be achieved without any significant increase in costs, it is too good a deal to pass up.

CHAPTER
31

Diversify Across Every Asset Class

Economists rightly expect that, over very long periods of time, stock investments will probably be the highest returning asset class. There are theoretical reasons why this should be so. This hypothesis is also borne out by a very long historical record. As a practical matter, if you have unlimited time, the best investment is likely to be a diversified portfolio of stock investments.

On the other hand, there is not a human being on earth who has unlimited time. That is not the nature of our lives. Most of us invest money hoping to grow it but with the intention of eventually spending it. For those who intend to use their money soon and thus have a limited investment time horizon, stocks are a potentially terrible investment. To put it more forcefully, stocks over short periods of time are nothing more than gambling.

This conundrum, stocks for the long haul but something less risky for shorter-term money, starts to shine a light on portfolio construction.[1] It is not difficult to construct a diversified portfolio, across all asset classes, based on what portion of your money will not be needed for a very long time.

For example, the Johnson family sought an investment plan that would deal with the need of two parents to retire in approximately 25 years, one child who would start college in 3 years, and another child who will not reach college for 14 years. They determined that 40 percent of their savings were for retirement, 30 percent for the older child's college education, 20 percent for the younger child's college needs, and 10 percent for a kitchen they had to have next year. With some guidance, the Johnsons built a portfolio with about 40 percent of their investments in diversified stock funds, approximately 30 percent in bonds expected to mature in three years, about 20 percent in balanced funds that approached a 55 percent stock/45 percent bond split, and 10 percent in cash equivalents. Of course, the Johnsons also wanted the portfolio to have exposure to all the other major asset classes, and that was dealt with by making small adjustments to the figures described above.

Be Honest with Yourself about Your Risk Tolerance

One of the greatest perils facing you as an investor is that your emotions will lead you to make wrong moves. In particular, human beings feel tremendous pressure to sell stocks when they are falling (and thus becoming more of a bargain) and to buy them when they are rising (and becoming more and more expensive). To the extent that you can somehow guarantee yourself that you will not panic and sell at the worst possible moment, a great emphasis on stocks may be warranted. Alas, it is easy on a sunny day to promise ourselves we will be calm in a storm. Our actual behavior in the churning waves and fierce winds may be a different story entirely. If, like Odysseus, you can find a way to tie yourself to the mast, then go ahead and put more into stock investments. On the other hand, consider this mantra often repeated at our firm: "If you have trouble sleeping well at night, you have too much risk in your portfolio."

Let's review the major asset classes that, together, comprise a well-diversified portfolio.

- U.S. stock investments (all sizes of companies)
- Foreign stock developed-markets investments (all sizes of companies)
- Emerging market stock investments (all sizes of companies)
- Real estate (both U.S. and international)
- U.S. bonds issued by many types of entities and with a broad range of maturities
- Foreign bond investments (including emerging markets)
- Inflation-protected bonds (TIPS)
- Commodities
- Money market funds and short-term bond investments

How to Achieve Diversification of an Investment Portfolio

Investment portfolios that are less than fully diversified carry more risk than necessary. A prudent investor will seek opportunities to diversify away some of it. Here is an example of how you might approach that.

Let's start by assuming that you have invested in a major oil company such as ExxonMobil. At this point, after buying only one stock, you are highly undiversified. You can increase diversification by purchasing shares in a number of major world oil companies, including Chevron and BP and Royal Dutch Shell. Now you have invested in the oil industry and reduced your investment risk by purchasing many companies within the industry, rather than a single stock. You have reduced specific company risk within that one industry.

That is one level of diversification. But why would you want to invest all your money in only one industry? You can further reduce risk by spreading out to other areas of the economy, such as technology companies, banks, utilities, consumer products companies, and retailers. The ultimate reduction in specific industry risk involves buying stocks in every recognized industry group.

Why invest in some companies in each industry group when you can choose to invest in all companies? This brings us to the topic of broad index funds. These are mutual funds that try to replicate a market rather than make selections in an attempt to beat that market. So, for example, a fund that replicates the S&P 500 index does not attempt to select companies among large-capitalization U.S. firms; rather, it buys them all in their proper market weights (meaning in proportion to their market capitalization). An index fund tied to a broader index, such as the Russell 3000, replicates the performance of just about the entire U.S. stock market.

Now that you effectively own all the stocks in all of the industries in the United States, it is appropriate to consider the rest of the world. You can seek to invest in stock of a broadly diversified group of companies from all over the globe. Traditionally, these have been broken into international stocks (the countries of the so-called developed economies) and emerging markets (the countries with less developed or emerging economies). Once again, use of very broad index funds will allow you to replicate almost the entirety of these two categories.

Stocks are often divided into two broad categories: growth stocks and value stocks. Growth stocks are those companies with rapidly growing profits whose prospects look bright. They would seem to be wonderful investments, except that their stocks are already very expensive due to all the optimism surrounding their future. Value stocks, on the other hand, are those companies whose shares are on sale for some reason, such as slowing growth, poor profitability, products with a dim future, or some sort of corporate catastrophe. As you know, a properly functioning liquid market contains no bargains, so it is difficult to predict which of these two groups will do better in the short or medium term. It is best to own both. Of course, very broad index funds will accomplish this for you.

Companies are also grouped by size. This is usually accomplished by looking at market capitalization, which is the number of shares outstanding times the price of a share. One could say that the market capitalization is the value that stock market investors have placed on the company. Financial folks speak of large caps (huge companies), mid caps (relatively big companies), small caps (smaller companies), and micro caps (the smallest of public companies). Professors Fama and French believe they have proven that small companies will do better than larger ones over very long periods of time, but, to reduce risk, you want to invest in companies of all sizes.[2]

At this point, we have built a portfolio containing stocks of all the different sizes of companies—large-cap, small-cap, mid-cap, micro-cap—within growth and value stock categories for the United States, the developed markets, and the emerging markets. This represents an extremely broad diversification across stocks.

Now we turn our attention to other asset classes.

Diversifying Asset Classes beyond Stocks

Broadly speaking, there are three types of things you can invest in. You can have an ownership interest in a company (stock), you can be a creditor of an institution (bond), or you can own a thing that you hope will appreciate in value (commodity). Of course, these very broad categories are further broken down in the investment world. Let's examine the investment asset classes that a prudent investor should seek to diversify across.

Bonds

You can invest in debt by buying a bond either from the original issuer (the borrower) or from another investor. There are a number of important distinctions between types of bonds. Let's examine them briefly.

Bonds are usually classified by the type of issuer. They are issued by governments, businesses, nonprofit institutions, and other entities. Other types of bonds worthy of their own individual categories are municipal bonds (because the interest they pay is federally tax free) and inflation-protected bonds (because their principal amount is adjusted upward for inflation).

As discussed earlier, bonds are subject to default risk and interest rate risk. The dangers associated with default risk are supposed to be analyzed and summed up by the rating agencies, which assign each bond a risk rating. The different ratings result in a sorting of bonds, with the safest ones called investment grade and the riskiest bonds labeled as junk. Interest rate risk increases with the length of time until the investor recovers her money. Thus, long bonds have very high interest rate risk and short bonds have very little. The prudent investor probably diversifies across all of these risk factors.

Inflation-Protected Bonds

In light of the cost-of-living increase in principal that is a feature of Treasury inflation-protected bonds (often referred to by the acronym TIPS), they should be considered a separate asset class. These TIPS can be expected to behave differently from traditional bonds in many economic climates. In particular, they perform significantly better in periods of high inflation. Thus, investment in TIPS is a method for diversifying away some of the bond risk associated with inflation. A wise investor owns both traditional bonds and TIPS.

Real Estate Investments

The various kinds of real estate are often considered another asset class. It may behave differently from stocks or bonds in certain economic or market conditions and, thus, is helpful in further diversifying an investment portfolio.

Many families own their home. For some, this is among the largest investments they have. In many cases, this is an appropriate level of real estate investment to achieve the desired diversification. For others, though, further exposure to the real estate asset class is desirable.

An investment vehicle called a real estate investment trust (REIT) affords an opportunity to easily invest in a broad (and sometimes diversified) collection of properties. Significantly greater diversification can be achieved by investing in a selection of different types of REITS or, perhaps, a mutual fund investing broadly in many different REITS.

Commodities

Human beings have a long history of investing in *things* with the hope that their value will rise and a profit can be realized. From tulip bulbs to baseball cards, investors have been tempted by rising valuations. Perhaps the single commodity that has the greatest history as an investment vehicle is gold. Let's use the example of gold to discuss the entire concept of commodities.

If the price of gold rises, an investor can make a profit. Furthermore, since gold has come to have almost the status of an alternative currency, it can hedge against the danger of declining currencies or rising inflation. There are some distinct negatives to investing in gold or similar commodities, though, and these should be considered. Unlike companies or debt or real estate, gold is not designed to bring in money. It draws no profits or interest or rents. It just sits there. Furthermore, an investment in the metal itself must be stored and insured. Thus, it costs money to hold gold.

Some of the problems of investing in actual gold can be ameliorated by investing in gold companies. In particular, firms that mine the metal are often an excellent proxy for an investment in gold itself. Applying our earlier learning, it is probably more prudent to invest in a broad range of gold miners than in a single one.

By the same principle of diversification, why invest in a single commodity when you can invest in a basketful of different commodities? The smartest way to invest in commodities is probably to buy a mutual fund that owns shares in a wide variety of mining and materials companies across the globe.

Cash

There is an asset class called cash. While individual dollar bills would qualify, that is not usually how an investment in cash is achieved. After all, the bills in your wallet do not bring any interest, whereas a bank account does.

Thus, there are a significant number of investments that are considered cash equivalents. Among these are certificates of deposit, Treasury bills, and money market mutual funds. Basically, any very-short-term debt instrument that has virtually no default risk will be considered a cash equivalent.

Although rare, there have been years when cash was among the very highest returning asset classes. This is likely to occur during a period of sharp declines for stocks, bonds, real estate, and other classes of investments.

Use Time to Further Diversify

If it is wise to divide your eggs into many baskets, it is also wise to place the eggs into those baskets over a period of time rather than all at once. This is sometimes called dollar cost averaging, and it is understood as the practice of buying an investment over time in regular, fixed intervals. Savvy investors routinely do this.

Consider this example: Instead of investing $12,000 in a broad stock market index fund on the day you finish this book, you decide to put $1,000 into the fund on the first of each month for a year. At the end of the year, you will have invested $12,000 into the fund. Rather than buying all your shares at one price, though, you will have purchased shares in 12 different lots at 12 different prices. The average price you paid for a share is likely to be similar to the average price of the fund over the course of the year. In doing this, you have decreased the risk that you might have bought at the very highest point. If a sharp drop in the price occurs at some point during the year, you will purchase further shares at a lower price in subsequent months.

If dollar cost averaging your way into investments is a wise practice that reduces risk, then dollar cost averaging your way out must be the same. And so it is. In particular, this is a good way for older folks to begin taking money out of their retirement portfolios for spending or investment in lower risk investment choices. Take a little out each month, rather than a large amount all at once.

If you think about it, a lot of dollar cost averaging happens automatically. The most common example is having an employer put money from every paycheck into a retirement plan. These investments are made regularly at the same interval as the paychecks.

At the other end, having money taken out of your plan and sent to you monthly will achieve the same effect: diversifying over time.

Use Index Mutual Funds to Create Very Broad Diversification

At first glance, it would seem difficult to construct such broadly diversified investment portfolios. They require investing in hundreds of individual securities in complex combinations. Furthermore, holding so many different individual investments would require more capital than most of us have. It would also cost a significant amount just for trading fees. As argued earlier, though, mutual funds and their progeny[3] have made this task quite easy. The desired diversification can be achieved by investing in just a handful of funds.

A vehicle that allows you to invest in hundreds of stocks with a single investment is just what the diversification doctor ordered. You can easily gain complete exposure to all of the asset classes and subclasses discussed here.

Once it is clear that mutual funds and their cousins[4] are the way to achieve your diversification goals, the question becomes what sort of mutual funds you should invest in.

Funds that are actively managed involve someone (or a group) running the fund and aggressively trying to decide which investments are best. At their worst, actively managed funds trade in and out of stocks often and generate large trading commission costs. They are expensive to operate—which cost is passed on to shareholders in a slightly clandestine way as operating expenses. They also create capital gains, if they are lucky, or capital losses that must be declared as taxable events. At their best, actively managed funds buy good stocks, trade only occasionally, and have expenses only double or triple those of the best index funds.

Index funds, on the other hand, skip the cost of having someone pick out individual investments. Rather, they buy all the stocks in a given index (such as the Standard & Poor's 500) in their correct proportions and accept the fact that they will perform no better than that index.

The Efficient Markets Hypothesis

The efficient markets hypothesis shows us why index funds are the wiser choice.[5] There has long been a great debate in the investment world regarding active versus passive funds. One of the fundamental contentions of this book is that the indexers are right, the active management crowd is mistaken, and the stakes for an investor are very significant.

If nobody can know in advance which stocks or investments will do better or which mutual funds will succeed in picking the best performers, it makes more sense to simply choose the index fund and accept the advantage of its extremely low costs. And because actively managed funds incur much higher costs, they have little hope of outperforming index funds over long periods. Index funds allow investors to play the odds the prudent way by holding investing costs to a minimum, being tax savvy, and acknowledging that there is no effective way to beat the market. They are the wisest method for pursuing your investment aims.

When comparing index funds, you can include exchange-traded funds (ETFs) in your research. These investment vehicles are, essentially, index funds that trade throughout the day like stocks. Because they were created to compete with index funds, they have extremely low operating costs, in some cases even lower than comparable index mutual funds. As a result, they are a valuable complement to traditional index funds and, notwithstanding all the hype, a worthwhile investment vehicle.

Some Practical Advice on Choosing Specific Categories of Index Funds

Some of you have picked up this book looking for specific and practical advice. This paragraph is for you. A good suggestion is to invest in a total U.S. stock market index fund and a total international stock index fund. To these you may wish to add an emerging markets stock index fund. With those three index funds, you will own a slice of the overwhelming majority of stocks that trade in the world. For bonds, use a total U.S. bond index fund, and supplement it with a foreign bond fund. For real estate, look for a U.S. REIT index fund and an international REIT index fund or a combined global REIT index. For inflation-protected bonds (TIPS), a number of fund companies offer these unique bonds. Finally, if you want to invest in some hard assets, consider a precious metals fund and a natural resources fund. Many investors access commodities by choosing funds that invest in the companies that mine or sell them. If you need something to hold in your hands besides your monthly statement, you may want to buy a few Canadian Maple Leaf gold coins and some pre-1965 U.S. dimes, quarters, and half-dollar coins.

In sum, you should have a portfolio of mutual funds that invest in all sectors of the U.S. and foreign stock markets in proportion to their overall market capitalizations. You should also hold funds that invest in the various types of bonds. Through other funds, you should add investments in foreign bonds, Treasury inflation-protected bonds, and diversified real estate. You may also consider a small fund investment that targets hard assets or precious metals. Almost all of these can be achieved through very-low-cost index funds (or ETFs), and that is usually the wisest choice.

Chapter Summary

- Consider stock investments only for long-term investments.
- Invest across all the recognized asset classes.
- Invest over intervals of time (rather than all at once) to further reduce risk.
- Build a diversified portfolio by using low-cost funds or ETFs.
- In most circumstances, choose index funds rather than actively managed funds.
- Avoid paying anyone to pick individual stocks and bonds— either directly or indirectly.

Notes

1. Jeremy Siegel, *Stocks for the Long Run*, 5th ed. (New York: McGraw-Hill, 2013).
2. Beverly Goodman, "Back to School: Fama, French Discuss Their Work," *Barron's*, January 4, 2014.
3. Mutual funds and more recently developed investment vehicles that share their characteristics and low costs. See comments in the next section that take favorable notice of ETFs.
4. Throughout this book, when I refer to index mutual funds, I am talking about all the investment vehicles that perform like those funds and have equally low costs. For example, I have referred to an investment that allows you to own a small slice of many stocks or bonds as a mutual fund. For many of us, though, much of our portfolio is held in tax-deferred vehicles such as a 401(k), IRA, or other pension plan, or a 529 or Education-IRA college savings plan. Such tax vehicles use different terminology for the same idea. Thus, your 401(k) may allow you choices that are extremely similar to (or the same as) a mutual fund company's offerings, but they go by different names. A rose is still a rose (and a dog remains a dog) regardless of the label, so you should use the logic of these chapters in the same way for your tax-deferred plans as for your normal (nonretirement) investments.
5. Eugene Fama, "Efficient Capital Markets: A Review of Theory and Empirical Work," *Journal of Finance* 25, no. 2 (May 1970): 383–417.

32

We Know What Has Happened in the Past

There's no mystery to past performance of investments that trade on major exchanges. Research tells us how stocks, bonds, and commodities have previously done. Between 1927 and 2012, the Standard & Poor's 500 Index returned 9.8 percent annually. A broader measure of the total U.S. stock market also returned 9.8 percent per year during that period.[1]

This statistic is not a very difficult one for economists to find. After all, careful records have been kept by most stock markets for a very long time. Indeed, since the computer age began, the study of historical pricing of stocks and markets has been pretty darned easy to do: The data are already in the computers and need only be retrieved and analyzed.

Based on that analysis, we know that 10 percent, give or take, is about as good as it gets over the long term. Although there have been wild swings up and down along the way, approximately 10 percent per year has been the historic stock market average return.[2] It is also not a bad number to use when guesstimating about your long-term return on stock investments going forward.

The Historical Average Return on Stock Investments Is a Very Good Result

The good news is that 10 percent is a wonderful rate of return. It will double your money in about seven years and (if you can live long enough and avoid taxation) grow your money to 128 times your initial investment over approximately half a century.

The other side of the coin is that all those ads and unsolicited calls and excited conversations with random stockbrokers, which often promise returns significantly better than 10 percent, are so much baloney. A call from somebody claiming to be able to provide dramatically better returns than that, without undue risk, is less a moment of opportunity than a warning bell telling you to walk away.

Seeking Higher Than Market Returns Is Called Gambling

Notice that I said "without undue risk" in denouncing promises of greater than historical returns. It is not hard to construct a portfolio (or even a single investment) that can return dramatically more than 10 percent per year if things go your way. The problem is that as the promise of return goes up, the level of risk goes higher, and thus the odds of things going your way grow longer and longer, or worse and worse. Eventually, you are facing a situation that is little different from somebody offering to take your money to Las Vegas and play roulette on your behalf.

Speaking of gambling, this idea of 10 percent returns on stock investments is *strictly* about average returns for long-term investments.[3] Nobody knows what stocks will do next month or next year, and, as a consequence, stock investments over shorter time periods are just plain gambling. You should no more put your short-term money into stock investments than take it to a casino.

To make this point more dramatic, let's look at three very big drops in stock market valuation. During a 694-day period in 1973 through 1974, stocks, as measured by the Dow Jones Industrial Average, lost a startling 45 percent of their value. In October 1987, the Dow Jones Industrial Average lost almost a third of its value in less than a month.[4] And by March 6, 2009, the Dow had dropped an astonishing 54 percent over a period of 17 months. These historical facts help remind us of the very great risk of stocks for the short term. Ignore that risk at your own peril.

Not only is 10 percent per year a reasonable rough target for long-term stock returns but also it can help you filter information. When approached by people selling investments they claim will appreciate at a considerably greater than historical rates, you should recognize them as the snake oil salesmen that they are. Thus can historical information be useful to you here and now.

Chapter Summary

- Long-term returns are easy to research.
- Although nobody can know future returns, the historical 10 percent figure forms a good basis for an educated guess.
- Investing in stocks over short periods is essentially gambling.
- People promising returns significantly above historical averages are best understood as snake oil salesmen.

Notes

1. Center for Research in Security Prices, University of Chicago.
2. For a careful and detailed discussion of historical returns, see the superb book by my colleague Jeremy J. Siegel, *Stocks for the Long Run*, 5th ed. (New York: McGraw-Hill, 2013).
3. Jeremy Siegel, *Stocks for the Long Run*, 5th ed. (New York: McGraw-Hill, 2013).
4. Burton Malkiel, *A Random Walk Down Wall Street: The Time-Tested Strategy for Successful Investing* (New York: W. W. Norton, 2007), 187.

33

Costs Are Important—They Reduce Your Returns

All investments have costs associated with them. The rule against free lunches is ever present, and nobody works without compensation. Thus, buying a stock, holding a mutual fund, taking out a CD from your bank, buying real estate, or keeping gold coins in a safe deposit box all cost money. These are the questions to focus on: (1) How much are we told these transactions will cost? (2) Are there hidden costs that we are not informed of or are somehow concealed from our view?

Higher Costs Result in Lower Returns

Economists know this simple truth: The more one spends on the making of investments, the correspondingly less is the return. Consider two mutual funds that invest in exactly the same way but charge different operating fees. If one charges 2 percent per year, the other charges 1 percent, and the returns from the underlying investments are the same, the first will have a real return that is 1 percent lower than the second.

This is easy to understand in the supermarket yet, somehow, more difficult to follow in the world of money. You wouldn't buy the apples from Chile at a higher price if the same type of apples, just as delicious, were in season locally and selling for a lower price. It stands to reason that you would not want to buy investment vehicles that have higher costs or fees if a very similar one imposing lower costs is available.

Just as you do in the grocery store, search for the better value when choosing where to put your money. Most investment vehicles have a number of very similar (or identical) cousins. Indeed, there are many instances where two equivalent investments differ primarily in the fees that each charges. The universe of things to invest in is smaller than it looks. It is true that there are thousands of companies to buy stock in, many countries you can lend your money to, plenty of real estate you can own, and a bunch of currencies, rare metals, and natural resources you can speculate on. The total number of possible investments is magnified many times over, though, by a vast army of investment vehicles that invest in essentially the same things.[1] This is an inconvenient truth for investment firms.

Thousands of financial jobs on Wall Street involve new ways to package or slice up the various real investments that already exist. Firms spend a lot of time explaining why three animals each with the head of a dog, the torso of a pig, and the tail of a fish are much better than one dog, one pig, and one fish. And they produce hundreds of so-called new investments each year. In examining their wares, though, extreme caution is called for. No matter which way the butcher slices a pound of baloney, it is still, in the end, just a pound of baloney.

Many Investments Carry Expenses That Are Just Too High to Be a Good Deal

It is fair to generalize that the more management, engineering, or salesmanship is involved in a complex investment, the higher its costs are likely to be. Indeed, some of these products carry such high fees that their sellers dare not be up front about them. Lots of investments have some (or all) of the costs hidden in various ways. As a general rule, investments with hidden costs are investments with costs that are too high.

One particular fee warrants special notice because it is critical to small investors. Many mutual funds are sold with sales charges called loads. These loads are often between 3 and 6 percent of the amount you are investing in the fund, above and beyond the underlying operating fees that all mutual funds charge. The load money does not go into your investment but, rather, compensates the people and companies that sold you the fund. There are other mutual funds that do not charge such loads and are known as "no-load" funds. Lots of studies have been done and economists are quite clear on this: Mutual funds with loads do not perform any better than no-load funds. Funds that charge high fees, such as sales loads and excessive brokerage charges, are almost guaranteed to underperform. After all, they must overcome the drag of those high costs just to stay even. One of the simplest and most profitable things you can do as an investor is work to avoid high costs.

Figure Out How Much You Are Paying to Those Who Lay Hands on Your Investments

Just how much are your investments costing you? It depends, of course, on how you invest and which companies you hire to handle your money. In some cases, though, the true costs of investments may be hidden far from view in operating expenses, trading fees, sales charges, management fees, 12(b)(1) charges, and on and on. Since economists tell us that such costs reduce returns dollar for dollar, it is very important to get a handle on the true price tag of what you are doing with your money.

How You Can Minimize Costs

There are several things you can do to hold down the costs of your investments. First, decline to do business with high-cost investment companies, including not only funds with high operating expenses and other charges but also tricky companies that appear to be concealing their true fees. If they seem to be hiding the ball from you on expenses, you can bet it is because their overall charges are higher than they ought to be. The second thing you can do is just say no to sales charges and loaded funds; stick to the no-loads. Third, avoid trading in your investment portfolio to sharply reduce your costs.

Wall Street has worked hard to instill in us the idea that trading is somehow a good idea. Actually, it is a terrible thing to do more than minimally. Purge the very word from your mind. You don't want to trade; you want to invest. And to do that prudently, you need to create a solid, diversified, low-cost portfolio and keep it. Of course, you will want to make minor adjustments as your circumstances change (and your circumstances *will* change; if nothing else, each year you are a little older and probably in need of a slightly more conservative asset allocation). Trading swells costs, causes tax recognition, and inappropriately wastes your mental energy. Economists know that we cannot better our overall situation by significant trading (it is, after all, an attempt to beat the market), and the trader must bear the extra costs.

There is another expense to trading, and this one is very well hidden. It's called the spread, and it exists on almost anything that is bought and sold. The spread is the difference between the price to buy and the price to sell. (By analogy, we might compare it to the difference between the wholesale price and the retail price.) Most of us understand when we buy a brand-new car that we cannot turn around and sell it for the dealer's price, but it is less obvious that a similar buy-sell disparity applies to financial assets we buy as investments. Take a look at your favorite stock right now; you will see a bid price and an ask price. The ask price is the amount you would have to pay (plus trading commission) to buy the stock right now. The bid price is the amount (plus commission, of course) to sell it right now. Notice that the ask price is higher than the bid price. Wall Street firms that make a market in the stock do very well by this spread; buyers and sellers do not. Somebody benefits when you trade a lot, but that somebody is not you.

Needless to say, the costs of trading are even higher if you are buying and selling anything that carries a (visible or hidden) sales charge. Be careful to avoid all the ways that the industry has found to hide those charges. For example, those who refuse to buy class A shares that have such sales loads (discussed earlier) are offered class B shares that do not, but the underlying fees on the B shares are marked up enough to more than make up for the lost sales commission in a few years. (That's right, the operating fees on a mutual fund sold as B shares are actually a lot higher than the regular operating fees, even though the costs of running the fund are exactly the same.) Sometimes new issues are sold as having "no sales charge," but their price is set so that it is 5.75 percent or 10 percent or 15 percent higher than the price it will sell for the day it begins trading on the open market. When the brightest guys on Wall Street set out to hide the sales charges from you, they can get pretty creative. *Caveat emptor.*

An article in the *Journal of Corporation Law*[2] stated that mutual fund fees are too high. The authors based this claim on their comparison of the difference between those fees and what some of the same companies charge large pension funds for essentially the same services. They pointed out that the pension funds were in a position to bargain knowledgably and hold down these costs. Mutual fund investors, on the other hand, are the victims of both a conflict of interest between themselves and the directors of their funds, and a lack of comprehensive knowledge. The article went on to suggest that the main reason investors do not have adequate knowledge about the overall costs of mutual funds is that the information is being hidden from them.[3] It gave examples where not only shareholders but also journalists, the Government Accounting Office, the Securities and Exchange Commission, and even fund directors themselves were unable to access or interpret information on mutual fund pricing.[4]

Finally, although I'm sure this point is obvious to you by now, you should never, ever pay a management or advisor fee to anyone who is in any way selling products or making any kind of commissions on the investments you make. By analogy, it is as if you went to the doctor's office only to be told that your physician was now charging a special fee for determining the best drugs for your treatment. At the same time, the pharmaceutical company manufacturing the drug was paying her a commission for every pill consumed by her patients. This situation could never be acceptable or considered fair. The incentives created by the commission work in direct conflict with the doctor's duty. Furthermore, you are already paying a fee to the doctor for her promise to fulfill that duty; she must use her expertise to select the very best drug for treating your ailment. Payment for "product placement" adds significant costs and is never going to be compatible with the use of professional judgment.

Chapter Summary

- Economists know that the cost of investments reduces their effective return.
- Keeping costs lower tends to raise returns.
- When comparing similar investments, consider relative costs and fees.
- More costly investments do not perform better than those with lower costs.
- You should minimize trading.
- Do not pay anyone a fee if they are steering you into things on which they make commissions or are otherwise compensated.

Notes

1. One example is funds that invest in mortgage-backed securities in the United States. (These are often called GNMA or "Ginnie Mae" funds, after the government-sponsored consolidator of mortgages.) There are several dozen mutual funds that invest in such mortgage loans. There are very slight differences in the overall interest rates, duration, and creditworthiness of their various portfolios. For the most part, though, these GNMA funds invest in more or less the same thing.
2. John P. Freeman and Stewart L. Brown, "Mutual Fund Advisory Fees: The Cost of Conflicts of Interest." *Journal of Corporation Law* 26, no. 3 (Spring 2001): 609.
3. Ibid., 662–670.
4. Ibid., 663–668.

34

Investments to Avoid

While there are countless investments for you to consider, some are better avoided altogether. I don't want to spend too much time on this subject, and certainly don't suggest that this list is comprehensive, but I did want to write briefly on some types of investments that you should steer clear of.

In every type, variation, and flavor of investment, some are better than others. However, the ones I list here are never a good idea.

Variable Annuities

Variable annuities are a terrible investment, expensive as the dickens, and wildly popular in America. What's wrong with them? For starters, they are loaded with costs and surrender charges. These are additional fees you must pay if you want to get at your money during a surrender period, typically in six to eight years. In addition, variable annuities turn long-term capital gains into regular income (a very bad thing from a tax point of view). Furthermore, they are sold as having an insurance component when, in fact, that insurance is a cruel hoax. Happily, you don't have to take my word for it; just see the issue of *Forbes* magazine dated February 9, 1998.[1] The cover of that magazine says it all: "Don't be a sucker! Variable annuities are a lousy investment."[2]

Hedge Funds

Hedge funds were the flavor of the week for quite a while, and though they have fallen slightly out of favor, are still prevalent.

They are also full of very troubling details. Supposedly, a major advantage of hedge funds is that they can make bets that investments will lose value (taking a short position), as well as the more traditional wager that their favorites will gain. That sounds good until you remember what economists know: If nobody can consistently pick what will go up, the exact same logic shows us that nobody can consistently choose what will go down, either. Hedge funds are extremely expensive: The manager is paid a fee to run the fund and then a big chunk of any profits (the going rate is 20 percent). Furthermore, hedge funds are not regulated by the government in the way that mutual funds and stock and bond investments are. (The governmental attitude on this seems to be that these investments are only for big boys and girls who can take care of themselves.) Thus, hedge funds are free to report their results, or not, as they see fit. It will come as no surprise that they tend to be more diligent about reporting when they have had a good year than when things have not gone their way.

Hedge funds are famous for making big bets, and this is part of the problem. Anyone can take another person's money and bet, for example, that oil[3] will go up. Through the use of leverage (borrowing), they can make a very big bet. If oil goes up, they look smart. If oil goes up a lot, they look like geniuses (and attract a lot more money to play with). And if oil goes down, they get wiped out, close up the fund, and walk away.[4] We note that they could make the same bet on oil going down, to the same effect. The key point is that hedge fund managers have nothing to lose in making such bets. You do. Be extremely wary of anyone who is betting other people's money and thus has an incentive to go for broke in this way.

Derivatives

Derivative is a catchall word for a bunch of investments, the values of which are derived from other investments. The most common of these are stock options. Using "puts" to bet a stock will go down and "calls" to bet on a rise is marketed heavily and appeals to folks who like to gamble. What these are, really, are the contractual rights to sell (put) or buy (call) the stock at a given price and date. Andrew Tobias offered this warning in a recent edition of his book, *The Only Investment Guide You'll Ever Need:* "Just remember this: it is a zero-sum game and the odds are definitely against you. Anything you do win is fully taxed as a short-term capital gain. There are no dividends, lots of commissions. It may be addictive."[5] My memory, though, was that he gave an even graver warning in an earlier edition with respect to the danger of playing with options: "For most people, the bottom line is this: it's an exciting game, but if you play long enough, you will lose all your money."[6]

Callable Bonds

What is a callable bond, and why would anyone choose to invest in one? The concept is pretty straightforward. While a traditional bond, such as most U.S. Treasury bonds, promises to pay you the stated interest rate until the maturity date, one that is callable is a bit more complex. A callable bond can be redeemed by the issuer prior to its maturity. In other words, if it suits the issuer, the bargain can be terminated early, and you get your money back.

Sometimes the return of principal includes a premium (extra money) to compensate for the fact that the redemption isn't so great for the bondholder. Sometimes it does not. That depends on the terms of the bond—which are the equivalent of a long and complex legal contract.

The primary reason such a bond is redeemed before its final maturity date is that interest rates have fallen. In such a situation, the issuer would be able to refinance the debt more favorably. The market price of the bond would almost surely have risen. And, of course, you as the bondholder are going to get your money back at a moment when only lower interest rates are available if you wish to reinvest on similar terms.

Thus, a callable or redeemable bond is structured so that the issuer has a choice as to whether to end the deal and give bondholders their money back at certain points in time. Bondholders, of course, are not offered this flexibility. It is not a fair or even deal. That should be okay, though, since the price of the bond is adjusted to reflect that this provision is a one-sided covenant in the issuer's favor.

A properly functioning and highly liquid marketplace will price these bonds correctly to adjust for this one-sided provision. But what if the marketplace for bonds is either not functioning properly or not highly liquid? This complexity in the structure and fairness of the bond is going to benefit the party who has more information. If both sides of the transaction are highly sophisticated bond experts, the whole thing is going to turn out fine. That, however, reflects the reality of neither the world generally nor the voracious financial industry. Rather, the information asymmetry will probably be used to take advantage of the party less able to protect its own interests in this deal. And that is going to be you.

At a conference I recently attended, a speaker was talking about bond market trading. In the middle of a discussion about deals between highly sophisticated institutional traders, someone asked a question about individual bond investors. The expert paused briefly and said, "Retail investors get slaughtered in the bond market." No explanation, no concern, and no further comment. He just offered it as a widely known and indisputable fact. Then he went back to what he had been talking about.

It's true. Small retail investors get slaughtered in the bond market. They are playing on a field they don't belong on, like a kitten on a superhighway. Unlike large-capitalization U.S. stocks, bonds are not traded in a properly functioning liquid market. Rather, small bond investors must rely on bond desks concerned with their own inventories, markups, and profitability. The small investor must contend with complexity, opaqueness, rent-seeking, and asymmetric information that all work against her.

The simple answer is to avoid callable bonds entirely. There are plenty of good alternatives. You can stick to bonds that are more straightforward. Even better, you can delegate the entire problem to a low-cost mutual fund or ETF. Perhaps better still is to invest in an index fund that eliminates entirely the question of which bond is better than another.

Having completely sidestepped the problem, all you need is a succinct answer as to why. When a friend, neighbor, or bond salesman asks you why you decline to invest in these bonds, your reply will be simple: "When the game is 'heads they win, tails I lose,' I prefer not to play."

Convertible Securities

Convertible securities are investments that have some of the characteristics of stocks and some of the attributes of bonds. At first glance, this can look like a nice compromise. On further reflection, though, it is a bad idea.

A stock is a piece of ownership in a company. Holding a share of stock brings with it a certain bundle of rights. A bond is an IOU from a company, government, or other entity. You have lent them money, and holding the bond entitles you to certain rights that include interest and the collection of your principal when the term is over. Now consider a preferred stock or convertible bond that gives you some of the rights—but not all—from each of those bundles. The rights and restrictions you receive are complex and difficult to understand. They are not a perfect split down the middle of the stockholder and bondholder privileges; rather, they are fashioned by the Wall Street financial engineers who created the security. Those folks charge dearly for their financial wizardry, and the instrument you bought must cover those costs. It is worse, though, in that such a hybrid security is invariably created by a firm that is looking out for its own interests. The creators will want to carve up the rights so that those remaining after the sale of the security are valuable to them.[7] By analogy, consider your local butcher.[8] He has a huge 20-pound roll of salami and a huge 20-pound roll of bologna. You tell him you want two pounds of a hybrid mixture of salami and bologna. Now you must wonder: Will he put the less desirable end pieces from each meat into your hybrid? Will he put less of the more expensive salami and more of the cheaper bologna? Will he use the highest quality brand of salami or one of those lesser brands? Will he put his finger down harder on the scale to compensate himself for his creativity? Instead of buying two individual items that you know how to measure and evaluate, you have asked him to create one hybrid that you have no idea how to assess. Wouldn't it have been wiser to simply buy one pound of salami and one pound of bologna? So it is with convertible securities.

As with callable bonds, convertible and hybrid securities have much in common with long and complex legal contracts. They are rife with conditions, trade-offs, preferences, and compromises that must be fully understood to ensure fairness. Once again, the asymmetry of information is going to benefit those who created the instrument and work to the disadvantage of those less able to protect their own interests. In other words, the average small investor is going to be the loser when complex investments are created out of relatively simpler ones.

High Costs, Complexity, and Creative Geniuses

Other investments to avoid include complex partnership deals (which can also give you fits at tax time), investments of one kind that are indexed to another (such as certificates of deposit that pay you some percentage of the gain on the stock market), and any kind of investment scheme that involves insurance.

This list of investments to avoid is far from complete. It is only a sampling of categories and types of investments that offer far greater peril than they do advantage. What they all have in common are high costs, complexity, and the burden of having been created by highly paid geniuses who are richly rewarded for their clever financial engineering. In general, it seems fair to say that complexity is not your friend as an investor. It invariably involves added costs, and it creates information asymmetries that will never be to your advantage. No amount of negotiating skill will enable you to completely erase these deficits. If you invest in any of these types of instruments, you start off behind the eight ball and are far less likely to do well.

Chapter Summary

- There are many categories of bad investments, and only some are mentioned in this chapter.
- Do not allow yourself to be sold a variable annuity product.
- Hedge funds are a great deal for the people running them but not for investors.
- Derivatives such as puts and calls are not a good idea.
- Complex bond structures that create one-sided advantages should be avoided.
- Complex partnership investments, schemes to invest via insurance contracts, and investments of one kind indexed to another should also be avoided.
- Steer clear of high costs, complexity, and products created by financial geniuses.

Notes

1. *Forbes*, February 9, 1998.
2. Consider the corporate courage of *Forbes* to print such a cover story: A tremendous number of their advertisers sell the very annuity products they were so prominently criticizing. Consider too, though, how bad these investments must be for *Forbes* to muster that much courage.
3. Or Microsoft stock, or the Thai baht, or almost anything else.
4. Some mutual fund companies have used the same logic to start new funds with records of fabulous returns. They incubate 10 funds, all making very

different bets, and see which one does well (one of them must). Then they can bring the big winner to market while folding up the other nine funds. Remember the story about a single person in the room flipping heads many times in a row.

5. Andrew Tobias, *The Only Investment Guide You'll Ever Need* (Orlando, FL: Harcourt, 2002), 185.

6. Andrew Tobias in an e-mail to the author, February 6, 2006.

7. Late in the roaring decade of the 1990s, an older friend of mine used to brag continuously that his broker was putting him in "high-quality preferreds." He would go on and on about the joys and value of high-quality preferreds. I often wondered to myself what "high-quality" meant in this context, but I didn't want to ask him. I assumed that this referred to the preferred stock of more established and less speculative companies. After all, preferred stock and convertible bonds are often used to raise capital for weak or very speculative companies. After the first few years of the twenty-first century, with its sharp stock market fall, I never heard another word from him about high-quality preferreds—or anything else about his investments. Later, though, a mutual friend told me that a significant number of those high-quality preferreds were issued by Enron.

8. Alas, few of us still have local butchers who own their own shops. On the other hand, such a butcher-businessman invariably was aware that his customers lived down the street and would be in to see him next week. This is in sharp contrast to the investment firm peddling hybrid securities that is unconcerned with its interaction with the retail customer.

CHAPTER 35

How Much Is at Stake?

The amount of money that is at stake for an individual investor is startling. By learning how to negotiate your investments effectively, including a strong knowledge of the economic truths in Part III of this book, you can put a remarkable amount of money into your own pockets. By the same token, the failure to pay attention, learn what economists can prove, and advocate effectively for your own interests will actually cost you a fortune over time.

Some years ago, I turned to one of my brightest Wharton students and said, "Make me a chart that shows exactly how much is being gained for any amount of additional return or reduced costs." (Their effect on your bottom line is the same.) He asked me to state a compounding rate or, to put it simply, a realistic estimate of how much the money would grow each year. Some basic research suggested 7 percent, so that is the return rate I asked him to use. Table 35.1 is what he came up with.

Table 35.1 is not hard to read. It starts with a $1 million portfolio. Running down the first column is the amount (expressed in percentages) that return is increased. (Or that costs are decreased. The effects are exactly the same.) The columns to the right of that show the resulting increases in portfolio value over a number of different time periods. Thus, if you go down to 2.00 percent (2 percent per year) and read across, you will see that at the end of 30 years, you would have $4,319,166 more than if you had lost out on 2 percent per year. It is a remarkable fact of compounding that this number is more than four times greater than the amount you started with.

Table 35.1 Percentage of Savings and Resulting Increases in Portfolio Holdings, Starting with $1,000,000

% Savings	1	5	10	15	20	25	30
0.10%	$1,000	$6,554	$18,385	$38,678	$72,331	$126,812	$213,434
0.20%	$2,000	$13,108	$36,770	$77,358	$144,668	$253,639	$426,906
0.30%	$3,000	$19,662	$55,155	$116,041	$217,016	$380,496	$640,453
0.40%	$4,000	$26,216	$73,541	$154,728	$289,380	$507,400	$854,115
0.50%	$5,000	$32,770	$91,929	$193,422	$361,765	$634,364	$1,067,927
0.60%	$6,000	$39,324	$110,318	$232,123	$434,178	$761,405	$1,281,929
0.70%	$7,000	$45,879	$128,709	$270,834	$506,623	$888,538	$1,496,158
0.80%	$8,000	$52,433	$147,101	$309,555	$579,105	$1,015,778	$1,710,652
0.90%	$9,000	$58,988	$165,496	$348,289	$651,631	$1,143,140	$1,925,450
1.00%	$10,000	$65,543	$183,894	$387,036	$724,206	$1,270,641	$2,140,589
1.50%	$15,000	$98,319	$275,931	$581,035	$1,087,999	$1,910,745	$3,222,739
2.00%	$20,000	$131,102	$368,077	$775,611	$1,453,822	$2,556,604	$4,319,166
2.50%	$25,000	$163,894	$460,368	$970,957	$1,822,356	$3,210,159	$5,434,714
3.00%	$30,000	$196,697	$552,839	$1,167,266	$2,194,289	$3,873,370	$6,574,300
3.50%	$35,000	$229,512	$645,527	$1,364,734	$2,570,309	$4,548,221	$7,742,934
4.00%	$40,000	$262,342	$738,469	$1,563,554	$2,951,113	$5,236,726	$8,945,736
4.50%	$45,000	$295,190	$831,701	$1,763,924	$3,337,406	$5,940,933	$10,187,956
5.00%	$50,000	$328,057	$925,258	$1,966,039	$3,729,898	$6,662,929	$11,474,995

*Assumes 7 percent average annual rate of return, so 1 percent savings is the difference between 7.5 anc 6.5 percent.

It is sometimes argued that these numbers will be accurate only if all money saved is immediately reinvested. That is true. I would point out, though, that in the case of a retirement plan such as a 401(k), it is surely the case that the money would indeed remain invested in the plan. Virtually nobody who noticed that their retirement plan was earning 2 percent more than expected would react by trying to pull money out. Remember, the law strongly incentivizes retirement savers to keep that money in. So at least in the case of retirement plans, it is safe to say that a penny earned is going to multiply as shown in this chart.

The Impact of the Fees You Pay for Advice

How is that possible, you may wonder, that so much money is at stake? Let's consider the fees you pay for investment and financial services. The services you are actually receiving may well be costing an amount far in excess of what is fair. For example, consider Sarah who asked us to estimate the overall costs and fees she paid to the advisory company she had previously worked with. Although some of those costs were deeply hidden, we were able to conclude that those services had been costing her a total of approximately 4.6 percent of her investment assets each year. Let's suppose that a fair fee for those services might have been 1.25 percent per year. She was losing out on 3.35 percent per year. It is fairly simple math to see that her $1 million portfolio was growing by $33,500 less each year than would be the case if she paid only a fair fee. Even in the short term, the difference in portfolio value as a result of higher fees is striking.

That sounds like a lot of money, but the long-term numbers get much more dramatic. That money would have been reinvested in her portfolio and remained there for 30 more years. Let's assume the overall return on her investments would be 7 percent per year except for the 3.35 percent of excessive fees. To see how much money she lost out on, we must calculate the return at 7 percent and then recalculate at 3.65 percent and compare the two totals. Once the calculation is completed, we see that her cost of doing business with those folks for 30 years would be more than $3.5 million.

Jack Bogle, the founder of the Vanguard Group and a noted critic of the financial services industry, estimates the cost of financial intermediation—that is, fees that financial middlemen

Table 35.2 Percentage of Savings and Resulting Increases in Portfolio Holdings, Starting with $100,000*

% Savings	Number of Years Invested						
	1	5	10	15	20	25	30
0.10%	$100.00	$655.40	$1,838.46	$3,867.83	$7,233.15	$12,681.17	$21,343.40
0.20%	$200.00	$1,310.80	$3,676.96	$7,735.81	$14,466.83	$25,363.87	$42,690.59
0.30%	$300.00	$1,966.20	$5,515.51	$11,604.10	$21,701.60	$38,049.63	$64,045.34
0.40%	$400.00	$2,621.61	$7,354.15	$15,472.84	$28,937.98	$50,739.97	$85,411.45
0.50%	$500.00	$3,277.03	$9,192.90	$19,342.21	$36,176.53	$63,436.43	$106,792.71
0.60%	$600.00	$3,932.45	$11,031.80	$23,212.34	$43,417.78	$76,140.54	$128,192.90
0.70%	$700.00	$4,587.88	$12,870.87	$27,083.40	$50,662.27	$88,853.82	$149,615.81
0.80%	$800.00	$5,243.33	$14,710.14	$30,955.53	$57,910.54	$101,577.81	$171,065.25
0.90%	$900.00	$5,898.79	$16,549.64	$34,828.89	$65,163.14	$114,314.04	$192,545.01
1.00%	$1,000.00	$6,554.27	$18,389.41	$38,703.63	$72,420.60	$127,064.05	$214,058.90
1.50%	$1,500.00	$9,831.94	$27,593.15	$58,103.51	$108,799.87	$191,074.51	$322,273.88
2.00%	$2,000.00	$13,110.25	$36,807.73	$77,561.09	$145,382.17	$255,660.45	$431,916.57
2.50%	$2,500.00	$16,389.42	$46,036.77	$97,095.68	$182,235.65	$321,015.94	$543,471.38
3.00%	$3,000.00	$19,669.67	$55,283.90	$116,726.64	$219,428.86	$387,337.00	$657,430.04
3.50%	$3,500.00	$22,951.20	$64,552.73	$136,473.38	$257,030.86	$454,822.09	$774,293.44
4.00%	$4,000.00	$26,234.24	$73,846.90	$156,355.43	$295,111.31	$523,672.57	$894,573.61
4.50%	$4,500.00	$29,518.99	$83,170.05	$176,392.38	$333,740.56	$594,093.27	$1,018,795.59
5.00%	$5,000.00	$32,805.68	$92,525.82	$196,603.95	$372,989.81	$666,292.92	$1,147,499.46

*Assumes 7 percent average annual rate of return, so 1 percent savings is the difference between 7.5 and 6.5 percent.

charge—for the average family is 2.4 percent per year.[1] Over the course of a lifetime, that amounts to a fortune lost.

Saving 1 percent per year on a $1 million portfolio will net you $2,140,589 after 30 years. Saving 2 percent on that same portfolio over the course of 30 years, you would have $4,319,166. Due to compounding, or interest generating even more interest earned, a small change in your investment performance can yield millions of dollars more in your lifetime.

If these numbers are too rich for you, consider the chart in Table 35.2. It is exactly the same as Table 35.1 but with $100,000 as the starting point instead of $1 million. Here, the effect of saving 1 percent (or increasing earnings by that much) each year brings you over $214,000 over 30 years.

The point I am making is obvious. In light of the effects of compounding, what might sound like a relatively small amount of money is actually huge over a significant length of time.

The Need for Action

This is the big message of this entire book. The amount at stake is far too great to ignore. As a teacher and writer, my greatest fear is that you will see that everything in this book is true and yet, somehow, conclude that these things are not too important. As this chapter demonstrates, though, the numbers are huge. The material in this book is what lies between you and a significantly better financial life. It is very important, and it deserves your attention today.

For most families, this information is worth several million dollars. That may seem exaggerated, but consider carefully. In addition to savings, most American families are depending on a retirement plan that requires making savvy investment decisions. We have moved from the old system of defined-benefit plans to a new world of defined-contribution plans. You get help from your employer and Uncle Sam with putting money in but, as far as making choices about how to invest the funds, you are pretty much on your own. Saving for college is, at least partially, moving in the same direction. Other parts of your financial life, such as insurance, also depend on your skill at understanding and holding your own in this complex financial system.

This is all to say that understanding the economics that underlie your investments, learning to be a strong negotiator when you invest, and avoiding being taken advantage of are far more important than you might have thought. The information in this book could be the most valuable contribution to your financial life that you have ever made.

Chapter Summary

- A great deal is at stake—perhaps several million dollars.
- Saving or negotiating even a 1 percent improvement in the performance of your investments can result in vast amounts of extra money over your lifetime.
- Get started now. Do not wait. Make the changes suggested so that the compounding of extra money can begin in your accounts.

Note

1. John Wasik, "Bogle's Blueprint for Enlightened Investing," *Chicago Tribune*, August 20, 2012.

Afterword: What Is a Good Outcome in Your Financial Life?

As we draw toward closing, we return to the beginning. This book started out asking you to think about a good outcome: how it is defined and what it might mean to you in a particular situation. Figuring this out is essential to real success in any negotiation. What do you really want? At the end of the first chapter, I suggested the answer might include that which increases your happiness, fulfillment, pleasure, achievement, delight, contentment, and peace. It is a good answer, but it is not *your* answer. The definition of a good outcome is utterly subjective. It has got to be your good outcome if it is to be of real use.

Part I proceeded to explore how the best negotiators go about thinking, preparing, and doing. The elements of a negotiation were identified and the phases explored. While the exact pattern of any given negotiation is unique, the general way surely is not. The teachers and practitioners who have come before us left a rather well-worn path that we can follow. My hope is that the first part of this book can stand alone as a guide to becoming a better negotiator.

Part II showed you that investing is merely another type of negotiation. The methods, concepts, and tools of the negotiator can be used to improve your investment results. Once again, you should start by determining what a good outcome looks like and work toward that goal. As with negotiating generally, investment negotiations typically follow recognizable patterns. The difficulties, problems, and crooked places have been highlighted by those who preceded you. Part II explored some particular challenges facing you as an investor-negotiator. Thereafter, it examined the elements and phases with special emphasis on negotiating with investment advisors and financial intermediaries. Ultimately, the second part of this book was designed to help you get better outcomes when you invest.

Throughout, I urged you to pursue the negotiation process with diligence. Your success will be increased by doing your homework.

In particular, improved outcomes are a product of preparation, exploration, thought, and discipline. A good negotiator learns the jargon, practices, and beliefs of those on the other side of the table and, when applicable, the arguments, rationalizations, and deceptions they may employ. So too, increasing subject matter knowledge and expertise will greatly advance your efforts.

If there is science, data, scholarship, or common sense to be mastered, it will serve you well to become totally familiar with them. In other words, the pursuit of a good outcome requires learning all that you can and using that knowledge in the negotiation process.

With that in mind, understanding and using economic facts is essential. There is great value in mastering the basics of what economists know; both to negotiate skillfully and to avoid being taken advantage of. Part III of this book considered some of the economic truths that will help to level the playing field. Among those is the extraordinary amount of money involved over the course of your lifetime.

In general, this book did not shy away from making opinionated suggestions concerning what might constitute a good outcome regarding your investments. Nor did it hesitate to preach about things to avoid, dangers to beware of, and bad outcomes generally. A great many of my own thoughts were offered up for your consideration.

In the end, though, it is not for me to define good investment outcomes. That job belongs to you. As this book has urged, you should be pondering it from the very beginning. It should remain a focus point throughout your negotiation. You should even keep it in mind when the entire process would seem to have reached its conclusion. All the while, you are adjusting and refining it, fending off developments that may interfere with it, and seeking to improve it by identifying an *even better* outcome. Can you come up with a more essential answer to the question, "What are you *really* trying to accomplish?" Your ability to name, envision, and work toward that good outcome will be the greatest factor in your success. At the end of the day, it is the most vital part of the task that lies before you.

It is my hope that the preceding pages gave you all the tools and guidance you need to turn your good outcome from idea to reality. I am confident that achieving it will greatly enrich your life. I wrote this book based on that belief. If I am right, and have done a good job guiding you, the result will be a big improvement in your financial circumstances. My fondest desire is that this work contributes to your greater well-being. If that turns out to be true, I will consider it a very good outcome indeed.

Selected Bibliography

Axelrod, Robert M. *The Evolution of Cooperation*. New York: Basic Books, 1984.

Beer, Jennifer E., and Eileen Stief. *The Mediator's Handbook*. Rev. and expanded 4th ed. Gabriola Island, BC: New Society Publishers, 1997.

Benton, Alan A., Harold H. Kelley, and Barry Liebling. "Effects of Extremity of Offers and Concession Rate on the Outcomes of Bargaining." *Journal of Personality and Social Psychology* 24, no. 1 (October 1972): 73–83.

Bogle, John C. *Bogle on Mutual Funds: New Perspectives for the Intelligent Investor*. Burr Ridge, IL: Irwin Professional Publishing, 1994.

Bogle, John C. *Character Counts: The Creation and Building of the Vanguard Group*. New York: McGraw-Hill, 2002.

Bogle, John C. *The Battle for the Soul of Capitalism*. New Haven, CT: Yale University Press, 2005.

Burrough, Bryan, and John Helyar. *Barbarians at the Gate: The Fall of RJR Nabisco*. New York: Harper & Row, 1990.

Cialdini, Robert B. *Influence: The Psychology of Persuasion*. New York: HarperBusiness, 2006.

Diamond, Stuart. *Getting More: How to Negotiate to Achieve Your Goals in the Real World*. New York: Crown Business, 2010.

Dimensional Fund Advisors. *Matrix Book 2013*. Austin, TX: Dimensional Fund Advisors, 2012.

Ellis, Charles D. *Winning the Loser's Game: Timeless Strategies for Successful Investing*. New York: McGraw-Hill Education, 2013.

Fama, Eugene. "Efficient Capital Markets: A Review of Theory and Empirical Work." *Journal of Finance* 25, no. 2 (May 1970): 383–417.

Fisher, Roger, Elizabeth Kopelman Borgwardt, and Andrea Kupfer Schneider. *Beyond Machiavelli: Tools for Coping with Conflict*. Cambridge, MA: Harvard University Press, 1994.

Fisher, Roger, and Scott Brown. *Getting Together*. London: Penguin Books, 1989.

Fisher, Roger, William Ury, and Bruce Patton. *Getting to Yes: Negotiating Agreement Without Giving In*. 2nd ed. New York: Penguin Books, 1991.

Freeman, John P., and Stewart L. Brown. "Mutual Fund Advisory Fees: The Cost of Conflicts of Interest." *Journal of Corporation Law* 26, no. 3 (Spring 2001).

Goldberg, Stephen B., Eric D. Green, and Frank E. A. Sander. *Dispute Resolution*. Boston: Little, Brown and Company, 1985.

Goleman, Daniel. *Emotional Intelligence*. New York: Bantam Books, 1995.

Grant, Adam. *Give and Take: A Revolutionary Approach to Success*. New York: Penguin, 2013.

Kolb, Deborah, and Judith Williams. *Everyday Negotiation: Navigating the Hidden Agendas in Bargaining.* San Francisco: Jossey-Bass, 2003.

Lathrope, Daniel J. *Selected Federal Taxation Statutes and Regulations.* San Francisco: Thomson/West, 2012.

Lax, David A., and James K. Sebenius. *The Manager as Negotiator: Bargaining for Cooperation and Competitive Gain.* New York: Free Press, 1986.

Levitt, Steven D., and Stephen J. Dubner. *Freakonomics: A Rogue Economist Explores the Hidden Side of Everything.* New York: William Morrow, 2005.

Lewicki, Roy J., Joseph August Litterer, John W. Minton, and David M. Saunders. *Negotiation.* 3rd ed. Homewood, IL: R. D. Irwin, 1985.

Lewis, Michael. *The Big Short: Inside the Doomsday Machine.* New York: W. W. Norton, 2010.

Malkiel, Burton Gordon. *A Random Walk Down Wall Street: The Time-Tested Strategy for Successful Investing.* Rev. and updated ed. New York: W. W. Norton, 2007.

Malkiel, Burton Gordon, and Charles D. Ellis. *The Elements of Investing.* Hoboken, NJ: John Wiley & Sons, 2010.

Mnookin, Robert H., Scott R. Peppet, and Andrew S. Tulumello. *Beyond Winning: Negotiating to Create Value in Deals and Disputes.* Cambridge, MA: Belknap Press of Harvard University Press, 2000.

Rackham, N., and J. Carlisle. "The Effective Negotiator—Part 1: The Behaviour of Successful Negotiators." *Journal of European Industrial Training* 2, no. 6 (1978): 6–11; Rackham, N., and J. Carlisle. "The Effective Negotiator—Part 2: Planning for Negotiations." *Journal of European Industrial Training* 2, no. 7 (1978): 2–5.

Raiffa, Howard. *The Art & Science of Negotiation.* Cambridge, MA: Belknap Press of Harvard University Press, 1982.

Schelling, Thomas C. *Micromotives and Macrobehavior.* New York: W. W. Norton, 1978.

Schelling, Thomas C. *Choice and Consequence: Perspectives of an Errant Economist.* Cambridge, MA: Harvard University Press, 1984.

Shapiro, Ronald M., Mark A. Jankowski, and Jim Dale. *The Power of Nice: How to Negotiate So Everyone Wins—Especially You!* New York: John Wiley & Sons, 1998.

Shell, G. Richard. *Bargaining for Advantage: Negotiation Strategies for Reasonable People.* New York: Viking, 1999.

Shropshire, Kenneth L. *Negotiate Like the Pros: A Top Sports Negotiator's Lessons for Making Deals, Building Relationships, and Getting What You Want.* New York: McGraw-Hill, 2009.

Siegel, Jeremy J. *Stocks for the Long Run: The Definitive Guide to Financial Market Returns and Long-Term Investment Strategies.* 2nd ed. New York: McGraw-Hill, 1998.

Stone, Douglas, Bruce Patton, and Sheila Heen. *Difficult Conversations: How to Discuss What Matters Most.* New York: Viking, 1999.

Susskind, Lawrence, and Jeffrey Cruikshank. *Breaking the Impasse: Consensual Approaches to Resolving Public Disputes.* New York: Basic Books, 1987.

Taleb, Nassim Nicholas. *The Black Swan: Second Edition: The Impact of the Highly Improbable.* New York: Random House, 2010.

Taleb, Nassim Nicholas. *Fooled by Randomness: The Hidden Role of Chance in Life and in the Market.* New York: Random House, 2010.

Thompson, Leigh L. *The Mind and Heart of the Negotiator.* 3rd ed. Upper Saddle River, NJ: Pearson Prentice Hall, 2005.

Tobias, Andrew. *The Only Investment Guide You'll Ever Need.* Rev. and updated. New York: Houghton Mifflin Harcourt, 2011.

Tversky, Amos, and Daniel Kahneman. "Judgment Under Uncertainty: Heuristics and Biases." *Science* 185, no. 4157 (September 27, 1974): 1124–1131.

Ury, William. *Getting Past No: Negotiating Your Way from Confrontation to Cooperation.* Rev. ed. New York: Bantam Books, 1993.

About the Author

Steven G. Blum, who holds two law degrees, has been guiding clients through all aspects of their financial lives for more than 30 years. In addition to maintaining a law practice, he is a principal at Steven G. Blum and Associates, LLC, which places a special emphasis on the ethics of the professional-client relationship. The firm is based near Philadelphia.

Blum has been teaching in the Department of Legal Studies and Business Ethics at the Wharton School of Business of the University of Pennsylvania since 1994 and was a visiting professor at the ALBA Graduate Business School in Athens, Greece, for more than a decade.

In addition to teaching semester-long courses for undergraduate and MBA students, Blum has taught in Wharton Executive Education programs, lectured and consulted widely, and frequently leads seminars and educational forums. He has led training sessions for a number of Fortune 100 companies as well as organizations of lawyers, physicians, accountants, and other professionals.

Of all the different aspects of his career, Blum takes tremendous pride in his role as teacher. He believes it is the highest calling in society. He has five times won the William G. Whitney Award for outstanding teaching at Wharton.

Blum holds a bachelor's degree from Wesleyan University, a law degree from Northeastern University School of Law, a master's degree in education from Harvard University, a certificate of specialization in negotiation and dispute resolution from Harvard University's Program on Negotiation, and a master's degree in the law of taxation from the New York University School of Law.

To read more of Blum's writings or to get further information, visit www.negotiatingtruth.com.

Index

Accountant, 86
Achievement, 4
Action, need for, 245–246
Active listening techniques, 34–35, 39
Adversary
  identification of, 122
  vs. partner, 165
Agents
  added knowledge of, 85
  agent employment foolishness, 86–87
  agent employment wisdom, 85–86
  conflicts of interest, 87
  extra drag of, 87
  interests and incentives, 88
  interests of, 87–89
  involvement of skilled, 89
  summary, 89
Aggressive approach, 51
Aggressive behavior, 35
Agreement, structure, 153
Agreement steps, 46–47
All or nothing, 47
Alternatives
  power from, 49
  use of from, 131
  when making direct investments, 132–137
Annuity, 100
Appearance, of good outcome, 7–10
Arbitration system, 185
Ask price, 230
Asking about needs, 68
Asset allocation, 229
Asset classes
  beyond stocks, 216–220
  diversification of, 213–214
  major, 214
Asymmetric information, 98, 121, 141–142, 177, 237
  knowledge, taking advantage of, 118–120
  tricks of trade imbalance, 117–118
  summary, 120
Atmosphere, interpersonal, 37
Atmosphere creation, 32–33
Authority, 37, 166

Avoiders, 62
Ayers, Leonard P., 211

Bad outcome, 4, 7–8
Bargaining, 72
Bargaining for Advantage (Shell), 16–17, 29, 57
Bargaining phase, 180
  about, 71
  concessions, slow and fair, 75–76
  conditional language usage in exploration, 73–74
  fair and favorable proposals, 75
  fair share insistence, 76–77
  pie increasing and sharing, 72–73
  summary, 77
Bartering, 14
BATNA (best alternative to a negotiated agreement), 131
  awareness of, 71
  identification, 51
  of other side's estimate, 53
  of other side's, weakening, 53–55
  vs. relationships, 56–57
  strengthening, 51–53
Bauer, Leigh, 155
Beardstown Ladies, 193–194
Berkshire Hathaway, 73, 76
Best agreement, 150
Best alternative, power from, 51–57
  perception shaping of others, 55–56
  possible alternative inventory, 49–50
  summary, 57–58
Best interests and trustworthiness, 123–124
Best investment deal among many, 151–153
Best possible price, 95
Better offer vs. more money, 50
Bias toward trusting, 122
Bid price, 99, 230
Biden, Joe, 30
Big-ticket negotiating similarity, 95–96
Binding, 41–44, 47
Blind trust, 167
Bogle, John, 158–159, 243

Bonding with others, 67–68
Bonds, 217
Brainstorming process, 44, 47
Broad index funds, 215
Brokers, investing through, 132
Brown, Scot, 37–38
Buffett, Warren, 72–73, 76, 183
Business model, 179
Buy-sell disparity, 230

Call (buy), 234
Callable bonds, 170, 235–236
Capital, controlling, 143–144
Capital calls, 184
Car sales, 96–98
Care, 141
Cash, 218–219
Cautions, 153–154
Caveat emptor, 119
Certificates of deposit, 219
Chamberlain, Neville, 79
Charges. *See* Costs and fees and charges
Checking and getting out ability, 183–184
Class A shares, 230
Class B shares, 230
Clients
　new and current, 144
　profitability from, 143
　retaining, 144
Closing and commitment phase, 183
　about, 79
　patience, 82
　promises that will be kept, 80
　scarcity as enhancement for deal, 80–82
　summary, 82–83
Closing window of opportunity, 80
Codes and expectations, 128
Cognitive dissonance, 36
Commission-based compensation, 112–113
Commissions and fees, 113. *See also* Costs
　and fees and charges
Commitments
　binding tightness, 41–43
　binding timing, 43–44
　degree of, 44–45, 47
　duration, 169
　little agreement steps, 46–47
　meter, 45
　in negotiations, 41–42
　thinking about, 41–47
　throughout the process, 46
　what and when, 169–172
　summary, 47
Commodities, 218
Communication
　failures, 34
　method of, 38–39

　monitoring efforts of, 34
　planning, 161–163
Compatible interests, 23
Competition, 7
Competitors, 62
Complexity, 182
Compounding, 159, 245
Compromise, 7
Compromisers, 62
Concessions, 71, 75–76
Conditional language, 73–74, 149
Confidence-building measures, 47
Conflict(s) of interest, 121, 141, 177, 179, 231
　about, 111–112
　agents, 87
　incentives, 112–113
　other than money, 113–114
　summary, 114–115
Confusion, 34
Contracts of adhesion, 156
Contractual agreement, one-sided, 156
Control, seizure of, 35
Conversation, 35, 37
Convertible securities, 236–237
Cooperation, 75
Coppola, Francis Ford, 54
Cost minimization, 229–231
Costs and fees and charges, 92, 108, 179
　advisor, 231
　of agents, 86
　awareness, 158–159
　brokerage charges, 229
　excessive, 158
　explanation of, 140
　of financial intermediation, 243
　hidden, 227–229
　hourly fees, 155
　management, 231
　negotiation over, 159
　sales charges, 230
　transparency of, 157
Currency risk, 208

Danger of lies, 69–70
Data gathering, 175–176
Data presentation, 37
Deal, new, 152
Deal improvement, 151
Deal structure, possible options for
　best investment deal among many,
　　151–153
　cautions, 153–154
　training interest of others vs. yours,
　　149–150
　working together to make packages, 150
　summary, 154

Dealers, investing through, 132
Deals, Pareto optimal, 18
Deciding
    consulting before, 37
    vs. inventing, 34
Default risk, 207–209, 217
Defense systems, 55
Defined-benefit plans, 245
Defined-contribution plans, 245
Demand response with confidence, 136–137
Derivatives, 234–235
Differential treatment, 37
Direct investments, when making
    about, 132–133
    alternatives when investing through
        intermediaries, 133–136
    demand response with confidence,
        136–137
Direct purchases, 132
Dirty tricks, 37
Distractions, 6
Distributive bargaining, 72, 74
Diversification
    about, 211
    of asset classes, 213–214
    asset classes beyond stocks, 216–220
    efficient markets hypothesis, 220–221
    further, 219–220
    index funds selection advice, 221–222
    in investment portfolio, 215–216
    and portfolio risk, 212
    risk tolerance and, 214
    summary, 212, 222
Documentation in writing, 184–187
Dodd-Frank law, 135
Dollar cost averaging, 219
Double meanings, 34
Dow Jones Industrial Average, 224
Dubner, Stephen, 89

Early exit penalty, 170
Economic truths for investor-negotiators,
    189
Efficient markets hypothesis, 191, 220–221
Ego, 147
E-mail, 31
Emerging market bonds, 209
Emerging market stock funds, 221
Ending focus, 59
Enemies, 122
Errors, 34
Even better outcome, 3
Exchange Traded Funds (EFTs), 236
Exit fees, 169
Expertise, 141
Experts, trust of, 127
Explanations, comprehensive, 140

Facebook, 133
Face-to-face cues, 31
Fact collecting, 68
Fair and favorable proposals, 75
Fair deal, 66
Fair division demands, 158
Fair profit, 158
Fairness, 61
    about, 25–27
    defined, 25
    definitions of, 156–157
    fair share, 76
    fair share insistence, 76–77
    fair standard, 181
    fairest solution, 27
    measurement beyond market value, 27
    norms of, 75
    outside measures of, 76
    understanding of, 65
    summary, 27–28
Fairness standards, insistence of use of,
        182–183
    beware of variances to, 156–157
    fair division demands, 158
    fees and costs awareness, 158–159
    measurement of, 155–157
    profitablity and transparency awareness,
        157–158
    value-providing services payment, 159–160
    summary, 160
Faithfulness, 128
Fama, Eugene, 216
Fee impacts, 243–245
Fee-only advisors, 113
Fees. See Costs and fees and charges
Fiduciary pledge, 182, 185
Financial advisors
    characteristics of, 148
    concerns about, 167
    investing through, 132
    questions for, 179
Financial experts, 93
Financial instrument, 95
Financial markets, nature of, 117
Financial practitioners, 144–146
Financial products, 143
Financial services firms, 142–144
Financial services industry, 109
Firm deadline, 44
Fisher, Roger, 11, 13, 19, 25–27, 37–38, 49,
        73, 163
529 College Savings Plan, 204
Fixed pie, 20
Flexibility, 57
    vs. binding, 43
    options, 44
Footdragging, 80

Forbes (magazine), 233, 238
Framework, 1
Fraud, legal definition of, 157
Freakonomics (Levitt and Dubner), 88
French, Ken, 216
Friendly in person, 162
Friendships, 146, 166
Front running, 118
Future dollars, 205

Gain, 4
Gambling, 105, 213
Gambling and market return, 224
Getting to Yes (Fisher, Ury and Patton), 11, 13
Getting Together (Fisher and Brown), 37–38
"The Gift of the Magi" (Henry), 34
Give and Take (Grant), 29, 62
Goals. *See also* Individual goals; Interests,
    options, and goals; Relationship goals
    reflection
    vs. relationships, 61–62
    setting, 17, 30, 62
    tentative, 62
The Godfather (movie), 52
Gold, 218
Goldman Sachs, 72–73, 76, 119
Good negotiating process, 35
Good outcome, 59
    about, 3–6, 104
    appearance of, 7–10
    vs. bad outcome, 7
    defined, 7–8
    identification of, 6–7
    for investor, 139
    of negotiations, 8–9
    process planning, 37–38
    and relationships, 60
    vs. winning, 6
    summary, 10
Good outcome regarding investments
    about, 103–104
    individual goals regarding, 104–108
    investment goals, 104, 108–109
    summary, 109
Google, 13
Grant, Adam, 29, 62
Growth stocks, 216

Haggling, 75
Hedge funds, 193, 233–234
Henry, O., 34
High costs. *See also* Costs and fees and
    charges
    complexity and creative genius, 237–238
    impacts, 227–228
Historical average stock return, 223–224
Historical professionals, 127–128
Hitler, Adolf, 79

Honest dealings, 140
Honesty, 180
Human behavior, 112

Ideal client, 143
Ideas, latching on, 44
If-then statements, 22, 149, 152, 181
Impatience, 69
Incentives, 112–113, 183
Index funds, 220–222, 236
Index mutual funds, 220
Individual goals
    about, 104
    investing to be clever, 105–106
    investing to be safe, 105
    investing to be wise, 106–107
    investing to feel connected to peers,
        107–108
Individual Retirement Account (IRA), 204
Industrial bonds, 210
Industry risk, 215
Inflation-protected bonds, 217
Influence, 85
Information
    access to, 196
    clarifying, 66
    on facts, 68
    factual, 68
    give-and-take, 33
    inside, 196–197
    of others, 62–63
Information exchange phase, 92, 177–178
    about, 65–66
    bonding with others, 67–68
    danger of lies, 69–70
    fact collecting, 68
    question asking, 66
    summary, 70
Information gathering, 62
Informational playing field, 118
Insurance companies, 134
Integrative bargaining, 72
Interest rate risk, 208, 217
Interest rate(s)
    principal loss risk investment, 209–210
    risk reflection in, 207–209
    summary, 210
Interests
    composition of, 12
    conflicting, 13
    defined, 12, 139
    different but compatible, 14
    knowledge, 139–148
    leading you astray, 146–147
    material, 15
    vs. positions, 12
    thinking about, 142–146
    trade of, 151

Interests, options, and goals
  about, 11–12
  needs of others, 18–20
  options, 17–18
  shared interests, 13–15
  underlying interests, 15–16
  value creation, 20–22
  wants, 12–13
  win-win settling, 16–17
  summary, 22–23
Intermediaries, when investing through,
    133–136
International stock market funds, 221
Internet communications, 31
Interpersonal atmosphere, 37
Inventing vs. deciding, 34, 73
Inverted yield curve, 208
Investing
  to be clever, 105–106
  to be safe, 105
  to be wise, 106–107
  to feel connected to peers, 107–108
  objective, 104
  reasons and goals, 104
  through financial entities, 132
Investing as type of negotiating
  big-ticket negotiating similarity, 95–96
  different types of, 98–101
  vs. other processes, 97–98
  summary, 101
Investment advisors, 136
Investment categories, 216
Investment choices, 131
Investment goal narrowing, 108–109
Investment goals, 104
Investment negotiation, phases of
  bargaining phase, 180
  checking and getting out ability,
    183–184
  closing and commitment phase, 183
  compromising limits communication, 182
  continuous data gathering, 175–176
  documentation in writing, 184–187
  information exchanging phase,
    177–178
  most important interest proposals,
    181–182
  planning for ease, 178–180
  preparation phase, 173–175
  salesmen skills concerns, 182–183
  summary, 187
Investment portfolio, diversification in,
    215–216
Investments
  comparison, 205–206
  costs of, 229
  goals, 109
  motivation driving, 108

Investments to avoid
  callable bonds, 235–236
  convertible securities, 236–237
  derivatives, 234–235
  hedge funds, 233–234
  high costs, complexity and creative genius,
    237–238
  variable annuities, 233
  summary, 238
Investor risk
  about, 241–243
  fee impacts, 243–245
  need for action, 245–246
  summary, 246
Investor-negotiator, 92–93, 112, 117, 119,
    134, 136, 155–156, 165–167, 169, 189
Issues
  lists of, 35
  process, 37

Jargon, 161
"Jay Gatsby" (character), 108
Journal of Corporation Law, 230–231
Junk bonds, 209

Khrushchev, Nikita, 32
Knowledge. See also Interests
  scientific, 141
  taking advantage of, 118–120

Labor negotiators, 86
Language problems, 34
Large caps, 216
Law of unintended consequences, 6
Lax, David, 22, 76, 158
Leverage, 134
Levitt, Steven, 89
Lies/liars, 69, 180
Life insurance, 204–205
Liquid markets, 98–99
Listening skills, 66
Loads, 228
Lobbyists, 85
Long-term stock returns, 224
Loss, 81
Loss aversion, 80–81
Low costs, 140
Loyalty, 87, 141
Luck, 105

Madoff, Bernie, 108, 118, 147
Making money, 145
Malkiel, Burton, 191
The Manager as Negotiator: Bargaining for
    Cooperation and Competitive Gain (Lax
    and Sebenius), 158
Manipulation, 146

Market average, 193
Market beating regularity
    market rationality, 191–192
    random chance vs. skill, 192–194
    stock research value, 195–198
    summary, 198
Market benchmarks, 198
Market capitalization, 216
Market rationality, 191–192
Marketing ploys, 147
Marx, Groucho, 107
Measurement
    beyond market value, 27
    of fairness standards, 155–157
Me-or-us, 15
Messaging, 31–32
Microcommunication, 39
Mid caps, 216
Miller, Bill, 194
Mini-communication, 46
Misinterpretation, 34
Mistrust, 34
Mix-ups, 34
Money market funds, 209, 219
Money-back guarantee, 205
Moral code, 118
More money vs. better offer, 50
Most important interest proposals, 181–182
Motivation, 111
Moynihan, Patrick, 180
Municipal bonds, 217
Municipal debt, 210
Mutual funds
    companies, 135, 219
    pricing, 231
Mutual gain, options for, 20
Mutual promises, 18

Natural resources funds, 221
Need for action, 245–246
Needs of others, 18–20
Negotiated outcomes, 8
Negotiating partner, outcome impact, 11
Negotiating poer, 50
Negotiating principles application to
    investing, 91–94
Negotiation
    about, 91
    with brokers, 142
    elements and stages, 2
    face-to-face, 31
    good outcome of, 103
    power in, 131
    preparation for, 63, 175–176
    situations, 92
    subjects of, 134
    ways, 33
Negotiation process, 46, 175

Negotiations, control of, 87
Negotiators
    concentration, 139
    path for partner, 16
    preparations taken by, 1
Negotiators' dilemma, 22
No-loads, 229
Noninvestment alternatives, 105
Nonparticipants, power of, 11–12
Nonverbal messages, 32

Obama, Barack, 30
Objective criteria, 155, 157
Obscurity issues, 157
Offers and counteroffers, 71
Online services, 147
The Only Investment Guide You'll Ever Need
    (Tobias), 234
Open structure, 74
Options, 17–18, 23, 149
    for mutual gain, 20
    very best, defined, 17
Overcommitment, 80–81

Pareto optimal deals, 18
Parties, relationships between, 59
Partners, 20
Passive acceptance, 36
Past history
    gambling and market return, 224
    historical average stock return,
        223–224
    summary, 225
Past performance vs. future results
    predictions, 201–202
    summary, 202
Patience, 82, 184
Patton, Bruce, 11, 13, 19, 25, 27, 49, 73
Perception, 55
Perception shaping of others, 55–56
Pie expansion, 20
Pie increasing and sharing, 72–73
Pie-in-the-sky goals, 17
Planning for ease, 178–180
Plans and alternatives, 39
Porter, William, 34
Portfolio
    construction, 213
    diversified, 213–214
Portfolio risk, 211–212
Portfolio theory, 212
Positions vs. interests, 12
Possible alternative inventory, 49–50
Power
    from alternatives, 49
    defined, 133
    use of from alternatives, 131
Power dynamics, 35–37, 39, 166–167

Power structure, 36
Precious metal funds, 221
Preparation
    checklist for, 173–174
    for negotiation, 63
    taken by negotiators, 1
Preparation phase, 173–175, 189
    ending focus, 59
    goal setting, 62
    goals vs. relationships, 61–62
    information of others, 62–63
    relationship issues, 60–61
    substantive issues, 60
    summary, 63
Present dollars, 205
Present value concept
    about, 203–204
    comparing investments, 205–206
    life insurance, 204–205
    money-back guarantee, 205
    tax deferral worth, 204
    summary, 206
Price gouging, 158
Primary interest, 181
Principal loss risk investment, 209–210
Private equity partnership, 170
Problem sharing, 20
Problem solvers, 62
Process issues, 37, 174
Professionalism
    issues, 177
    reclaiming of, 129
Professionalism, why and who
    society's need for, 127–128
    traditional professionals, 127–128
    summary, 130
Professionals
    engaging, 93
    traditional, 127–128
Profitability
    from clients, 143
    and transparency awareness, 157–158
Promises that will be kept, 80
Proposals, fair and favorable, 75
Prospectuses, 201
Put (sell), 234
Pyrrhic victory, 5–6, 9, 103

Question asking, 66
Questions, 52
Quotas, 145

Random chance vs. skill, 192–194
A Random Walk Down Wall Street
    (Malkiel), 191
Rapport, 70
Rating agencies, 210

Rational market theory, 191–192
Reagan, Ronald, 167
Real estate
    brokers, 96
    deals, 96
    investments, 217–218
Real estate investment trust (REIT), 218
Realtor's incentives, 88
Reciprocity, norm of, 74
Redeemable bonds, 235
Referrals, 144, 181
REIT index fund, 221
Relationship goals reflection
    financial advisors, concerns about, 167
    personal nature of, 165–166
    power dynamics, 166–167
    summary, 167
Relationship issues, 60–61, 174
Relationships
    adversarial, 38
    future, 61
    good, 29
    and good outcome, 60
    with negotiators, 146
    between parties, 59, 67
    personal nature of, 165–166
    positive, 38
Relationships and communication
    about, 29
    active listening techniques, 34–35
    atmosphere creation, 32–33
    focus on, 33–34
    goal setting, 30
    good negotiating process, 35
    good outcome, process planning for,
        37–38
    power dynamics, 35–37
    tool selection for, 30–32
    summary, 37–39
Relative strength, 55
Reputations, 8
Research, 176
Retirement plan, 243
Returns and costs. See also Costs and
        fees and charges
    cost minimization, 229–231
    degree of, 229
    high costs impacts, 227–228
    impact of, on deal, 228–229
    summary, 231
Right price, 132
Risk, 224
Risk aversion, 105
Risk reflection, 207–209
Risk tolerance, diversification
        and, 214
Rule of 72, 206
Russell 3000, 215

Sales loads, 228–229
Salesmen skills concerns, 182–183
Scarcity as enhancement for deal, 80–82
Scarcity principle, 80–82, 184
Scientific knowledge, 141
Sebenius, James, 22, 76, 158
Securities, hybrid or convertible, 237
Self-esteem, 147
Self-evaluators, 56
Self-understanding, 35
Setting, a tone, 32
Settling, consequences of, 50
Shared interests, 13–15
Shell, Richard, 7, 16–17, 29, 34, 57, 59, 62, 71, 75, 80
Short-term stock investment, 224
Signing, 171, 183
Similarity principle, 67
Sinclair, Upton, 114
Skill, 141
Small caps, 216
Smart money, 108
Social exchange, 75
Social skills, 67
Spice Girls, 12
Standard & Poors, 194
Standard & Poors 500 Index, 215, 221–223
Stock exchange, 100
Stock market
   average return, 223
   investment, 99
Stock options, 234
Stock picking, 192–193, 201
Stock price, 195
Stock research value, 195–198
Stocks vs. bonds, 210
Stone Soup story, 160
Substantive issues, 60, 174
Sunk costs, 81

Takes-no-prisoner bargaining style, 88
Tax deferral worth, 204
Telephony, 31
Them (others), 15
Third parties, 11, 23
Time, 145–146
Time is money, 87
Time value of money, 206
Tobias, Andrew, 192, 234
Tone, 32, 37
Tool selection, 30–32
Trade-offs, 18
Trading, 229
   expense to, 230
   frequent, 147
Traditional professionals
   efforts and goals of, 128

professionalism, why and who, 127–128
   society's need for, 127–128
   teaching of, 129
Training interest of others vs. yours, 149–150
Transaction costs, 100. *See also* Costs and fees and charges
Transparency, 183
Treasury bills, 219
Treasury inflation-protected bonds (TIPS), 217, 221
Trickery, 171
Tricks of trade imbalance, 117–118
Trust, 39, 124, 127
Trust, with whom and why
   best interests and trustworthiness, 123–124
   care and degree of, 121–123
   working well without, 123
   summary, 125
Trustworthiness issues, 177

Underlying interests, 11, 15–16
Understanding your own interests, 139–142
Ury, William, 11, 13, 19, 25, 27, 49, 73
U.S. bond index fund, 221
U.S. National Highway Traffic Safety Administration (NHTSA), 5
U.S. stock market funds, 221
U.S. Treasury bonds, 209, 235

Value concept, 22
Value creation, 20–23
Value stocks, 216
Value-providing services payment, 159–160
Variable annuities, 233
Vigilance, 123
Visibility issues, 157

Walkaway, 183–184
Wall Street Journal, 160
Wall Street norms, 156
Wants, 12–13
Well being, defined, 9
Winners' curse, 7
Winning, 145
   vs. good outcome, 6
Win-win lose, 21
Win-win settling, 16–17, 21
Working together to make packages, 150
Writing, unyielding in, 162
Written agreement, 184–186
Written words, 32

Zero-sum game, 20